Sta

Nina Kaye is a contemporary romance author who writes warm, witty and uplifting reads with a deeper edge. She lives in Edinburgh with her husband and much adored side-kick, James. In addition to writing, Nina enjoys swimming, gin and karaoke (preferably all enjoyed together in a sunny, seaside destination). Nina has previously published *The Gin Lover's Guide to Dating* and has also been a contender for the RNA Joan Hessayson Award.

Also by Nina Kaye

NINA KAYE

STAND UP GUY

CANELO

First published in the United Kingdom in 2024 by

Canelo
Unit 9, 5th Floor
Cargo Works, 1–2 Hatfields
London SE1 9PG
United Kingdom

A CIP catalogue record for this book is available from the British Library.

Print ISBN 978 1 80436 632 5
Ebook ISBN 978 1 80436 633 2

Cover design by Emily Courdelle

Look for more great books at www.canelo.co

Printed and bound in Great Britain by Clays Ltd, Elcograf S.p.A.

1

To Angela and Geraldine

Chapter 1

'Are you about finished for the day, Lea?' My colleague, Tanya, appears next to me. 'I know how committed you are to this work, and it's greatly appreciated, but it's nearly six p.m. on a Friday. Surely, you have somewhere else you'd rather be?'

'Oh, uh, is that the time?' I glance at my watch. 'I didn't realise it was so late. I'd better get out of here.'

My foot catches on the strap of my bag as I jump out of my seat, causing me to stumble.

'Careful.' Tanya reaches out to steady me. 'You don't want to ruin your weekend plans by breaking your ankle.'

'Obviously not.' I flash her a grateful smile while pulling on my jacket.

'Well, whatever you're doing, make the most of it. Before you know it, you'll be married with three sulky teenagers – one of them being the man you married – and the highlight of your weekend will be cleaning the bathroom with the music on full blast.'

I chuckle, taking in her almost haughty expression. Tanya is the research fellow on the project I'm working on and she's the human embodiment of an oxymoron. On the outside she's well-polished and articulate, with a slightly plummy-sounding voice. You might expect her to be a bit prim and dull, and hyper-politically correct, but she's actually the complete opposite.

'That doesn't sound so bad,' I say.

'You're just being kind.' She light-heartedly narrows her eyes at me over the top of her rimless spectacles. 'I'd sell my family to be your age again.'

'I'm sure they'd be delighted to hear that.' I raise an eyebrow and chuckle.

'I'm serious, I would. Now, off you pop and have a wonderful time with those gal pals of yours. I want to hear all about your adventures on Monday.'

Saying goodbye, I hurry out of the lab and through the clinical-looking hallways of the university campus building where I work. Then, once I'm outside and well out of range of Tanya, I slow to an aimless wander. Instead of delightedly breathing in the humid early-August air, and enjoying the feeling of freedom the weekend brings, I give a loaded sigh at the gloominess that's already settling over me like the many-a-summer-day-ruining Edinburgh *haar*. Though I know there will be nothing of interest on my phone, I pull it out of my bag anyway, always hopeful that I'll be proved wrong.

I'm not.

Scrolling absently through my social media feeds, I take as long as is humanly possible to traipse to the bus stop. At least out here, with the commuters rushing by, I'm not alone – not in a physical sense anyway. It's going to be another long evening of just me and my streaming services, but at least I have a date to look forward to tomorrow – with a guy I actually see some potential with.

–

I spend Saturday morning thoroughly cleaning my two-bedroom Marchmont-based tenement flat, which my great-aunt Lizbeth left me in her will. Not because it's particularly dirty, but because it's something to do to pass the time, and because I'm also hopeful that tomorrow I won't be waking up alone. Once there's nothing left to dust, wipe, hoover or polish, I have some lunch and take a walk to the corner shop on Marchmont Road.

My thinking is that if Paul does stay over, I can tempt him to stick around by serving something tasty for breakfast. Not that he's needed much tempting so far. We're nine dates in (yes, I am counting) and he's stayed at mine four times. So, I'm hoping for another sleepover at the very least, and perhaps even spending Sunday afternoon together, if things go really well.

Paul is super dreamy. He's like a cross between Shawn Mendes and Robert Pattinson, is scarily intelligent, plays rugby, is always dressed impeccably, and he has this sexy Borders accent that makes me want to maul him (in a good way) every time he opens his mouth. In a word, he's H-O-T.

After getting breakfast supplies in, I find myself at a loose end, neither able to concentrate on the witty romance novel I'm halfway through, nor on the Netflix series I'm binge watching. Instead, I resort once again to looking at my social media feeds, trying hard not to feel like the only person in the world who doesn't have an amazing social life. I'm paying little attention, scrolling in that dead-behind-the-eyes zombie-esque way that means you've lost control of your thumb, when I see a familiar face float across my phone.

'Ooh, Paul, what are you up to?' I peer at the photo of my current love interest, who's grinning like he's won the lottery while holding up a document from the Australian Government titled: 'Visa Grant Notice'.

It takes a moment and a read of the caption below the photo to realise what's going on, and when I do, I jolt with horror and disbelief.

'*You're moving to Australia?*' I shriek at my phone. 'Are you bloody kidding me?!'

Surely not. Something as significant as this would have to have come up in conversation before now. Wouldn't it? Plus, he's blurred out the key information on the document, so there's no saying that's even *his* visa confirmation. He must be playing a prank on someone. He's mentioned his mates are the boisterous type, so perhaps it's to wind one of them up.

I quickly tap out a WhatsApp message.

> Hi Paul, your post about moving to
> Australia just came up on my Insta feed.
> Am I right in thinking this is a joke you're
> playing on someone? xx

I see that he reads my message straight away, then the status bar at the top of the screen says he's typing. My heart is in my throat, hoping for a confirmation that will surely come imminently. While I'm staring at the screen, willing him to hurry up, he stops typing and appears to go offline.

'No, don't do that,' I plead with him. 'Just tell me we're all good so I can get on with… well, not doing very much.'

Puffing out my cheeks, I look around my pristine flat, seeking something to distract me while I wait for him to respond. But this isn't necessary, because by the time my attention has returned to my phone, he's replied. Drinking in his words like a parched gun dog, every ounce of me instantly deflates.

> Oops. Had to brag about it. Maybe should
> have waited till I'd told you tonight. X

'Damn right, you should have.' Tears of hurt and injustice prick at the corners of my eyes, but I force them back.

Then, on cue, my naturally analytical brain goes into overdrive. Why did he not tell me about this? How, even? Nine dates, we've been on. He's had *nine* opportunities to bring it up – yet, he hasn't. How is that even possible if he's this excited about it? The chances of him just blurting something out during conversation or making an unintended remark must have been high. Unless…

Now pacing back and forth across my living-room floor, I rack my smarting brain for some other explanation, but come up empty-handed, meaning I have no choice but to face the grim reality of this situation. All the little signals he's been sending me, leading me to think we were going somewhere, were fake. He's been using me. I was his last Scottish hurrah: someone to get his end away with until he packed his bags and flew off down under.

'*You total knob end,*' I spit at his WhatsApp profile picture on my phone, having lost any sense of myself or the fact that having it out with a phone app won't really achieve anything. 'You're so not just getting an "Oh, OK, then. Wish things could have been different for us and hope you have a wonderful life". Nope. You need to know what a complete cock you are.'

I furiously type out a response to his non-apology.

You think?! Or how about you should have told me you were planning to skip the country on maybe… our first date?? Or our second or third at the very least. That's what any decent human being would have done. Let me decide if I wanted to spend any more time with you, which by the way, I wouldn't have done, because I'm looking for a real relationship. You knew that and you intentionally led me on. I feel sorry for the Australian women who will have the displeasure of making your acquaintance. I also hope you catch something nasty and your dick falls off.

Having at least the presence of mind to read back what I've written, I delete the last sentence to retain the moral high ground, before jabbing angrily at the send button. I then can't help but watch to see when he reads the message, imagining his conscience – if he has one – kicking into gear and making him write me an actual apology. He starts typing again and I wonder if 'schooling' him has in fact made a positive difference. Maybe the women of Australia are safer now I've called him out on this.

His message pops up on my screen, and it takes all of half a second to realise I should never have been so naïve as to mistake Paul for a human being.

All right, calm yourself. We never made anything official and I didn't lie to you. It just didn't come up. Never had you pegged as a bunny boiler but guess they come in all shapes and forms. Was about to say good thing I loosened you up a bit, but it's clear you're frigid as they come. Probably why you're such a crap lay. Laters.

His message is cruelly punctuated with a waving-hand emoji, making me want to immediately reply with one giving him the finger. His reply gives me an insight into who Paul really is: a nasty, misogynistic, egotistical arse-hole. I should be lauding my lucky escape, but even with his true colours proudly on display on my phone screen, I can't help feeling like I'm the one who is deficient and who has lost out. While unconscionable Paul is heading down under to chase the 'better life' that's heralded on British daytime TV shows, I'm left staring at the nicely painted but suffocating walls of my flat, dreading the emptiness of not just this evening and tomorrow, but every evening and weekend for the foreseeable future.

I really don't want to cry over this bastard – crying means he wins – so I text the two people I know I can talk to about this stuff and who will be on my side: my friend from university, Katie, who lives on the outskirts of Edinburgh with her husband and two adorable but demanding toddlers, and my oldest friend, Jill, who swapped her life in Scotland for the Netherlands first chance she got after a long and very boozy weekend in Amsterdam.

Pinging them each a message, asking if they're around for a chat (I'm doubling up because I don't like my

7

chances), I anxiously await their replies. The first comes from Jill, who is permanently glued to her phone.

> Sorry sweetz, I'm out with the Amsterdam crew. It's been an all-day affair (beer gardens are the best!) and we've just scored VIP tickets for the hottest club. I'll try and call tomorrow… if I'm in any fit state. Luv ya! xxxx

Then, moments later, Katie, replies.

> Soz, Lea. Up to my stinking unwashed pits in a double nappy explosion. Another stomach virus doing the rounds at the nursery. Call you next weekend?

Katie's message is followed by an entire row of vomiting emojis, which theoretically should make me feel better about my own situation, but it really doesn't.

Flopping onto my large navy-blue sofa, I discard my phone and my resolve to keep a stiff upper lip, and dissolve into tears. Tears that are not just about Paul having used and discarded me like a wet dishcloth. They come from the sense of inadequacy I try so hard to keep buried, because I'm in the prime of my life (as Tanya incessantly reminds me) and at the age where I should be living it up, making amazing memories to look back on fondly. I do love my job as a research assistant and the career I'm building for myself, and there's nowhere I'd rather live than this amazing city, but the fact is: I have no one to hang out with and I'm desperately lonely.

Chapter 2

After a good long cry, I spend a further forty-five minutes lying on my sofa, staring at my ornately corniced ceiling, listening to the skeleton wall clock in the hallway ticking away as if counting down to the end of my existence. It takes a while longer for me to come around from the blow Paul's cruel words have inflicted on me, and when I do, I decide I can't bear to be here like this any longer. Right now, my flat feels more like a prison than a home, especially as it's August and, seemingly, the whole world has descended on the city to be part of the iconic Edinburgh festival (which is actually a handful of different festivals that run largely in parallel to each other).

'OK, Lea.' I haul myself to a sitting position, my fingers drumming anxiously against my thigh. 'Suck it up and go do something. Anything.'

Changing out of my 'comfies' into a casual summer dress and my favourite sandals, I quickly apply some mascara and smooth out my long, straight, chestnut brown hair, before perching my sunnies on the top of my head.

'There you go. That's a bit better,' I say soothingly to my red, puffy-eyed reflection in the hallway mirror, trying to ignore the sadness that's so evident in my grey-blue eyes. 'You don't *need* a man in your life. And you can still have fun on your own.'

Cringing at my mirror image, I ponder for the gazil-lionth time whether talking to myself makes me weird. I've been caught doing it at work on the odd occasion, with the jovial 'first sign of madness' comment having inevitably followed. My view is that, whoever made up that saying must have been lucky enough to have a lot of people in their life. I'd also add that they were a bit lacking in sensitivity. When you spend a disproportionate amount of time on your own, you crave human interaction in a way that some might never understand – and sometimes your own reflection is as good as it gets.

'If it makes me mad then so be it.' I shrug at myself, then with one last check of my appearance, I lock up my flat and make my way down the echoing stone staircase to the beautiful, breezy afternoon outside.

I roam the Old Town and surrounding areas for a good hour, battling my way through the hordes of groups that have descended on the city for some festival fun, but this only makes me feel more alone. Having reached the conclusion that returning to my flat might actually be a less painful experience, I'm making my way along Crichton Street in the direction of The Meadows, when I'm accosted by a cheery young bloke brandishing a pile of flyers.

'Fancy a free show?' He practically shoves one of them into my hand before I can even respond. 'This one's a dinger. Do you like cats?'

'Why? Do I look like a "cat lady"?' Though affronted, I'm starting to wonder if that's the life I'm doomed to.

'No.' He bellows with laughter, obviously unaware of what's at the root of my irrational response. 'It's a comedy show about cats. All the ups and downs of humanity's relationship with what the comedian calls the "world's most devious critter". The guy who does it is really funny. You'll love it.'

I'm tempted to hand the flyer back, particularly because I'm in no frame of mind to stomach any 'cat lady' jokes if they do come up, but then I realise this is exactly how I can spend the evening out by myself, without feeling like a loser. I can go to some free shows and be invisible in the audience.

'Ah, hell, why not.' I smile at the guy, who looks mighty pleased to have recruited an audience member. 'When does it start and where is it?'

'In an hour. Just over on West Nicolson Street in a bar called The Smiling Bull.' He vaguely points in what I know to be the right direction. 'Fringe venue 259. Make sure you're there ten minutes before so you get a seat. It's a small room.'

Leaving the leaflet guy to scope out further victims, I scan my surroundings, wondering how to pass the time until the show, and my eyes land on the outdoor bar in Bristo Square that skirts the McEwan Hall. I could definitely enjoy a glass of prosecco before the show – might even help me get through it if it's crap.

I start towards the bar, then hesitate. I've never gone drinking on my own. Not that this is 'going drinking' as such. Will I look like a saddo? Because I really couldn't cope with 'judgy' eyes on me today of all days.

I'm about to back off from the idea and go find a bench, when my mind suggests I reconsider. Will anyone really care? I could be waiting for someone who's late. Why wouldn't I grab a drink for myself in that situation? And surely there must be plenty of people who visit the Fringe alone. I can't be the only one.

Before my befuddled brain can talk itself out of what it's just talked itself into, I stride across to the busy outdoor bar area, which has several pop-up stalls. A couple of them are serving food, and a couple more are offering beer and the usual range of drinks – I'm pleased to see there's also an Edinburgh Gin stall and one serving prosecco out of what looks like a glammed-up horsebox.

After a moment of indecision – I'm almost now wishing there was time for a drink from each – I opt for an elderflower gin cocktail and decant to a standing table, taking a long sip of my drink, which is divine. It's fruity and light and bubbly, with just the right amount of alcoholic heat.

Smiling to myself while sipping – actually, more like glugging – at my drink, I'm almost content. It's certainly a reassuring feeling, knowing I have purpose to my presence here. But my comfort blanket of a cocktail is gone too soon and, not wanting to risk standing here looking like the local weirdo, I decide I'll have that second drink after all.

When I return to my spot armed with a beautifully chilled, fizzing glass of prosecco, I remind myself that I need to make this one last longer, otherwise I'll turn up at the show not just alone, but also hammered. Not being the world's biggest drinker – more due to a lack of social life than choice – I'm already beginning to feel the effects from my cocktail. Which leads me to…

Sod Paul, the absolute arsehole! Anyone who allows a person to develop feelings for them when they have no intention of taking things further deserves that label and more. He let me think we were going somewhere and he didn't do that by accident. It might be that my pain is just numbed by the alcohol, but I can now see that I have not lost out, nor am I a lesser being than Paul; I am actually better than him.

And while I'm in a rare moment of bravery and defiance, why shouldn't I go out and enjoy myself, just because I don't happen to have a social circle in the city? Maybe I should do this more often. I'm actually quite good company, if I may say so myself.

Uninhibited thoughts continue to swirl in my mind, acting as an inner pep talk. They include a daydream about Paul's dick actually falling off after being bitten by some scary-ass Australian spider. I snicker to myself, attracting the attention of a man drinking a beer at a table not far from mine, and my alcohol-fuelled courage has me immediately alert and ready to hit back if he dares to judge me. But he doesn't. He simply gives what appears to be a sad smile before returning his attention to his pint.

Cocking my head, I watch him for a moment. He's around five foot ten, with a slender build and floppy dark brown hair that falls into his eyes while he's looking down, making me want to walk over there and push it to the side so he can see better. With his head bowed like that, it's hard to get much more of a sense of his appearance. But there's one thing that I don't need a better view to figure out, because his stance and body language say it all: he looks utterly miserable. And he's also alone.

I surreptitiously keep an eye on the man while sipping at my drink, waiting for him to be joined by a sulky girlfriend he's had a fight with, or a banterous group of lads who'll cheer him up. However, after about ten minutes, he's still standing alone, staring into his pint, which he has barely touched in that time.

Checking my phone, I can see it's nearly time for me to leave for the show, but that's going to be a challenge because I'm transfixed. There's something about this guy that's tugging at my heartstrings, since I know better than anyone how isolating it feels to be in a bad place and have no one to talk to.

Looking at him, it's like seeing my own loneliness and feelings of inadequacy reflected right back at me. And knowing how awful that is, I so badly want to go across and offer to be the shoulder he needs.

Aware that I'm now in danger of missing out on a seat, or of not getting into the show altogether, I have a decision to make. I either prise myself away from this all-too-familiar scene in front of me or go speak to him.

The two drinks I've had get the final vote and – no real surprise – they opt for the latter.

Sinking the last mouthful of my prosecco, I abandon my glass and approach the man with an air of confidence I most certainly do not demonstrate in my day-to-day life.

'Excuse me?'

'Yeah?' He looks up from his pint, making eye contact for a split second before angling his gaze over my shoulder, his expression remaining deeply pained.

Seeing him properly for the first time, I note that he's quite good-looking, though not at all my type. With his dark hair, green eyes and a kind of puppy-dog look about him, he reminds me of a younger – and very unhappy-looking – Paul Rudd.

'I couldn't help but notice that you look upset.' I smile at him compassionately. 'Are you OK?'

For a moment, it's as though he hasn't heard me, then he looks at me properly.

'I'm fine. Thanks for your concern.' His accent is unmistakably Northern Irish.

He gives me the same sad-looking smile he did before, and although I don't know him, I feel an inappropriate urge to give him a hug and reassure him that everything will be all right.

'Are you sure?' I persist. 'You don't seem OK. Is there someone here with you?'

'No, it's just me, but I'm fine, honestly. I'm sure you've got better things to do than pick up the pieces of some lad you don't know.'

'Actually, I don't…' I almost blurt out that I'm as miserable and alone as him, but manage to stop myself in time. 'I don't… um… have much time. I'm heading to a show.'

'Right, that's nice.' The man nods. 'Have a good time then.'

'Thank you. I will. At least I hope I will. It's a free one, so you never know. Could be the worst zero pounds I've ever spent.'

He half-chuckles in response to my lame joke, then returns to staring into his beer.

Hovering for a moment, I'm unsure what to do, but the man doesn't look up again, so I turn and leave. However, a full thirty seconds later, as I'm walking in the direction of West Nicolson Street, the man is still on my mind. He looked so lost and, really, it was a bit rude of me to say that I had somewhere else to be. Plus, he might have said he was all right, but it obviously wasn't true. He probably just didn't want to burden anyone else with his woes.

Well, he can burden me all he wants, I suddenly decide. Performing an abrupt U-turn that causes a gaggle of Japanese tourists behind me to leap out of my way, I march back into the outdoor bar area and right up to the man.

'I can skip my show.'

'Sorry, what?' He looks up at me once again and blinks.

'I can give the show a miss. I mean, how funny can a comedy show about cats be, right?'

'Right.' His expression turns to one of bemusement, making me realise I haven't actually contextualised my point.

I give an exaggerated, alcohol-fuelled facepalm. 'Sorry, I'm not making myself clear. What I mean is, the show is not important. You said that I must have better things to do than pick up the pieces of someone I've never met, but I don't.'

'Course you don't,' he mutters, which momentarily throws me, but I recover almost instantly.

'No, I don't. Wouldn't it be a sad world if we all chose having a good time over helping someone in need?'

'I'm not sure I said I was in need.'

'Of course you didn't.' I adopt a warm-hearted tone. 'Nobody wants to admit that, which is why it's important to notice what's going on around us. Now, what can I get you? Another pint, maybe? That one must be flat by now. Then you can tell me all about it.' I reach into my handbag for my purse.

'No, thanks.'

'Oh, right.' I bounce my knuckles off the side of my head, communicating my moment of idiocy. 'Probably not a great idea to self-medicate with booze, eh?'

'Actually, I meant no thanks to your proposal in its entirety.' His eyes narrow slightly. 'I don't want another pint and I definitely don't want to talk.'

'Ah…' I hesitate, struggling to get a read on the situation. 'Then maybe you could join me for the show? If we go quickly, we can still make it. A good laugh should help cheer you up – if the show's funny, that is. You know how it goes with these free ones, they're so hit and miss.

Mainly "miss" in my experience, but that might just be my crappy luck.' I roll my eyes. 'So, what do you say?'

'What do I say…?' The man screws up his face thoughtfully. 'How about this? I'm not sure where you got the idea that I want your company, but to be clear, I don't. When I said you must have better things to do, it was my polite way of saying I wanted you to leave me alone. Am I having a shit day? Yes. But the last thing I want is to be picked up by some weird loner chick who sees me as an easy score.'

I give a startled gasp at the harshness of his words.

'So, if you don't mind…' he continues with a slightly mocking tone to his voice, '…I'd like to return to staring into my pint – which, compared to the excruciating five minutes I've had to spend with you, seems like a top night out.'

Stunned into silence, I have no words. Not even a catty, petty response. I stand stock-still for a few seconds, as if trying to process what's just happened, then as the raw humiliation stings my eyes, I slowly turn and walk away.

Chapter 3

Big fat tears roll down my cheeks as I hurry across Bristo Square, having forgotten in my emotional state that it would have been quicker to cut round by George Square to get to my flat. Excitable festivalgoers pass me in their droves, some shooting me sympathetic looks, which is kind of them but really quite intolerable in my fragile state. Unable to keep my head down due to the crowd, I pull my sunglasses down from the top of my head to hide my eyes.

Despite my upset, I still don't want to go home. My flat will seem even bleaker now I've been shat on by two blokes in one day – and one of them I wasn't even interested in in that way. I was just trying to be a decent human being. However, I'm not in the mood for a comedy show now and, let's face it, it would be a bit of a downer for the rest of the audience if I sobbed my way through it.

Finding myself at a loss, I slow my pace and wander across to the bus stop on Forrest Road, where I sit on the metal bench while I gather myself together and decide what to do. I also quickly cotton on to the advantage of being at a bus stop: people don't tend to hang around for long and they often travel alone, so no one's likely to notice me – provided I keep my sunglasses on and cry quietly.

Rummaging in my handbag in the hope of finding a stray tissue to blow my snotty nose, I curse myself for not being the type of person who always carries a pack. But then, I'm not normally the kind of person who weeps in public. This is a new experience, and quite frankly, one I don't want to repeat. As I'm starting to think I need to venture out of my new-found comfort zone in search of a convenience store, a distinctive Northern Irish accent comes from above me.

'I assume this is what you're looking for.'

I stop rummaging and lift my head, finding myself face to face with the rude man from the bar. He's holding out a folded clean tissue; one that's obviously come straight out of a pack.

'No, thanks.' I jump to my feet and stomp off, while praying that the snot threatening to drip from my nose will stay put a bit longer.

'*Wait.*' He comes after me, overtaking me and bringing me to a halt by standing right in front of me.

'Get out of my way,' I hiss at him, attracting the attention of the bus stop's current occupiers.

'Will you please take the tissue?' he pleads. 'You've got a little something…' He indicates towards my nostril with his forefinger, gritting his teeth squeamishly as he does.

'Fine.' I grab it from his hand and blow my nose hard. 'Now will you leave me alone? In fact, why am I even asking, when only minutes ago you told me to get lost. You were a dick to me, so I'll be one to you. Piss off and get out of my face.'

'That's fair.' He holds up his hands in an apparent admission of guilt, as I try and fail to go around him. 'But, in my defence, I've had a shitter of a day. I'm normally much more pleasant to be around. Think… guinea pigs and fluffy bunnies.'

'Guinea pigs and fluffy bunnies may be friendly, but they obviously don't know how to apologise.'

I try to go around him again, but he darts in front of me with a pathetic grin.

'*Seriously?*' I let out a cry of frustration. 'Will you get *out* of my way.'

'I'm sorry.' He puts his hands together in a prayer-like gesture. 'I'm truly sorry. You did not deserve to be spoken to like that.'

'Well, at least we agree on something.' I stop trying to escape and fold my arms across my chest, prepared to hear him out, but most certainly not showing any sign of forgiveness. 'You're not the only person in the world who has bad days, you know. But people like me try to get on with things without making someone else's already bad day ten times worse.'

He ups the ante on his plea to me. 'I know. Will you *please* let me buy you a drink as an apology and I'll explain myself properly. Wait… did you mean you're having a bad day too? Maybe we can compare notes? Start up a support group or something?'

I snort with amusement. 'You're full of shit, aren't you?'

'I really am.' He nods earnestly. 'I make a living out of it. Or at least I try to. So, are we on?'

'Only if we go back to that bar and you buy me the most expensive gin cocktail on the drinks menu.'

'Done.' He slaps a triumphant hand on his thigh, then holds the other one out in the direction of Bristo Square. 'Lead the way, fine lady.'

Shaking my head at his gall, I march back in the direction of the outdoor bar, leaving him attempting to make conversation from behind.

'I'm Shep, by the way. And you are…?'

'Lea. I'd say it's a pleasure to meet you, but I think the jury's still out on that one.'

'Ha, you're funny! I like a girl with a sense of humour. The drier the better.'

'Watch it.' I aim a warning shot over my shoulder. 'We're barely on speaking terms, so I'd hold off flirting for now if I were you. Plus, you're not really my type.'

'Ouch.' Shep makes no secret of being stung by my burn. 'That was acidic. Scars for life, that stuff, you know.'

'Oh, I know. I received my own dose of it earlier.'

'Shit, yeah, I'm sorry about that. I was out of order. You're not a "weird loner chick". You were really kind, trying to help me like that.'

'Yeah, well, you can't take all the credit, I'm afraid. You weren't the first arsehole to ruin my day.'

'Ah, I'm sorry. I really am.' Shep finally catches up with me, rubbing his forehead exhaustedly. 'I'm not proud of myself, but unfortunately your comment was a bit close to the bone, so I lashed out.'

'My comment?' I give him a confused side-glance.

'Let's get the drinks in and I'll explain all.'

Chapter 4

'So, what's your war story?' Shep hands me my gin cock-tail and we commandeer the same standing table where he was moping before, in the outdoor bar.

As it is now Saturday evening, the place is becoming packed out, with a livelier atmosphere, so we have to share the table with a couple who are talking in frustrated-sounding hushed tones and appear to be having a minor tiff.

'Uh-uh.' I shake my head. 'You first.'

'Thought you might say that.' He takes a slug from his pint, his floppy hair nearly taking a bath as he does. 'All right, here goes. But do me a favour and don't take the piss.'

'OK.' I'm slightly bemused by this request.

'I'm not from here. I'm a stand-up comedian. Came to the festival to try and make it big.'

'Oh, that's cool. Say something funny.'

'Really?' Shep gives me a withering look. 'Literally every person I meet does that. I'm a comic, not a performing monkey.'

'Sorry.' I chuckle, not sorry at all. 'Why did you think I would mock you for being a comedian? I think that's well brave, and you're in the right place for it. There are some well-known names who got their big breaks from doing the Fringe. Billy Connolly and Stephen Fry spring to mind. And didn't Graham Norton as well? I'm sure I read that somewhere.'

'You seem to know your stand-up trivia. There are some greats who have made it, all right, but also many who haven't.'

'I'm sure. Trying to make people laugh for a living must be a tough gig, if you excuse the pun.' I take a deep, satisfying mouthful of my drink, eyeing his grimace, though it's unclear whether it was a reaction to the pun or to the truth of my words. 'One miscalculated joke to an unforgiving audience and it's death by social media. No way I could make myself the sacrificial lamb in that way. I'm a lab rat through and through — more than happy to spend every day with my nose in my research.'

'You're a researcher? Like at a university — this one, perchance?' He jabs his thumb over his shoulder in the direction of the University of Edinburgh's Informatics Forum building.

'Research assistant,' I clarify. 'And no, I work at Edinburgh Simpson University, which is less prestigious than Edinburgh Uni, but our research has a solid reputation. Anyway, back to you. I'm not letting you off the hook with this one, so don't try to divert my attention.'

'A researcher and a hard taskmaster by the sounds of it. What have I let myself in for?' Shep theatrically raises his eyes to the sky, making me smile.

'So?' I prompt him.

'All right, all right. The reason I asked you not to take the piss is because I'm doing free shows.'

'Oh? *Oh.*' Realisation bites as my earlier comment flits through my mind. 'I called them "hit and miss"… "mostly miss".'

'You did. Which is why I had a go at you.'

'I'm sorry. That was a throwaway comment. I was talking nonsense. I'd also sunk two drinks in about half an hour and I'm a lightweight.'

'Good to know I won't have to shell out for another.' He gives me a cheeky wink.

'I was only trying to get you to speak to me,' I continue my apology, cringing with guilt. 'There was no real substance to what I said. I really am sorry.'

'Forget it. Anyway, you don't owe me any apology. I was the one who was out of order. So, cheers, it's nice to meet you and thank you for caring.' He raises his plastic pint glass and I tap it with my own.

'And now we're at the part where you tell me why you were so down earlier.' I raise my eyebrows at him expectantly. 'You've explained why you bit my head off, but there's clearly a considerable chunk of this story still missing.'

'Because that's the bit that's harder to share.'

The lighter mood we've enjoyed is chased away by a heavy sigh and a hardening of Shep's expression. He goes quiet and stares down into his pint like before, which I'm now realising must be his way of trying to escape his current reality. Rather than giving him another prod, I wait patiently for him to continue – not for fear that he'll turn on me again, but out of respect for him, and the fact that whatever this is, it's difficult for him to face.

'I'm broke,' he says eventually.

'Ah.' My mouth pinches sympathetically. 'How bad is it?'

'Bad enough that my dream is over. I'm having to cancel my shows and go home. Didn't even get close to a full week of performances, which is such a kick in the teeth, because the ones I did were actually really well

24

received. I wasn't getting many people through the door – there are just so many shows to choose from – but word of mouth could have changed that.'

He produces a flyer from his pocket and hands it to me. Unfolding it, I see that it has his name on it and the show itself is called Caught In The Act.

'If you don't mind me asking, what changed? I mean, you obviously came here thinking you could do the full month.'

Shep furrows his brow, his expression pained. 'That's a matter of interpretation. I certainly came here *hoping* I could do it. I managed to get accommodation for next to nothing. However, my hosts – through no fault of their own – have had to end my arrangement with them. They've had a real harrowing family tragedy.'

'Oh, that's awful.' I put my hand to my mouth with great sadness for these people whom I don't even know.

'It is.' He nods. 'I could tell they felt terrible about asking me to leave, but it was the right thing to do. They need their space.'

'Of course. But it obviously means you have nowhere to stay, and if you're broke, you're not going to be able to pay for accommodation. I assume you don't get much by way of donations through your free shows.'

'Even if I could afford something cheap, I'd be lucky to find a cheap room anywhere in the city at this time of year.'

'And you have no one you can ask for some financial help?'

'That's the best bit.' Shep looks up from his pint grimly. 'My family could help me, but they won't. I come from a family of medics. My brother and sister followed the path to righteousness and got their MDs, whereas

I apparently lost my way. They'd happily shell out if I suddenly announced I wanted to do a medical degree, but for this, not a chance. They take every opportunity they can find to ridicule my choice of career and make digs at my lack of success. I'm meant to be the funny guy, but I'm the family joke.'

'Shep, I'm so sorry.' I reach out and touch him gently on the arm. 'That's really rough. I don't understand why some people have to be so cruel, especially to their own flesh and blood.'

'Thanks, I appreciate it. That's why I came after you. With everything that's happened, I couldn't allow my last memory of this experience to be upsetting someone who was just trying to be nice. That's not the person I am. I'm not like my family. It's gonna be a right bundle of laughs going home with my tail between my legs.' Shep drinks the last mouthful of his beer glumly.

'I can imagine.' I grimace, wishing there was something I could do to help. 'Can I get you another pint? I know it's not the answer in these situations, but I'd like to reciprocate, especially as you've been so kind as to buy me a drink when you're skint. I also feel guilty that I made you buy me the most expensive one here.'

'Not quite. Last girl I offered to buy a drink for asked for a bottle of prosecco and a straw.'

'*What?*' My mouth falls open in astonishment.

'I'm kidding.' He gives a weak smile and I chuckle at having been caught out. 'You don't owe me anything, Lea. I'm not destitute. I just can't afford to stay in the city, and having your company right now means it's a tenner well spent.'

'That makes me feel a little better, but unless you think having another pint will do you more harm than good, I'd still like to buy you one. Please?'

'Go for it.' Shep gives an easy wave of his hand. 'It's not like I'm in a rush to get to the airport.'

'You're leaving tonight?' I feel an unexpected rush of disappointment. 'Where's all your stuff?'

'In a luggage locker at Waverley Station. I'm on a late flight, so I thought I'd come up here to drown my sorrows—'

'And the beer fog would make leaving less painful.'

'Got it in one.' Shep gives a sheepish grin. 'Clever one, you are. Makes sense you're an academic.'

'It was hardly a Mensa puzzle.' I rummage in my bag for my purse then head for the bar.

Relaying my order to the guy who's serving, my mind ticks over what Shep's just told me. What a crappy situation to be in. And what rubbish parents he has, unwilling to support him with his dreams. They might not like the path he's chosen, but to ridicule him for it, that's another thing altogether. Glancing across at him, I can see how he's already regressed to the same stance and expression from when I first spotted him, rubbing his face in that 'stressy' way that's reserved for only the biggest and most painful of life's dilemmas. I'm well aware that it won't just be returning home that Shep's dreading; he'll probably face interrogations about what's next for him and be pushed even harder towards getting a 'real job'.

Turning back to pay the barman for the drinks, I'm more grateful than ever for the parents I have. They can be a bit overprotective and stifling at times, but I know they would support me with anything I wanted to do in life. Even after they divorced – reasonably amicably, thankfully

– they remained fully aligned on one thing: my safety, wellbeing and career dreams came first. Shep deserves that same support. His parents could bail him out and help him achieve his dream, but they won't – and probably purely because they want to be right.

Well, if they won't help him, I will, a voice in my head unexpectedly pipes up.

'What?' I accidently vocalise my response to this.

'Were you speaking to me?' The barman, who had gone to chat to a colleague, makes his way back across to me. 'Is everything OK with your drinks?'

'Eh, yeah, sorry.' I bite my lip in embarrassment and pick up the two plastic glasses he's served me. 'I was… talking to myself.'

'Right.' He gives me an odd look. 'Well, enjoy your drinks.'

Glancing back across at Shep, who's still lost in his thoughts, I set the drinks down on the bar for a moment to give myself space to think.

It's not the worst idea in the world, is it? Helping Shep out. He seems like a decent guy, and I've got a spare room. I've also seen the flyer for his show, so unless he's made all this up and used some random comedian's leaflet, he must be genuine. Plus, he didn't seek me out initially – I approached him and he palmed me off. Would a conman do that? OK, possibly. How would I know? But Shep seems like the real deal. If he's not, then he's a bloody good actor and he should consider the big screen as an alternative career path.

Anyway, the point is, I can do some good here. I can give this guy a chance at his big break, and in the process, it would mean I'd have some company for a few weeks. It would certainly be a welcome change not to spend every waking hour outside of work on my own. Not that that's why I'm doing it. Obviously. I've tried having flatmates to fill that gap in my life and it's never ended well, but this is just temporary. It's for Shep. And it's the right thing to do.

My mind made up, I pick up our drinks and head back across to our table.

Chapter 5

Handing a grateful Shep his pint, I plonk my own G&T on the table and look at him earnestly.

'I have an idea.'

'An idea about what?' He tips his glass in my direction, which I interpret as a combined 'cheers and thanks'.

'I have an idea that could solve your problem.'

'Of being broke?' He looks immediately sceptical. 'Don't tell me… you're a psychic and you've had a vision about tonight's lottery numbers.'

I frown. 'No.'

'You're secretly a gangster and you're gonna hold my folks at gunpoint until they cough up?'

'That's ridiculously unrealistic and over the top.'

'But the lottery one was perfectly believable?' He raises an eyebrow. 'Interesting where you draw the line.'

'Ha ha, funny man.' I stick my tongue out at him. 'Good to see your sense of humour isn't completely shot by all this, but how about you shut up and listen?'

'Sorry. I won't say another word.'

'Thank you. I have a proposition for you.'

'Now it's getting interesting.' His eyes widen and he snickers. 'Yes, I will sleep with you for money. I'm that desperate.'

'*Seriously?*' I eyeball him. 'This isn't some *Indecent Proposal* moment, and what happened to not saying another word? You're making me question my judgement here.'

'Again, sorry. Keeping quiet at key moments has never been my strong point.'

'Well, you must be a delight in bed.'

'*Ha!* Good one. Maybe I should have you write some material for me.' He clocks the look I'm giving him. 'But for now, I'll just shut up.'

'Wise choice. OK, so my proposition is this: I have a flat with a spare room just a five minute walk from here. Why don't you come and stay with me, so you can do your festival shows and have your shot at that big break you're seeking?'

Shep looks stunned. 'Are you for real?'

'Why not?' I shrug. 'I have the space and you need a temporary home. I can be your new festival host.'

'But... you don't know me... and you don't know you're safe with me. I could be some crazed lunatic who made up this sob story to prey on a vulnerable woman.'

'Don't you be getting all sexist now.' I tut at him.

'Ah, shit, I didn't mean it like that.'

'No, I mean *I* could be some crazed lunatic who preys on vulnerable guys. Is that not what you basically accused me of before? For all you know, you might not be safe with *me*.' I waggle my eyebrows, casting him a mischievous grin.

He blanches, and at first, I can't tell whether this is a genuine reaction to my bolshiness, or him playing along with my jokey insinuation that I might be the serial killer out of the two of us.

'Holy shit, I've met my match,' he pretty much announces to the whole bar, then lowers his voice when he notices people in the vicinity looking at us curiously.

'You did say you work in a lab. You could easily chop me up and liquify me, and no one would be any the wiser.'

'Exactly.' My eyes glint wickedly. 'So, shall we discuss whether you want to take your chances at mine for the next three or so weeks?'

'Listen, there's nothing to talk about. If you're absolutely sure about this offer, I'm gonna bite your bloody hand off.'

'Of course I'm sure. I wouldn't have offered if I wasn't.' I sip at my G&T casually. 'Anyway, you'll be kind of doing me a favour, so it's win–win.'

'How's that?' Shep's expression turns to one of interest as it dawns on me what I've let slip. I've clearly had too many drinks.

'How's what?' I go for ignorance to try and gloss over my faux pas.

'How will I be helping you out?'

'Did I say that?' I'm suddenly very interested in my surroundings.

'You did, and now you're acting like you don't know what I'm talking about. Don't you gaslight me, Lea. That's no way to treat a roomie.'

I snort. 'You've been my roomie for all of ninety seconds. I've had a longer relationship with a packet of crisps. Plus, that special status will not be awarded until your luggage is in my spare room.'

'Is that right? Well, in that case, I expect a ceremony, flag raising, drinks reception... the full shebang.'

Shep attempts to make eye contact with me, but I avoid him, knowing full well that he's trying to wear me down.

'Lea, Lea, Lea,' he coaxes me, turning serious. 'You've done an incredibly generous thing for me, and you have no idea how grateful I am. There's obviously something going on with you as well, so why not let me help you.'

I chew my lip apprehensively. Shep is such a character. He's probably someone with scores of mates, who's never short of someone to enjoy a night out with, and he likely wouldn't understand my predicament. Having made this positive connection with him after our rocky start, I don't want to risk putting him off again, because I'm now really looking forward to having him as a temporary roommate. He might be desperate for somewhere to stay, but that could quickly change – especially if he comes to the conclusion that he was right about me in the first place.

'Come on.' He gives me a friendly nudge. 'Whatever it is, you can tell me and I'll never breathe a word of it. You've basically saved my arse, so I'm forever indebted to you now. What's going on with you?'

'OK...' I take a deep breath, hesitating before I start to share. 'My day was shit because I found out through Instagram that the guy I've been seeing is moving to Australia.'

'That's harsh. What a dick.'

'That's what I thought. Told him as much, as well. We'd been seeing each other for about six weeks, which I know isn't long, but I honestly thought it was going somewhere – he even said stuff to make me think that way, I didn't just dream it up in my head. Turns out he was using me the whole time.'

'I'm sorry, Lea.' With our roles having reversed, it's now Shep's turn to offer the sympathy. 'Some people can be right arseholes when it comes to sex and relationships. So, is that how I'm helping you out? By taking your mind off him?'

'Eh… yeah, that's it.' I jump on the out he's handed me. 'We were meant to have a date tonight. I couldn't bear sitting in by myself, knowing he'd be out celebrating with his rugby mates, so—'

'That's total crap,' Shep interrupts me. 'You think I didn't spot that junction to easy street you just veered off at?'

'What are you talking about?' I do my best to look innocent, but I can feel my face flush.

'One thing you clearly don't realise, Lea, is that to be a comedian, you need to pay close attention to people. You have to master the art of reading them, so you can rib them at the right moments and spot when to back the hell off.'

'Nothing gets past you, does it?' I grumble.

'No, it doesn't. So, you may as well tell me what's really going on. Warts and all.'

With his appraising eyes on me, I feel way too exposed. I don't want to have to watch as he goes through the reactions of disbelief, then pity, then becoming freaked out as he inevitably lands on the assumption that he's been recruited to be my 'friend'. He'll be landing back on 'weird loner chick' before we've even finished our drinks.

'Do you not need to go and get your stuff from the station?' I make one last desperate attempt at a diversion. 'And what about your show? Do you not need to let the Fringe organisers know it's back on?'

'Nice try.' Shep shoots me a look and sinks the last of his pint. 'I haven't cancelled it yet – couldn't bring myself to do it – and this is the one night of the week it doesn't run. I was gonna ring the Fringe office tomorrow morning to let them know.'

'Denial was in full swing, then.'

'Something like that. Anyway, I can tell that whatever this is, it's too difficult for you to share, so I'm gonna back the hell off. How about you give me your address and I'll go get my stuff, then meet you back at yours? If I walk there and grab a taxi back, I should be with you in about an hour, say around nine p.m.?'

Relief washes over me as it becomes clear I'm off the hook – at least for now. 'Sounds like a plan. I'll go get your room ready.'

By nine p.m., I've made up my spare room and I'm lounging on the sofa watching *Friends* while waiting for Shep to appear. Thanks to my earlier cleaning spree, the flat is immaculate, so I haven't had to do much in preparation for his arrival – and thanks to Paul being a total wanker, I can even offer Shep a decent breakfast in the morning.

Although it feels a little sad to think it 'out loud', I'm really looking forward to having Shep here. He seems like great fun and we appear to have hit it off right away. Not in a romantic sense, obviously. He's definitely not my type, which is a good thing, because that kind of 'hitting it off' could get messy quickly with a temporary live-in arrangement in the mix. It will just be so nice to have someone around to chat to – and even better that it's someone I think I'll get on well with.

My previous failed attempts at having flatmates haunt me to this day. One turned out to be a creep who regularly wandered around in a towel, flexing his abs and making suggestive remarks. Another would have the noisiest sex I've ever heard. I swear she sounded like a piglet having its tail cut off very slowly with a pair of scissors. Then the last one – before I finally admitted to myself it was not a good idea to live with strangers – would bring random drunk folk he met at the pub back for late-night parties. Each time it was a complete mare trying to get rid of them, and somehow, I was left feeling like the bad one. All because it's my flat and I had to ask them to leave – it's not like I had the option to go myself.

It's taking longer than I would have expected for Shep to walk down to Waverley and get a taxi back to mine, as per his plan. So much so that I start to wonder if he's even going to turn up. As it gets close to two hours since we parted ways, I become immune to the jokes of New York's funniest friendship group and find myself increasingly fidgety. Getting up from the sofa, I go to the window and look down to the street, but apart from an elderly man walking a dog and a group of boisterous teenagers noisily making their way along the road, there's no one around.

A nagging sensation rises within me. What if Shep changed his mind and went to the airport after all? What if, after giving it some proper thought, he decided it was too weird staying with some random woman for the best part of a month? He said he was skilled at reading people, so maybe he clocked that I was desperate for company and used picking up his stuff as an excuse to get away. All he took was my address. We didn't swap phone numbers, which now seems odd. If he had got lost, how would he contact me to find his way here?

Moving away from the window, I wander aimlessly around my flat, re-organising things that really don't need to be re-organised. It's an anxious habit, I'm aware of this, but I can never seem to stop myself in the moment.

Would Shep really do that? Especially after I told him how I'd been dumped that day. Surely, he wouldn't be that cruel. But then what do I know about him? He's basically a stranger who knew all the right things to say. That doesn't mean he isn't another Paul. And to be honest, if he was picking up the 'lonely' vibes from me, could I really blame him for doing a runner?

By the time the clock in the hallway hits ten thirty, I've accepted that he's not coming.

'What did you expect, you idiot?' I berate my reflection in the hall mirror. 'You can't go inviting some bloke to stay, then tell him you've just been dumped. Think about it.'

Shaking my head at my reflection, I return to the sofa and switch *Friends* back on, then about three seconds later, my flat buzzer sounds.

'Oh my gosh, he's actually here,' I announce in surprise to the empty room.

Hopping back off the sofa, I pad across to the door and lift the intercom handset.

'Hello?'

'Hi, I'm here to see my mum who's unwell, but she's not answering,' a female voice says in my ear. 'Think her buzzer's broken. Can you let me in?'

My heart sinks. 'Oh, erm… of course.'

I press the door release button to let her in and listen – just to make sure she is who she says she is – as she ascends the staircase and knocks on the door of a flat one floor down from mine. My elderly neighbour greets her in familiar tones, making me comfortable that I haven't let anyone unsavoury into the building. However, with that temporary distraction out of the way, my focus is now back on who wasn't at the door.

Returning to the living room, tears well as I think about how daft and naïve I've been. I was so excited by the thought of having someone around, I didn't even consider that Shep might not show up. What was I even thinking, inviting him to stay like that? He must think I'm such a loser.

This is all it takes for my mind to run away from me and the tears to spill over, all rational thought having exited stage left. I imagine him returning home and telling his friends about me, then adding this experience to one of his future stand-up shows locally. After trying to be kind, though not without my own – quite harmless – personal intent, it really stings that, for him, I'll be nothing more than some great material and one hell of a punchline.

Chapter 6

By the time my apartment buzzer sounds for the second time at around 11:45 p.m., I've cleaned myself up and got ready for bed. Assuming it's just someone else asking to be let into the building, I ignore it at first, leaving them to try another flat. For reasons of security, I'm not supposed to let in people I don't know, anyway. However, after a minute or so, the buzzer blares through my hallway again.

'Oh, for goodness' sake,' I mutter. 'It's nearly midnight.'

Lifting the handset, I bark an unwelcoming, 'Hello?' into it.

'Lea, is that you?'

'Shep?'

'Yeah, it's me. Sorry I took so long.'

Pursing my lips, I'm unsure whether to be pleased or annoyed. This wasn't our agreement and the last thing I want is to invite someone into my home who's going to be elusive and unreliable. Unpleasant thoughts of how this guy could turn out to be yet another nightmare roommate – even if only for a few weeks – descend on me like those scary-ass, cat-sized seagulls on a discarded kebab. I do not want to feel like an enemy in my own home again. But then, shouldn't I give Shep the benefit of the doubt and at least let him explain why he's only turning up now – nearly three hours after he said he would?

Buzzing him into the stairwell, I open the door and listen to the echoing sound of him climbing the stone steps to my third-floor flat. Though I can't see him, I can tell from the pattern of his movements and the odd grunt of exertion that he's carrying something bulky. When he finally does appear, he's panting heavily and carrying an oversized black holdall.

'That's one steep set of stairs.' He grins at me, trying to catch his breath. 'Reckon I've just put my back out.'

'I'm sure you'll live.' I open the door wide to let him inside, without returning his warmth.

'How glad am I to finally put this thing down.' He lugs his holdall inside, dumps it on the floor and appears to wince in pain as he does so. He then looks at me properly for the first time and his grin falters. 'Ah, you're pissed at me, aren't you?'

I purse my lips in a thin line. 'I don't know, what do you think? You've just turned up hours later than we agreed and without a care in the world.'

Shep's shoulders slump. 'Shit, I'm sorry, Lea. I meant to get here sooner, but things didn't go to plan.'

'Meaning?'

'How about we grab a cup of tea and I'll fill you in on what happened?'

This time it's me that hesitates. If I agree to this request, I'm essentially inviting him to make himself at home and letting him off the hook, when I have no idea if I can actually trust him. And there's a part of me that still wants to send him packing.

'Actually... I'd rather you fill me in straight away.' I briefly meet his gaze, before my eyes dart to the kitchen, my brain cataloguing its contents for items that might help with self-defence.

Shep follows my line of sight and his face falls. 'I'm not a danger to you, Lea, I promise.'

Wincing at his ability to read me so easily, I force myself to look him in the eye. 'OK… then tell me why you didn't turn up when you said you would, and why I should trust you.'

'Of course. You deserve that.'

Shep shifts his stance as if preparing to explain, folding his arms, then unfolding them again. It's clear that he's tired and desperate for a seat, but I'm not wavering on this one. Having already had one guy take the piss out of me today, I'm not going to add another to the pile if I can help it.

'Go on, then.' I prompt him, my courage returning, most likely through adrenaline from my protective instincts kicking in.

'All right. When I left you, I went to the station to get my stuff as planned. I picked up my bag and was about to jump in a taxi, when I got a call from the owner of the pub I'm doing my show in. He asked me to swing by when I had a minute, and as I was not far away, I said I'd pop straight over.'

'So that's where you've been all this time? The pub.'

His eyes go to the floor. 'Yes, but not in the way you think. I took what I thought was a shortcut from the station, through one of those narrow closes, and… I got mugged.'

'*What?*' My hand flies to my mouth in shock.

My brain is firing out a raft of unpleasant thoughts and questions about what happened next. At the same time, there's a tiny part of me that's questioning Shep's story, wondering if what he's telling me is true – or whether it's part of his own plan to do me over.

'What did they take from you?' I ask. 'And are you OK?'

Showing signs of what appears to be genuine distress, Shep presses his palms against the sides of his head, wincing in pain again as he does.

'There were three of them. It seemed opportunistic, not planned or anything. They took my phone, wallet and watch.'

'You're kidding.' I shake my head in disgust.

'Unfortunately, I'm not. When they ran off, not only did I not have any money for a taxi, but I also realised your address was in my phone and I could only remember part of it.'

'But wait, if you didn't have my address, how did you find me?'

'I knew enough to get to this street and I could remember it was flat eleven, just not the building number.'

I let out a snort of disbelief. 'So how many of my neighbours have you pissed off in your quest to find me?'

'About fifteen to seventeen, give or take.' He gives a sheepish smile.

'Oh… my goodness.'

I rub at my tired eyes, trying to take this all in. It's such an elaborate story, I'm now pretty convinced Shep hasn't made it up, but there's still some lingering doubt I need to address.

'Look, I don't mean to be disrespectful here, but—'

'How do you know I'm legit and you're not gonna wake up to find your stuff gone in the morning?'

'Well, yeah.' I shrug, almost apologetically.

'You can search me if you like. You won't find a phone or a wallet on me, or in my bag.' He spreads his arms, inviting me to do so, and I shake my head.

'I'm not going to pat you down.'

'There's also this...' He lifts his T-shirt and I gasp with horror as I find myself looking at a huge, fresh reddish-purple bruise that's developing on his right side, running from his ribcage down towards his hip.

'Oh, Shep! Did they do that to you? I've always thought of Edinburgh as being quite a safe place.'

'Every city has its bad actors. This is what I got for trying to reason with them. It's partly why I'm so late. I needed to get my breath back before I felt up to the walk, so I stayed in the pub for a bit.'

'Did the pub owner not offer to get you a cab after what you'd been through?'

He cringes. 'I didn't tell him. Call it male pride.'

'You need to call the police.' I step forward to inspect his injury. 'You should also go to the hospital and get checked out in case you've a cracked rib – or something worse. I can drive you.'

'Tomorrow, maybe.' He waves away my concerns. 'Right now, I could really murder a cup of tea.'

'Absolutely.' I give him a sympathetic smile, then beckon him to follow me into the kitchen, feeling immensely guilty that I made him stand there and explain himself after what he'd just been through.

Chapter 7

On waking the next morning, I'm groggy and disorient-
ated from my late night. Reaching for my phone, my first
thought is to check the time, but before I can do that, my
brain kicks into high gear and demands that I leap out of
bed to check everything is in order. As much as I want to
believe every word Shep told me – and I generally think
the best of people until they give me a solid reason to
think otherwise – he's still a stranger and someone I know
next to nothing about.

'Please don't have robbed me,' I chunter to myself,
while pulling on a pair of trackie bottoms and a hoodie.
'That, I would never recover from.'

Quietly pulling open the door to my bedroom, I
stick my head out into the hallway to see if there's any
sign of Shep, but the flat is silent. A little too silent.
Tiptoeing across the hallway, my bare feet cool against
the natural wooden floorboards, I check the living room,
then the kitchen, both of which are in the state they were
left the previous evening. The TV, my Bose Bluetooth
speaker (a much-loved Christmas gift from my parents),
the microwave and all other portable electronics are sitting
snugly in their rightful places, which is certainly an
encouraging sign. It's also enough of a positive indicator
for me to instruct the paranoid part of my brain to pipe
down. What there is no sign of, though, is Shep. I can see

he's not in the bathroom, because the door is wide open, meaning the only place left to check is the spare room.

Creeping back across the hallway, careful to avoid the floorboards I know will creak and give me away, I put my ear up against the closed door, but there's not a sound coming from within. Maybe he's still asleep, I think to myself, then balk as I look over my shoulder at the skeleton clock and discover it's gone midday. I can't remember the last time I slept that late. Though, saying that, I can't remember the last time I stayed up till two a.m. – sad as that might sound coming from someone who's constantly reminded of how much partying she should be doing at her age. Returning my attention to my spare room and what might be going on inside it, I misjudge how close I am to the door and accidently headbutt it, causing a 'thunk' that's definitely loud enough to attract the attention of my new roommate.

'*Shit, shit, shit.*' I dance around in panic, before realising the only thing I can do to avoid it looking like I was spying on him (which, to be fair, I was) is to make out that I was knocking on the door.

Gathering myself together, I close my eyes for a moment, then knock twice.

'*Shep?* Just wondering how you are this morning, and if you'd like any breakfast?'

There's no response, so I try once more, louder this time. Again, there's no answer. At a loss as to what to do, my mind goes into overdrive. Why hasn't he answered? Surely if he had been asleep, he would have woken up by now. Oh crap, what if he's dead? What if he had internal bleeding after all, and now my guest bed is occupied by a corpse? If there's any chance that's the case, the last thing I want to do is enter the room; however, if he is dead, then

45

I'm going to have a bigger issue on my hands the longer I leave it.

Whipping myself into a panicked frenzy, I realise I have no option but to open the door and face whatever's inside. 'Just *effing* do it,' I chide myself, pushing open the door and anxiously peering into the room – only becoming aware that I'm holding my breath when I see that everything is in order.

Sagging against the wall with relief, I give a shaky laugh. However, this positive sensation is short-lived, because while Shep might not be dead, he's also not here. And neither is any of his stuff. This can only mean one thing: he's done a bolt.

Disappointment washes over me, followed by a rapid re-emergence of my suspicions. If he's gone, then why has he gone? If it were for any innocent reason, wouldn't he have waited to say goodbye? Which means he either decided our arrangement wasn't going to work out, and didn't have the guts to tell me, or...

Returning to the hallway, my eyes land on my handbag, which is sitting on the floor at the bottom of the coat stand – exactly where I dump it every day when I arrive home. This habit is fine when I'm living alone, but having impulsively invited some random bloke to stay, it's not such a wise move.

'*Oh, no.* Please, no.' I rush across the room, drop to my knees and rifle through the contents, looking for my purse. 'Oh shit, it's not here. It's gone. It's *bloody* gone. You are a total idiot, Lea. A completely naïve and stupid—'

'Why are you being so unkind to my landlady?' a male voice cuts through my distressed ramblings.

My head shoots round in surprise to discover Shep standing there, watching me quizzically, the front door of the flat wide open behind him.

'I… um…' I'm so blindsided by his sudden reappearance that I don't know what to say or do, but as my fingers finally locate my purse, one thing's for sure: he's not a thief.

'Shep, good morning.' I smile up at him, tugging at my hoodie guiltily. 'Where have you been? I was just… I mean, I thought—'

'You thought I'd done a runner with your purse.' He steps forward and helps me to my feet.

'What? No.'

'You're really gonna deny it?'

'OK, yes, I'm sorry.' I wring my hands in shame. 'I guess… I mean, I was comfortable enough with my decision of inviting you to stay while I was tanked up on gin, but I've had a few moments since when I've wondered if it was stupid and/or risky. While I'm apologising for jumping to the conclusion that you might be a thief, I don't think I should be apologising for being vigilant.'

'Definitely not.' He hands me a carrier bag with some groceries in it. 'I don't blame you one bit for questioning your decision. It was risky. I could have been a scammer pretending to be Shep the comedian, so it's lucky for you I'm just a regular guy down on his luck. But let's not forget that it was also a generous and selfless gesture.'

'Well, when you put it like that…' I offer him a toothy smile, while cringing a little at his use of the word 'selfless': it's a stark reminder of the fact that I went into this arrangement also seeking something for myself, and I

47

haven't shared that side of things with him (though, who can blame me?). 'Then we're good?'

'We're good.' He gives me a little wink. 'I only nipped out because I was gonna cook us some breakfast, then I clocked that you're low on milk and you didn't have any soda bread.'

'Oh, right. And soda bread is important?'

'It's like a comedian without a decent punchline. Everything falls flat.'

I tip my head back in amusement. 'Noted. So, are you still going to make that breakfast, then? Though I'm not sure I'm in any position to ask.'

'That's enough, you.' Shep gives me a jovial nudge. 'I've got to earn my keep somehow. You up for playing sous-chef?'

'Absolutely.' I clap my hands enthusiastically. 'What does that involve?'

'Making the tea and toast.'

'Think I can manage that.' I head into the kitchen, with him following behind. 'By the way, how did you get back in? You don't have a key… And I thought all your money was stolen?'

'I had some cash stashed away in my holdall, and I left the two doors on the snib. Was only for a few minutes, hope that's not a problem.'

'No, it's fine. But also, where's all your stuff? The spare room is empty.'

He looks at me and chuckles. 'Ever heard of a wardrobe?'

'Obviously.' I facepalm, wishing I'd had the presence of mind to think of that.

After a leisurely breakfast, which by definition turns into brunch, Shep and I hit the sofa with full bellies that leave us capable of doing little else. In addition to checking on his injury from the evening before and trying to persuade him to get it looked at, we've had more of a 'getting to know each other' chat than the day before. I've learned that his real name is actually Ciaran Shepperd (Shep being a nickname he acquired at school), he comes from a small town near Belfast, and his parents, brother and sister still live in that town, just a few streets away from each other. They also all work in the same hospital.

Although I don't like spending so much time alone, the thought of that is suffocating. My parents would have happily kept me at home, commuting to the nearest university, but I knew there was no way I could do that without killing them (not literally, to be clear). It would have been too much at a time when I was finding my independence, so I can fully understand Shep's need to follow his own path, even if that makes him the outcast of the family.

I also learned that he was the class clown in school – so basically a stand-up comedian with an audience since before he hit puberty – and he's been doing gigs in Belfast comedy clubs for eight years, while working as a customer service advisor for a bank. The latter he took on so he could afford to rent a small flat in the city and get away from the 'parental glare', as he calls it.

It was so lovely to have someone to chew the fat with, and I couldn't help but beam with delight in between mouthfuls of my food. It reminded me of my uni days, when there was always someone around to hang out with.

And not only did I have company, but I also learned something new: fried soda bread is indeed the *pièce de résistance* of a cooked breakfast. Who'd have thought it?

'Are you sure you don't want me to take you to the hospital for a check-up?' I say once again to Shep as we're clearing up in the kitchen a bit later on. 'That injury looked bad.'

'I'm grand, honestly,' he replies. 'It's just bruised. Looks worse than it is, and it's not as painful today.'

'OK, but if anything changes you need to let me know. And you need to go to the police and report it. You can't let those thugs get away with what they did.'

Shep shrugs. 'I don't expect the police will do much. They've much bigger issues to deal with.'

'Hmm.' I narrow my eyes at him, aware that some of that self-confessed male pride might be holding him back from coming forward as a victim of violence, but I don't want to push it too hard. 'I hope you will,' I add and then change the subject. 'So, I know I'm not allowed to request comedy on-demand, but I'm super curious about your stand-up career. It's just so different to what I do.'

'What do you want to know?' He hands me the tomato ketchup, which I put back in the fridge, then I pick up the empty egg box from the countertop.

'I don't know... like, where do you get your inspiration from? And what's your on-stage persona or whatever? I won't be using the right lingo, but you know what I mean, right?'

Shep grins at me. 'If you're that keen to see me in action, why don't you come to my show? I think you'll enjoy it. It's great craic.'

I pause, halfway to the recycling bin. 'Really? You'd be OK with that?'

'Why wouldn't I be?'

'I don't know. I wondered if maybe it would be off-putting having someone you know there.'

He laughs loudly. 'Says the woman who keeps reminding me I'm a stranger, and who has on two occasions suspected me of being a conman.'

'That's not entirely true.' I pull a pouty face. 'I only once thought you were a conman. The other time I just thought you'd gone home to Belfast without telling me, and then when you did turn up, I had you pegged as an unreliable roommate.'

'Ah, that's totally different, then.' He mocks me lightly, earning a tea towel in the face as a response. 'Lea, you're fine. You're not gonna put me off. Not unless you're one of those hecklers who make it their mission to destroy comedy careers purely so they can look smart – which they don't. They look like the tools that they are, ruining everyone else's fun.'

'That sounds like a voice of experience.' I load the final dishes into the dishwasher and set it off. 'I don't think you have any worries there.'

'Then you're more than welcome. It's good to know I'll have an audience of at least one tonight – and that I can look forward to your sizeable donation at the end of the show.'

'Oh, you're a cheeky one. A rent-free room isn't enough of a donation?'

'You make a good point. I'll just use you in my show instead, then.' He gives me a cheeky wink and I gulp, wondering what I've just let myself in for.

Chapter 8

Shep's show runs twice a day – once at 4:30 p.m. and then again at 7:30p.m. in a pub near the bottom of the Royal Mile called The Canongate Tavern. At his suggestion, I decide I'll attend the later one, which – based on the handful he's done so far – is apparently a bit livelier. It makes sense, I guess. The later the slot, the more likely it is the audience will have got boozed-up beforehand.

Shep leaves my flat around three p.m. to go and do whatever it is he does to prepare. For all I know, that might be rehearsing his delivery in front of a mirror, practising mindfulness or drinking a couple of pints to take the edge off his nerves – if he has any, as I've seen no sign of that so far. Once he's gone, I use the time to do boring stuff like driving to the supermarket for my weekly shop and doing my laundry. I also get some extra food in for him, so he has something to eat before heading out each day (I offered to do this, and he insisted he'll pay me back once his new bank card arrives).

At around 6:45 p.m., I lock up my flat and pace across The Meadows towards the Old Town. The weather isn't quite as nice as the day before. It's become cloudy and muggy, as if there's a thunderstorm, or at the very least a sizeable downpour, on the way. The air is perfectly still, though, and I enjoy breathing it in, a lightness settling over me that I haven't experienced in some time. I might be heading out alone again this evening, but I do have purpose to my outing, and that makes me feel like I'm leaps and bounds ahead of where I was yesterday.

Keen to soak in the festival atmosphere, I take the scenic route across George IV Bridge and down the cobbled High Street, past the magnificent St Giles' Cathedral and Edinburgh City Chambers, pausing a couple of times to watch the street performers as I go. The area is bursting at the seams with a melting pot of noisy, happy revellers, and in contrast to my lonesome walk the day before, I almost feel part of things as I take in the different accents and cultural backgrounds of the visitors who have travelled here from all over the world.

Arriving at The Canongate Tavern, a traditional-style pub that's had a modern refit of sleek laminate flooring, modish lighting and leather upholstered booths, I order a lime and soda at the bar, then follow the Fringe venue signs through to the back room where Shep's show must be taking place. It looks like the type of space that's normally used for private events – birthdays, leaving dos, that sort of thing. There are several rows of chairs, about sixty seats in total, split by an aisle down the middle of the room, and there's a microphone perched in a stand at the front, ready and waiting for Shep's arrival. Although I'm here fifteen minutes early – heeding the advice of the flyer guy in Bristo Square the day before – I'm pleased to see that I'm not the first. There are already two couples talking in muted tones, and three burly blokes sitting in the front row on the left-hand side. It's clear they've been on the pints pre-show, perhaps all day from the look and sound of them. I find myself thinking that they could be a tough crowd, and hoping they won't give Shep too hard a time. Then my next thought is how odd it is that I've known Shep for little more than twenty-four hours, and I'm already protective of him.

I hesitate, unsure where to sit. If I go for the front row, it'll be a clear show of support for Shep, but at the same time, I'll make myself an easy target for him. I'm not sure whether he was joking earlier when he said he would use me in his show, but I certainly don't want to encourage him. Deciding that he's a big boy with plenty of experience, who doesn't need me there to metaphorically hold his hand, I opt for a seat near the back instead. If I'm lucky, he might not spot me or he might even forget that I was coming along tonight.

By the time the show is about to start, the room is half-full, which isn't too bad. At least it means Shep has a decent enough crowd to do his thing in front of. Waiting for him to make his entrance and take his place behind the mic stand, I'm excited about seeing him in action. But I also feel a bit nervous on his behalf, which I know is stupid, because I'm seeing this situation through my own aversion to being the centre of attention. He clearly loves this world.

Though I should be expecting it, I start when a voice suddenly booms from behind the curtain at the front of the room.

'Ladies and gentlemen, can I please ask you to give a warm Edinburgh welcome to… Shep!'

I giggle as I clock that he's doing his own intro. He might have tried to disguise his voice, but I know it's him. Ah, well, it's not like someone doing free shows can afford to hire an MC for a *Live at the Apollo*-style opener.

Everyone in the room breaks into polite applause as Shep energetically bounds out from behind the curtain, grabbing the mic out of its cradle.

'Good evening, how're you all doing? It's great to see you.' He paces back and forth, smiling at us, no doubt checking out who's in the room and who can be picked on. 'So, I'm a comedian… *obviously*…'

He pauses briefly, still scanning his audience, and I wonder if this might be his way of covering up a faltering start, but then he goes into full flow.

'It's not like you lot have rocked up expecting to see a taxidermist at work. That would be pretty boring, wouldn't it? And a bit creepy. Though the Edinburgh festival has all sorts, so if there is in fact a taxidermy-themed show, don't tell them I said that. I might end up as one of the exhibits.'

A light chuckle ripples through the room.

'You're probably also not used to people announcing their occupations to you like I have. "Hello, nice to see you, I'm comedian." Like when you get on the bus, you don't expect the bus driver to greet you with: "Welcome aboard, I'm a bus driver." I'd say his role in the public transport system is fairly clear, as is mine. No, the reason I'm making a point of saying that I'm a comedian is because the rest of my family, you see… they're all doctors.'

'*Oh.*' A woman in the audience shakes her head sympathetically.

'There we are, right there.' Shep pounces on her. 'What was with the "oh"?'

I feel for her as she squirms in her seat, glancing around uncomfortably. 'Because… you're the odd one out. And no offence, but being a comedian doesn't earn you the same high regard, unless you're on the telly.'

'Exactly that!' Shep points to the woman triumphantly. 'And what's your name?'

'Beth.'

'It's nice to meet you, Beth. Thanks for your honesty.' He smiles at her and then returns his attention to the audience as a whole. 'What Beth here has put way more diplomatically and eloquently than I'm about to is that I'm the outcast of my family... the embarrassment, the one that didn't get a real job, the one that you pretend doesn't exist. Basically, I'm the floating turd of the Shepperd family.'

The audience snickers and I can already tell they're enjoying Shep's dry sense of humour. Sitting forward in my seat, I grin from ear to ear, now imbued with a sense of pride, which again is ridiculous. It's not like he's my son, or my brother or boyfriend. He's just my temporary lodger.

'This week my Fringe accommodation went down the pan,' Shep continues. 'Through no fault of my hosts, they're lovely people, and I send my deepest condolences to them. But I found myself with nowhere to stay, broke, almost cancelling my show. Did my family step up? Did they hell.'

There's a collective 'boo'.

'Oh, don't be so judgemental, I never actually told them about it.' There's a swell of groans at being caught out and Shep chuckles to himself. 'But if I had, I know what the answer would have been. No, the reason I'm still here is because I've got a new landlady and I don't even have to sleep with her to keep my bed.'

'Is she hot?' shouts one of the burly guys from the front row.

'Shall I let you be the judge of that? She's sitting here at the back.' Shep homes in on him, and despite being well-oiled, the man looks mortified but in a taking-the-teasing-well kind of way.

'Lea, why don't you say hello.' Shep's impish gaze lands on me and my face immediately flames as all eyes in the room turn towards me.

'Hi.' I give a self-conscious wave.

'Lea is an angel,' Shep tells the room. 'She's opened up her home to me in my time of need, and she's only accused me of being a criminal once since I moved in. Isn't that lovely?'

The thirty-strong audience laughs while I turn beetroot.

'She also thought I was dead this morning, but that's a story for another time. Give a round of applause to my new landlady.'

Everyone claps and cheers obligingly, while I sink into my seat.

'Sorry, Lea, but you knew you weren't gonna get off scott-free tonight.' Shep grins at me then gets back on track with his set. 'So where were we... ah yes, my doting family. I've actually turned their mockery of me into a sport. You know how, during the pandemic, video-call bingo became a thing? You know, like: "You're on mute again, Moira, you look like a cast member of *The Muppets*." And: "Can everyone see my screen?". "No, we can't but we've got a decent view of your black-heads, have you heard of exfoliator?" Then there's my personal favourite... when someone goes on and on about how wonderful their child is, then said child appears in the background having a really good dig up their nose and snacking on what they find. And we got to enjoy this entertainment even more by marking each of these moments on a bingo card behind our colleagues' backs.'

'Best part of the working day!' another one of the burly guys from the front row calls out.

'I wholeheartedly agree...' Shep nods at the guy. 'Which is why I've started playing "Shep bingo" with my family. It's my way of giving them the finger when they start on about my life choices, without having to lower myself to the level of actually doing it. In fact, I've got so into this game format that I've designed a supersized bingo card for us to use tonight. This one's called "comedy audience bingo".'

The moment he says this, the room fills with yet more groans as everyone, including me, realises they're about to be part of the show.

For the best part of an hour, the room is totally immersed in Shep's performance, getting boisterous and embarrassed in equal measures, picking on each other as part of the bingo game, whooping with awkward laughter at his more controversial jokes, and clapping at the moments we identify with most. He covers everything from being a gawky teenager to the latest political scandals, weaving his stories into each other perfectly and then into a brilliantly clever finale. By the end of it, I really am a beacon of pride as the audience members praise his performance while throwing their donations in the bucket he's holding on their way out.

'Thanks a million,' Shep calls after the last couple as they leave. 'Make sure you tell your friends about me.'

Once everyone has gone, I step forward to congratulate him.

'That was amazing!' I hold a hand to my heart in fangirling adoration. 'You're a total natural.'

'You're saying that 'cause you think you have to. You don't, by the way.'

'I'm not, honestly. My face actually aches. I'm not used to laughing that much.'

'Unsurprising in your line of work,' he deadpans.

'Careful,' I warn him light-heartedly, enjoying the banter. 'Remember I'm the keeper of the keys to your Fringe experience.'

'That, I am acutely aware of. Though I'm guessing from the smile on your face that I got away with ribbing you.'

'I'll overlook it, given it was funny and I was pre-warned.'

There's no way I'm letting on that, when I thought he'd taken off to Belfast without a word, I had a much worse vision of how he might use me in his show.

'Thanks.' He looks into the bucket he's holding to see how generous his audience members have been. 'Geez, they were a great audience but tight as hell. I'll be lucky if that works out as two quid a person.'

'Well, I haven't given my donation yet.' I pull my purse out of my handbag.

'I thought we agreed you giving me a bed for the month was enough.'

'Nonsense. You just put on a belter of a show that was better than some of the ones I've paid for—'

'Just some?'

'Don't push it. You might be the next Dara Ó Briain, but right now you're playing in the little league.'

'Ouch.' He clutches his stomach as if I've physically wounded him. 'Say it how it is, why don't you?'

'I didn't mean it like that. What I mean is that you're good. Really good. And you deserve proper payment for your work.' I take a tenner out of my purse and drop it in his bucket.

'Aww, thanks, Lea. You're a wee star. And I get what you were saying, by the way. I've got a way to go yet.'

'A "way to go" is better than a dead end.'

'I'll drink to that.' Shep lifts his chin as if rising to the challenge. 'Come on, let's get a beer in to celebrate my return to the stage.'

I raise an eyebrow. 'Did you not tell me you never cancelled your show?'

'It's symbolic, Lea. Get with the programme.'

Chapter 9

After enjoying a drink together while dissecting the show
– me playing back the parts I found the funniest and Shep
doing a self-critique of his performance – we head back
to mine, again via the High Street.

Despite the fading light, the long, steep cobbled road
is still bursting with energetic, excitable tourists. It's quite
different to an average Sunday night in Edinburgh, and I
take great pleasure from soaking it all in. It's so lovely to
be out and about on a 'school night', rather than holed
up in my flat, waiting to go to bed. In fact, it's so alien for
me to be doing this that it almost feels a bit naughty to
still be out at ten p.m.

Shep is like a people magnet. He's already made
friends with the bar staff at his Fringe venue, despite only
knowing them about a week, and he even gets chatting
to a group of tipsy women. It doesn't seem to be just his
banter that draws them in, I realise, when one of them
looks me up and down jealously, making it obvious she'd
like to take my place. Which is daft, because Shep and I
are not even together – not that I'm going to let her know
that. The last thing I want is a repeat of the squealing piglet
orgasms that echoed through my flat and that – I swear –
still haunt me in my nightmares.

Making our way along the lit path that crosses The
Meadows, there's a temporary lull in the conversation,

which might have been uncomfortable with someone else, but with Shep it isn't. It's companionable. Glancing across at him, I can tell that there's something ticking through his mind, so I keep quiet, allowing him to process whatever it is he's working through. Instead, I focus on how calm and peaceful The Meadows are at night when you're not rushing through them as a lone female. Not that it's a dangerous place as such, but bad things can happen anywhere (they happened to Shep only the night before), and it can make me feel a bit vulnerable.

'Lea, I can't thank you enough for this.' Shep eventually breaks his silence. 'Thanks for letting me stay.'

'No problem.' My response is breezy and casual. 'I'm happy to help. Probably most people would if they could.'

'But that's the thing, isn't it?' He stops suddenly and I follow suit. 'Most people probably wouldn't help. Because most people wouldn't have approached me in the first place.'

I shrug. 'Maybe you're right. Maybe most people wouldn't have offered to help, but you only needed one person to do that, and I did. So, all is well and good with the world.'

I start walking again, assuming that what I've said will be enough for Shep, but as he grabs me lightly by the hand and our eyes meet, I have a moment of slight panic that he's going to try to kiss me.

'Lea, I'm serious.' His gaze is still on mine and I want to break the moment, but I'm afraid of offending him and making things difficult between us. 'You're treating this as if you've put a fiver in a pot for a workmate's birthday, or thrown some money into a charity bucket. It's way bigger than that. You've given me a chance that my own family wouldn't even give me.'

'To be fair, it didn't involve me shelling out any money like they'd have to, so I'd hardly say it's a direct comparison.'

As soon as I've said this, I wish I could take it back. I'm not one to make insensitive comments, but I'm not exactly thinking straight – I fear that Shep's about to seek my permission to pull me into an embrace and lock his lips on mine, in what would likely be a full-blown case of 'rescue romance'. Wincing, I watch for his reaction, but he doesn't seem remotely fazed by my clumsy comment, which could be a good or a bad thing.

'The level of comparison is irrelevant.' He reaches out and gently takes my other hand in his as well. 'What you've done for me is huge, and no matter what happens with my comedy career, I'll never forget it. I promise you that.'

'OK, sure.' I nod my understanding.

Just as the level of eye contact is burning my retinas to an unbearable level, and my brain is frantically flicking through ways to brush him off without causing too much upset, he lets my hands drop and gestures for us to walk on.

This sudden change of direction from where I thought things were headed throws me, but luckily, I have enough presence of mind not to breathe a ridiculously loud sigh of relief. That's not to say I wouldn't be flattered if Shep did find me attractive enough to want to kiss me; it's just that I don't feel a connection with him in that way, and I think we could become great friends. I really wouldn't want to ruin that by rejecting him, nor would I want the next three-and-a-bit weeks to be super awkward, with us going out of our way to avoid each other. Especially as that's nigh on impossible in a two-bedroom flat.

When we get back to mine, I say good night to Shep and get ready for bed. Then, as I'm lying under the covers, waiting for sleep to come, a thought pops into my mind and my eyes spring open. What if Shep *was* going to kiss me, but he sensed that I wasn't into it? He's told me he's really good at reading people. Did he read my dread? And if so, was he hurt by it? Because hurting him is the last thing I'd want to do.

–

The next morning, I'm back at work with a genuine spring in my step. Not that I don't normally enjoy my job. I do. And I probably spend too much time there – though that's mainly because I don't have much else going on in my life.

Only, now I do! I have a real life, funny as hell comedian as a lodger who, despite me not wanting to kiss him, already has the potential to be an important person in my life – and that's regardless of whether we do or don't stay in contact beyond the end of this month. Because Shep is going to be the next big thing, and when he appears on *Live at the Apollo* and all sorts of humorous panel shows on the telly, I'll be bursting with pride, knowing that I did my bit to help him get there.

OK, maybe that's me getting slightly carried away. A half-full room at the back of a pub doesn't immediately equate to success on a national scale, but those people *were* laughing – a lot. That's got to be a positive indicator. It feels great to be helping Shep go for his dreams, and as a bonus, I have his company for the next few weeks. Thanks to him, Paul the wanker is already a long-forgotten blip on my shabby dating record. Well, 'forgotten' in the sense that I've realised I'm definitely better off without him. However, the humiliation of being used like that, and then verbally attacked for standing up to him, does still hurt.

'Ah, Lea. Paul is a self-serving, morally bankrupt arse-hole. Forget about him,' I scold myself, while perched at the table in the centre of the lab, reviewing my data sets on my laptop.

'Is that you talking to yourself again, Lea?' Tanya suddenly appears from the other side of the lab, scaring the bejesus out of me.

'Oh, my goodness, Tanya! I didn't know you were around. Were you in the other room?'

Please let her have been next door.

'Sorry, no. I've been hiding out, trying to get ahead with the paperwork for the next stage of our research.'

I blanch. She must have heard what I said, and having thought I was alone, it's unlikely that my critique of Paul is all I've vocalised since I got here.

'So, what did Paul do, and do we need to roast his testicles with a Bunsen burner?' Tanya waggles her eyebrows devilishly.

'If only.' I scoff. 'It would certainly stop him bedding poor unassuming women for sport.'

'He doesn't deserve you. On to the next, I always say. There are far too many XY chromosomes in the world to waste time over any one of them. How was your girls' night out on Friday?'

'Oh… eh, Friday turned into a quiet one.' I shift in my seat, uncomfortable about letting my boss think I do stuff I don't, but at the same time not wanting to admit the truth. 'But Saturday was interesting… after I got unceremoniously dumped by the world's biggest… um—'

'Arsehole. Yes, you said. We could always upgrade from the Bunsen burner. I've got a hefty blowtorch in the storage room that would do the job nicely.' Tanya leans in to inspect something in the data set on my screen. 'So, why was Saturday so interesting? Go on, indulge me. You never tell me about your escapades.'

'OK, sure, if you have time.'

'Actually, shall we do it over a coffee? I'm in need of a caffeine boost.'

We make our way along the clinical corridors of the university building to the main cafeteria, which is a large high-ceilinged space with a sea of tables, walls as white and drab as the corridors, and overhead lighting that gives you a headache after five minutes of being there. Queuing up behind a few other staff members I vaguely recognise, Tanya asks me what I'd like and insists on paying for our drinks. She then gestures for me to grab a table, which surprises me, because we normally do takeaway and head straight back to the lab.

A few minutes later, she joins me, carrying a tray laden with two medium Americanos, a couple of sugar sachets and a jug of cold milk.

'We'll call this a review meeting if anyone asks.' She flashes me a conspiratorial smile as she places the tray on the table and slides into the seat opposite me. 'We've been working our socks off lately – you in particular, with all the extra hours you put in – so I think we deserve the occasional coffee break.'

'Fine by me. Thanks for this.' I gingerly take the cup and saucer from the tray, careful not to spill its hot contents, then pour in some milk and give it a stir.

'Come on, then. What was so good about Saturday?' Tanya prompts me. 'I spent mine elbows deep in laundry, some of which would have been better in an incinerator – I have a fifteen-year-old son, if you get what I mean – and arguing with my daughter over the latest body piercing she wants and is *definitely* not getting.'

I chuckle. 'I don't envy you. That doesn't sound like much fun.'

'It isn't, which is why I need to live vicariously through you and the other whippersnappers in this place.' She cocks her head expectantly, her spectacles slipping down her nose as she does.

'Right, well, I'd better give you what you're looking for, then.' I smile and tuck a stray lock of hair behind my ear. 'I was meant to see Paul, but obviously that didn't pan out, as you already know, so I decided to go for a walk, and I met a guy while I was out and about.'

'Ooh. Tell me more.'

'Don't get too excited, because it wasn't that kind of meeting. It was more of a rescue situation. You see, he's a comedian at the Fringe, and he was about to have to pack it all in…'

I tell a riveted Tanya the whole story, including the weird moment between Shep and I the evening before, while she listens intently, sipping at her coffee. I wasn't initially going to mention the was-he-or-wasn't-he-going-to-kiss-me part, but having lain awake fretting over it for too long last night, I've decided I need another opinion. When I've finished telling her everything, Tanya sits back thoughtfully, pondering what I've shared as if considering what scientific-based conclusions she can draw from it.

'You're saying you're not attracted to this man at all. Yet you spent half the night worrying that you'd hurt him?'

She narrows her eyes, as if not quite buying my position on this.

'Yes. I mean, no.' I shake my head and take a sip of my coffee. 'I'm not attracted to him but I still wouldn't want to hurt him. Obviously.'

'Obviously.' Tanya raises an appraising eyebrow.

'I mean it. He's really lovely, and he has a cool Northern Irish accent, but he's not my type.'

'If I may ask, what is your type?'

'Tall, broad and muscular, normally blond or there-abouts. Someone who just needs to look at me and I'm a goner.'

'And how has that worked out for you?' Tanya's mouth twitches at the corners.

I sigh. 'Not well. They generally turn out to be vain and self-involved, and they never stick around. Literally, every guy I've met and liked seems to be just passing through – like Edinburgh is just a stopgap for them. Or I am.'

Tanya gives me a sympathetic look. 'If they always turn out like that, why do you go back for more of the same?'

'Honestly? I don't know. Maybe because each time, I hope it will be different. Or maybe it's a hangover from high school. I wasn't popular and then when I went to uni, I suddenly seemed to be attractive—'

'I'm sure you've always been attractive.' Tanya cuts across me. 'You're a beautiful woman, Lea. Don't doubt that.'

'I mean attractive to that type of guy. You know, the hot sporty ones. The ones who never so much as looked at me before.' I wrinkle my nose, realising how this sounds. 'I've tried to date other blokes. I even went out with a few scientists, thinking there might be more potential with men I have stuff in common with, but we always ended up talking shop. I might love my job, but I also want a life outside of intellectually stimulating conversation. Sometimes I just want to let my hair down and have a laugh.'

'Is there anyone better than a comedian to meet that need?'

'Eh… I guess not.' I deflate all of a sudden.

'Oh, I'm sorry.' Tanya pats my arm in a way that's more akin to soothing a distressed pet than a person. 'I didn't mean to overstep. All I'm saying is that if you're looking for a man who ticks every box in the looks, personality and morals department, you might find yourself on an endless quest.'

'Surely I shouldn't settle, though, either.'

Tanya frowns. 'No one said anything about settling. It's more about being realistic. Does our research ever give us exactly the answers we want?'

'No.'

'Then why would you expect that from your romantic life? The world is a messy place. You're young and aspirational, but what comes with grey-haired wisdom like mine is the knowledge that finding a life partner is more about who you can face life's struggles with – and maybe even laugh about them together in the process – than who fits the right "profile".'

'You don't have grey hair.' I knit my eyebrows together.

'Because I have an excellent hairdresser.' Tanya runs her fingers through her blonde bob as if to highlight this, then drains her coffee at the same time as I also finish mine. 'All I'm saying, Lea, is don't discount a perfectly good option just because you wouldn't ordinarily choose it. Open yourself up to possibilities. That's what a great researcher does, especially when the answers are not forth-coming. Perhaps this young man has everything you never knew you were looking for, but you've got yourself so blinkered you can't see it. Now, shall we get back to the lab?'

Chapter 10

Heading home on the bus after work on Monday evening, I'm pretty beat, not just from my cumulative lack of sleep from the weekend, but because my brain has been working with endless data sets all day. On top of that, Tanya's 'life lesson' from earlier has been rattling round my head, alongside the question of 'did Shep want to kiss me last night?' – and I'm not even sure why I care so much about that. It's all just a bit much, really.

I've tried to see the world through Tanya's eyes, I really have, but no matter which way I cut it, I'm struggling to get to a place where I can imagine Shep's arms around me, never mind swapping saliva and rolling around in bed together. No, this does not seem like an eventuality for us, and the more I consider it, the more I'm convinced I read that situation completely wrong. Shep just wanted to say a meaningful thank you. That's all. There's zero chemistry between us, and if I can see that, then he must be able to as well.

As I walk along my street at around 6:30 p.m., I'm actually quite relieved that Shep won't be there. As much as I'm really enjoying having him around, and will continue to do so, I need to get past these ridiculous inner ramblings about him. A good sleep should do that, so I'll go to bed early, while Shep is still out, and leave him a note saying

I'll see him tomorrow. Then all will be well with our set-up again.

On reaching the main entrance to my building, I insert my key into the lock at the same time as the door is unexpectedly hauled open, taking my hand with it and causing me to stumble forward.

'Shit, sorry, Lea,' Shep's voice greets me, while I re-orient myself and end up face to face with him. 'That was bad timing. You OK?'

'I'm fine.' I smile, trying to hide my awkwardness. 'It's a hazard I'm not unfamiliar with, living in a tenement building.'

'You just getting home from work?' He looks at his wrist, obviously out of habit, because he no longer has a watch to check the time.

'Yes, I work quite long hours.'

'By choice or because you've got a nasty boss?'

'Oh, by choice, for sure. She's great, my boss, though I wouldn't even really call her that. She's a senior colleague who's leading our research project.' I hesitate, unsure what to say next. 'I… um… wasn't expecting to see you here. Thought you'd stay in town between shows.'

'That would be easier, but on my budget, I need to be eating out of a fridge at least some of the time. Plus, if I have too much fish and chips, I'll be developing a pair of gills – and a blocked artery.' Shep taps his chest humorously.

'Fair enough.' I grin at him. 'Are the keys I gave you working all right? I remember one of my previous flat-mates used to complain that the one for the main door would stick in the lock.'

'It is a bit tricky but it's been grand so far. Thanks for trusting me with them, by the way. I know that takes a lot, and it's handy to be able to come and go as I want.'

'No probs. It seemed more logical than kicking you out on the street each morning when I leave for work. Plus, it would have been a right pain trying to co-ordinate our movements, especially when you don't have a phone.'

'I'm getting a new one tomorrow, actually. Was chatting to one of the bar staff earlier and she said she has a spare I can use.'

'That was nice of her. Was that the girl who served us last night?' There's an unpleasant stirring in my gut as I ask this, though I have no idea why.

He shakes his head. 'Nah, that was Jonie. It's Kira who's giving me the phone. She was off last night, but I'm sure you'll meet her at some point, if you can bear to come along to my show again.'

'Are you kidding? Of course I'll come again. I loved it.'

I also want to check out this Kira, a rogue thought hijacks me out of nowhere, causing me to do what can be most accurately described as an inner double-take. Where did that come from? What do I care if there's more than just kindness behind Kira's offer of a phone? It must be the squealing piglet thing haunting me again. Clearly, I don't want Shep for myself, but I also don't want him hooking up with anyone else – because I've agreed that he can stay with me, not him plus one. Is that selfish? Or reasonable?

'Earth to Lea?' Shep nudges my elbow. 'I said you should come again this week, then, if you've not already got plans.'

73

I drag myself back to the present moment. 'Eh… sure, I can come on… um… Wednesday… Yes, that sounds good.'

'OK, great. I'll see you later then, unless you're planning an early night?'

'Early night?' I scoff, feeling myself redden. 'What do you take me for? I'll see you when you get back. Break a leg, eh?'

'Cheers, have a good one.' He starts down the short garden path towards the street, then stops and turns back towards me as I'm about to head inside. 'By the way, I've left you something on the kitchen counter.'

'Oh?' I throw him a quizzical look.

'Just a wee token of my appreciation.' He gives me a little wink then disappears off down the street.

My curiosity piqued, I quickly climb the stairs, unlock the door and go straight to the kitchen, where there's a scrawled note lying on the countertop.

'*Hey, Lea. Thought you could enjoy these with your muckers (that's your closest mates by the way),*' I read aloud, then look around me, puzzled. 'Enjoy what? I don't see anything.'

Aware that I'm missing something, but unable to put my finger on what it is, I pick up the note to see if he's written anything on the back, and when I do, I clock the Fringe tickets hiding underneath.

'Oh, wow.' I pick them up and inspect them.

They're for a comedy show at nine p.m. on Saturday night. The comedian is not a name I know, but I expect Shep will have chosen someone he considers to be good, given he's in the business.

'Well, you're a bit of a sweetheart, aren't you, Shep?' I place a hand on my heart, deeply touched – and a little bit giddy? – by his thoughtfulness.

In fact, I'm so touched by this gesture that it takes a couple of minutes for my mind to catch up on the practicalities of the situation. There are three tickets, and while it was probably quite reasonable for Shep to assume I have friends I can invite along, the reality is that I don't. I could ask Shep himself – but I am so not doing that, because that's about the saddest thing ever. 'Eh, thanks so much for the tickets, Shep. Can you also come with me so I don't have to sit next to two empty seats?' Ugh, no way.

Holding the tickets in my hand, I feel a sense of duty to at least try to use them in the way Shep intended, so I dig my phone out of my bag and ping a WhatsApp to Katie.

> Hiya, don't suppose you and Guy can find a babysitter for Saturday night? I have two extra tickets for a comedy show at 9pm if you fancy joining me? xx

She doesn't reply immediately, which is no surprise, given she'll be in the throes of pre-bedtime activities with her kids. Hopefully, she'll get back to me later, when they're asleep.

Setting the tickets back down on the counter, my next instinct is to thank Shep for such a sweet gesture, but as he doesn't have a phone at the moment, I'm unable to do this. Instead, I get changed and make a poached salmon salad for my dinner, then settle down in front of the television and put on a new psychological thriller series that's trending on Netflix. However, I only make it ten minutes in before my dilemma about Shep's gift starts weighing on my mind again, making it impossible to focus on the plot. This, alongside Tanya's suggestion that Shep could have 'everything I never knew I was looking for' – seriously? – and unexpected musings of who this Kira is, and whether she and Shep have a thing for each other. The latter is purely out of concern that there could soon be a woman I don't know wandering around my flat, and I might become the third wheel in my own home. It's nothing more than that – obviously.

Chapter 11

Tuesday passes more slowly than any day I can remember in my job. Or any job. Or actually any day in my life.

I'm all but totally absent during our morning session to map out the next stage of our research study, and my afternoon is taken up by a disproportionate amount of mind wandering and jumping to unvalidated conclusions about Shep. It's really not like me and, whatever is going on, I need to get on top of it and back on my game before Tanya and the wider group of team members notice.

Except, if I'm honest with myself, I know exactly what's going on. I did go to bed before Shep got back last night, but not because I had an early night as originally planned. No, I stayed up waiting for him to return from his performance because I wanted to thank him for the tickets and check he could actually afford them. I was keen to make sure he wasn't skipping meals or sacrificing other life essentials in an attempt to make up for encroaching on my space. Because he's really not. I also wanted to make sure he knows I don't want or need anything from him in return – except maybe a bit of company, but I'm never going to say that out loud. Only, I never got to say any of it.

I waited up till ten thirty, by which point it had become blatantly obvious that Shep was not just delayed getting home from his show. He was probably out with people or another person – this Kira woman? – and my waiting up for him made me feel like an overprotective parent. So, I went to bed and it took way too long to fall asleep, because every time the door to the main building slammed shut – an annoying habit of some of the night owl-ish residents – I wondered if it was him. Then I would hear the door to one of the other flats close, making it clear it wasn't.

Eventually, I did fall asleep, and was woken at around five a.m. by the sound of Shep tiptoeing around on the creaky wooden floorboards before heading for bed. After that, I lay awake for nearly an hour, wondering where he'd been. I wasn't annoyed that he'd come back so late – how could I be? I'm not his mum or his girlfriend – but I was smarting a little over who he might have been with. Was it Kira? Was it one of his adoring fans?

'*Really*, Lea?' I'd then chided myself (quietly). 'If you don't want him in that way, you need to get the hell out of his business.'

That evening, I return home from work at my usual time, and while it's no different to every other day, my flat feels empty, like something's missing – or rather, someone – which is daft, because Shep's only been staying with me for three nights. It's not like I've had time to get used to him being around. And based on his movements last night, I probably shouldn't expect to. This thought disheartens me a little.

While I'm pottering around, making my dinner, my phone lights up on the kitchen counter, alerting me to an incoming call. Tapping the screen to accept it, I switch it straight to speakerphone.

'Hi, Mum. How you doing?'

'I'm good, honey, how are you?' Her soothing voice fills the kitchen. 'Thought I'd give you a call as I haven't heard from you in a week or so. Is everything OK?'

'Yeah, sorry, I've had a lot going on.'

I normally call my parents every weekend, and also sometimes during the week, so I'm not surprised my mum has picked up on this anomaly. I'm probably more surprised that she's waited until today to check in on me.

'Too much to call your old mum?' she queries, but I know she's being light-hearted and her question comes from a place of concern.

'You're hardly old.' I scoff. 'No, I just had a full weekend and it totally slipped my mind to call. Sorry if I made you worry.'

'I wasn't too concerned. Well, maybe a little. It was your dad… He called and said he hadn't heard from you either, so we thought it might be wise for me to give you a wee bell.'

Her tone is almost apologetic, as if she really didn't want to chase me, but at the same time, her and Dad's protective instincts have overridden any desire to leave me in peace and trust that I'd be in touch soon.

'Mum, it's fine,' I reassure her, while stirring the pasta and sauce I have in separate saucepans on the hob. 'I'm glad you called.'

'Thanks, honey. That's nice to hear. What were you up to at the weekend that kept you so busy?'

I hesitate. Despite knowing what they're like, I never really considered how my parents would react to me inviting a complete stranger to stay with me. It was an in-the-moment decision that's now creating a dilemma for me. While I don't want to lie, I know that telling them about Shep really isn't a good idea either. If I do, they'll be over like a shot, sniffing around him and causing me no end of embarrassment.

'Sorry, give me two secs, I'm just making my dinner while I chat to you.' I stall for time with more pot stirring, while considering the quandary I'm in. 'I... um... My weekend was busy in that I was out and about at the Fringe. The city is hoatching right now.'

'Of course,' says my mum. 'I forgot it's that time of year.'

'Oh, and things didn't work out with the guy I was seeing.' I drain my pasta and dump it in the simmering pan of tomato and basil sauce.

'Did they not? You seemed to like that one... Paul, was it? I'm sorry.'

'Don't be. I'm not. Well, I was at first, but he turned out to be a right piece of work...'

I fill my mum in on the cruel end to my fleeting relationship with Paul the wanker (the censored version, of course), which actually turns out to be a moment of enlightenment for me. It makes me realise that neither Paul nor any of the idiots that came before him would ever have surprised me with Fringe tickets – or even a cheap bunch of flowers, for that matter. Thankfully, this topic of conversation, along with some work chat, keeps her well occupied, meaning I don't need to go anywhere near the whole broke-Fringe-comedian-in-my-spare-room thing. We continue to chat away while I eat my dinner, before eventually saying our goodbyes, with me promising not to miss another weekend call – or to message if I'm busy.

After we hang up, I read my book for a while, then resume the gritty thriller series I only got ten minutes into on my last attempt at watching it. It certainly seems engaging enough and is heralded as having an 'enthralling twisty plot', but despite this, I find myself twitchy and constantly checking the time on my phone.

'Stop it!' I eventually scold myself. 'He might not be back at all this evening, so just get a hold of yourself.'

Hopping off the sofa, I take my phone into the hallway and ditch it on the table there to keep it well out of my sight and reach.

'Why do you care so much anyway?' I berate myself as I return to the living room.

'Why do you care so much about what?' a voice unexpectedly comes from behind me, making me jump.

Spinning round on the spot, I see Shep standing in front of the open front door, which I didn't hear him open, due to being so lost in myself and my stupid thoughts. I really need to fit a bell on that, or something, so I can know when he's there and stop embarrassing myself.

'Eh… hi. I was… just talking to myself.'

'I've noticed you do that. It's kind of cute.' He grins at me and I turn beetroot.

'Perils of living alone.' I try to wave off his comment, but my face is telling another story entirely. 'How were your shows? Good turnout?'

'Better. They're picking up, but I've still a way to go to get a full house.'

'You'll get there. You want some pasta? I cooked extra in case you came back and were hungry. Or are you going straight back out again?'

Please don't be going out. Especially not to meet Kira. Oh, *shut up*, Lea.

'Pasta would hit the spot.' He follows me into the kitchen and leans on the countertop. 'I haven't eaten since breakfast.'

I purse my lips uncomfortably on hearing this, sincerely hoping he didn't go without food because he couldn't afford any. Then I remember about his gift.

'Thank you so much for the show tickets.' I take the extra plate of pasta out of the fridge and put it in the microwave, then turn to him. 'That was really kind of you but totally unnecessary. I want you to know that you don't owe me anything, Shep, and I hope you didn't—'

'Break the bank?' Shep finishes my sentence for me. 'Don't you worry about that. I'm broke, but I'm not that broke. And if you're wondering how I paid for them – not having a bank card and all – Kira ordered them and I transferred the money to her via online banking.'

'I wasn't wondering that.' I try not to have a visible reaction at the mention of Kira's name.

'Anyway, you're welcome. I know you don't want me to feel like I owe you for this, but I wanted to repay your kindness somehow. She's a really funny comedian. Like take-a-change-of-underwear funny.'

'Right. Noted.' I grate some cheese on his pasta then hand it to him.

'Cheers for this.' He grabs a fork out of the drawer and we go through to the living room to sit.

There's a natural lull in our conversation while he tucks into his food, so I switch off my paused thriller and put on *Friends* instead.

'This show's great craic.' Shep is immediately engrossed and I can't help smiling to myself as I watch him guffawing loudly at Ross and Chandler's antics.

This is why the place felt empty. It may only have been three days, but Shep's personality and presence is so big that it fills a room – and it leaves you wanting more when he's not there. It's such a stark contrast to the world I was living in, and if I'm honest, I already never want to go back.

'What's up?' He picks up on me watching him, even though his eyes are still on the TV.

'Nothing.' I bite my lip, becoming aware for the first time that there's a teeny-tiny chance the pull I'm experiencing towards him is about more than just enjoying his company. 'You… um… just have an infectious laugh. I expect that's a helpful characteristic doing stand-up.'

He looks at me. 'Very shrewd. You've spotted my secret weapon.'

'I have?'

'Nah. Though I do turn up the funny when I'm in front of a tougher crowd and it does seem to help. Laughter is infectious, generally, so by enjoying myself while doing a routine, I engage better with my audience and they're more likely to respond positively to my jokes.'

'Really? Is that scientifically proven?'

'Check you, Miss Scientist. Straight on to the validity of my statement.' He gives me a little wink and I blush.

'I'm not doubting you. I'm genuinely interested.'

'Let's say it comes from a single subject study.'

'You mean it's your opinion.' I raise an eyebrow.

'Based on my many years of experience in the field, you cheeky mare.'

'I'm not sure that would withstand much scrutiny, though there have been studies that show that laughter is actually "contagious", so to speak.'

'See, I'm not talking shite.' He holds up his cutlery-wielding hands as if to punctuate this statement.

'I never said you were, and I was only kidding. I get what you mean. The likes of Kevin Bridges and Romesh Ranganathan, they laugh a lot during their stand-up routines. It's almost wicked laughter – and it does draw you in.'

'Two legends. Role models of mine, all right.'

Falling silent again, our attention returns to the TV, and while Shep becomes immediately re-immersed, belly laughing at the comical goings-on, my mind starts to tick over. It's so lovely, sitting here like this, hanging out and sharing a bit of banter. So comfortable and companionable. It feels just right. Almost like we're a perfect match – as roomies anyway.

Where were you last night, Shep? my brain suddenly asks out of nowhere. Were you with a woman? Was it Kira? Will this be a regular thing?

'You're still looking at me,' says Shep out of the corner of his mouth.

'Oh… uh… sorry.' I give my head a little shake to dispel my renegade thoughts which, to my chagrin, seem to deepen my earlier moment of confusion about how I view Shep. 'I'm obviously tired.'

'Maybe get an early night, then? I'm sure me staying here will have knocked your routine a bit.'

He drags his attention away from the screen and as his gaze locks on mine, something seems to pass between us that throws me off course even more: a sort of turbo-charged look that, if I didn't know better, I could mistake for a moment.

'I'm OK.' I break the eye contact between us and tell my befuddled brain to shut the hell up, then I settle back on the sofa beside Shep. 'All I need is a relaxing evening, exactly like this.'

Chapter 12

On Wednesday morning, I find another handwritten note on the countertop when I go through to the kitchen to make my breakfast. This time it's Shep asking if I want to meet him before the show for a fish supper, which makes me smile, because now he has a phone again and we've swapped numbers, he could have just messaged me. Nevertheless, I'm delighted by this invitation, which – not being one for early rises – he must have left there the night before, and I leave him one in return, saying I'll meet him outside The Canongate Tavern at 5:45p.m.

After what feels like the second longest day ever at work, I take the bus into town as planned and arrive at the pub nearly ten minutes late.

'How's about you?' Shep greets me with a laddish grin then spots my confused expression. 'I'm asking how you are.'

'Oh, right… Good, thanks.' I mirror his wide smile. 'Sorry I'm late. Damn rush-hour buses.'

'Are you late? I didn't notice.'

'Oh, well, that's good. I… um…' I continue to smile at him, and suddenly feel myself becoming tongue-tied and unable to finish my sentence.

He gives me an odd look. 'Shall we go get some food, then?'

'Yes. Definitely. Where shall we go? I don't often eat fish and chips, so I don't know where's good.'

'There's a place on South Bridge that's not bad.'

'Great.' I fiddle with my hair, less at ease in Shep's company than I've been previously.

What the hell is wrong with me? I was all weird last night and now this. Am I catching real feelings for him? Was Tanya right? Because all the things that seem to be drawing me to Shep are not the usual magnetics that get me hooked on a guy – like height and 'smoothness' and smouldering rugby-player good looks. Or is it simply that the tables have turned and he doesn't need me so much anymore? Am I now the one needing him? Sad lonely Lea, who just wants someone to hang out with. I grimace at this self-criticism, not liking what it says about me, but at the same time finding it difficult to refute.

'Are you all right, Lea?' Shep peers at me. 'You seem a bit off.'

'Eh, I'm fine.' I force the smile I was wearing before to return to my lips. 'Let's go eat.'

We snake our way through the never-ending flow of tourists to the takeaway on South Bridge. Then, armed with two fish suppers, drowned in salt and sauce, we head across the road to Hunter Square, where we're lucky enough to find a rare space on the steps at the back of the Tron Kirk to devour our food. The lack of interaction caused by my mind having crashed like a faulty laptop isn't much of a problem while we're getting our food and finding somewhere to eat it. However, once we're seated among a sea of happy, chatty people, the conversational lull between us becomes quite obvious.

Munching away on a chip, I try to think of a topic of conversation with some longevity, or even just something semi-interesting to mention, but it's like my brain has gone on strike. It's also clear that Shep has picked up on my strange behaviour and is unsure how to manage this.

'You've never really told me anything about your family.' He finally breaks the silence between us, much to my relief. 'What's your backstory? Better than mine, I hope.'

'There's not that much to tell, to be honest.' I shrug, and unless I'm imagining things, he looks slightly concerned that this is all I'm going to say on the matter. 'I'm an only child, so no brothers or sisters. Growing up, it was just me, my mum and dad... until they split up.'

'Ah, shit. Child of a messy divorce?'

'Yes and no. My parents fought a lot when they were together. I used to sit in my room and cry while they were at each other's throats for hours on end.'

'That's rough.' Shep looks gutted for me.

'It was, but believe it or not, it's not what dominates my childhood memories. One day, I got brave and I came out of my room and shouted at them... like, really went for it. I told them if they hated each other that much, they should get a divorce. So they did. And apart from being constantly shipped back and forth between two homes, it was kind of happy ever after from there.'

'Really?'

'No, not quite.' I chuckle. 'I'm sure they still argued after that, but never again in my presence. They even went to a marriage counsellor at one point, while they were still working through things. Apparently, it helped them see that they still had something major in common – me – and that they could be a strong parental unit, even if they weren't together anymore.'

'Did that work?' Shep glugs from his can of juice.

'It did. The counsellor gave them a "toolkit", which they followed religiously – I think mainly out of guilt that they had caused me hurt – and I swear they then got on better than they ever did. So, really, them splitting up was the best thing that could have happened.'

'That's great that they were able to put you first. It sounds like a no-brainer, but from what I've heard from friends whose folks have divorced, it's often not pretty at all.'

'I've heard similar stories, so I consider myself lucky.' I stab at my fish with my wooden fork, trying to separate off a piece small enough to pop in my mouth. 'It was even quite cool having two bedrooms. The only negative by-product of it all was that, with their focus being entirely on me, they became overprotective and kind of stifled me.'

Shep gives a reflective nod. 'That's not the worst, so long as you still had a chance to spread your wings, so to speak.'

'I did when I moved here. They still worry about me, but they've finally accepted they need to do that from a distance. They're fab parents, really. In the grand scheme of things, I think I've done well with them.'

'Sounds like it. Think I'd rather have what you have than the shitshow that is my family.'

'Yeah, I'm sorry about that.' I furrow my brow sympathetically.

'Don't be.' He nudges me affectionately, making me feel kind of warm and fuzzy, and comfortable in his company again. 'It is what it is. Tell me, do your folks know about me staying with you?'

'Take a guess.'

'That's what I thought. Have they any plans to visit in the immediate future? Not sure I want knocked into next week so soon after last time.'

'Aww, no, don't worry about that.' I giggle lightly, nudging him back. 'My dad works away a lot – I think he's somewhere in Europe at the moment – and my mum would never turn up without making an arrangement first.'

'Good to know.' Shep looks relieved by this. 'Hey, I never asked you if you know Cath Armstrong, the comedian I got you the tickets for?'

I shake my head. 'I don't. But I looked her up on my lunch break and I see she's been likened to Sarah Millican. I *love* Sarah Millican, so that's a good sign.'

'Great, I expect you'll like her, then. Kira's seen her live and thought she was hilarious. It was actually her suggestion to go for that show.'

And just like that, my mood plummets. Nothing could take the shine off Shep's kind and thoughtful gesture more than knowing that his new 'girlfriend' was involved in cooking it up, probably in between making out and doing all sorts that I don't want to think too deeply about.

–

With so much confusion rattling round my head, I'm not able to enjoy Shep's show as much as I did the first time. In fact, I have a hard time paying it any attention at all. This is everything to do with my issues and nothing to do with his delivery, which is as seamless as it was last time. When it's over, I consider heading straight home without waiting around, but I don't want to be rude, so I hang back like I did before.

'Great show, once again.' I touch his arm gently as he waves off his final audience members. 'And almost a full house. That's got to be a good sign.'

'I reckon so. Things are definitely picking up.' He tips his donations bucket towards me and I see that there are several banknotes in there, a far healthier picture than before.

'I'm so pleased for you.'

Despite my low mood, I do 100 per cent mean this.

'So, what are you up to now?' I ask. 'Are you heading back to the flat?'

'Uh, no. I thought I'd hang around for a drink or two. Kira's getting off shift shortly, so I said I'd have a beer with her… um… Do you wanna join us?'

He rubs the back of his neck, which I read as him giving away his discomfort in making this invitation, perhaps because he was planning to spend their time together with his tongue down her throat. My sitting with them like a lemon would ruin that opportunity and probably also the mood. I'm a bit winded by this thought, and it leaves me in no doubt as to what my answer should be.

'Thanks, but no, I'll head off home and leave you to it. I'll see you later – or tomorrow – yeah?'

To my horror, hot tears prick at my eyes, and I find myself praying I can get out of here with my dignity intact.

'Aye, OK.' Shep's forehead creases with what I assume is a guilty conscience.

Quickly turning away before I make a fool of myself, I scuttle through the pub towards the exit, glancing across at the bar as I go. There's a young woman there pulling a pint while chatting to a punter, and as the other servers are both men, it makes sense that this must be the infamous

Kira. Seeing how pretty she is, with perfectly tonged, glossy dark-chocolate hair, full red lips and beautifully applied eye makeup, I make a last-ditch attempt to swallow down my hurt before my face crumples, and I rush out onto the street, letting the door slam shut behind me as I do.

Relentless tears flow down my cheeks while I swipe at them, humiliated by my own behaviour. Pacing up the street, I'm unable to keep my head down as I navigate my way past the other pedestrians, meaning I see all the curious, sympathetic and even pitying looks I'm attracting by being in such a state – again. Eventually, the eyes of the tourists become too much to bear, so I duck inside the entrance to one of the Royal Mile's many old closes to get a hold of myself.

Why am I even crying? Because my temporary lodger has found himself a girlfriend? That's utterly ridiculous. I know I'm lonely and I've latched onto Shep as a short-term relief from the emptiness in my life, but is that really what this is all about?

Or is it that I have actually found 'everything I never knew I was looking for', as Tanya suggested, and realised too late? I mean, Shep is funny – obviously – and great company. He's really thoughtful and good-looking in a non-sporty kind of way, but that's not what I go for – not normally, anyway.

Though right now, I have to admit, I feel far less of an aversion to the idea of kissing him. Actually, I'm almost wishing that he had come after me and swept me into his arms. I'm also now realising that I don't just hate the idea of Kira strutting around my apartment because I don't want to feel like a spare part in my own home – I'm actually suffering from full-on jealousy. I don't want her around, because I think I want Shep for myself.

Wait, that can't be right. How can I have U-turned in this way in just three days? Could I be experiencing similar 'rescue romance' feelings to those I thought Shep might be having for me on Sunday night? Like, because I've been enjoying his company and I'm less lonely, I'm now mistaking these positive sensations for a romantic connection?

'*Arghh*, I don't know,' I wail, attracting the attention of a few people passing the close.

'Lea?' Shep suddenly appears out of nowhere, joining me just inside the entranceway. 'Hey, what's with you? Janusz from the bar just told me you ran out of the place in tears.'

'Nothing. It's nothing, I'm just being daft.' I dab at my eyes with my sleeve.

'This is not nothing. Something's clearly up if you're crying. How can I help you?'

'You can't. Look, I'm fine, really.'

He digs in his pockets, producing a pack of tissues, which he hands to me. 'Here. I'm always prepared thanks to the crappy invention of hay fever.'

'I wouldn't say hay fever was "invented" as such.' I smile pathetically at him through my tears.

'Don't you be going all scientist on me.' He frowns, but his eyes remain kind and caring. 'Especially if you're using it as a diversion tactic. I know when someone's giving me the runaround, so be warned.'

I let out a half-laugh, half-cough as he steps forward and offers me a hug, which I melt into. It feels so warm and comforting, and as he lets me go, I notice for the first time how green his eyes are, and that they sort of glint like emeralds in the half-light. His teeth are so lovely and white as well, and he has this adorable dimple hiding in among his days-old stubble.

'Now, are you gonna tell me what's wrong, or do I have to force it out of you?' He keeps one arm around me, tucking me into his armpit, while I snuggle into him, enjoying this moment of human closeness, despite the turmoil of my emotions.

Realising that I probably shouldn't vocalise anything about being attracted to him until I figure out if these feelings are real, I don't know what to say. The last thing Shep needs right now is further complication in his life, and to be honest, why would he ever choose me over the raven-haired, doe-eyed beauty that is Kira?

'Come on, you,' he coaxes me. 'Don't go disappearing into that head of yours like you did earlier.'

I consider telling him about the fact that I have no one to go to the comedy show with on Saturday, as a way of getting out of admitting what's really going on, but the can of worms that would open would be equally, if not more, painful. I'm terrified he'll think I'm a loser for having no friends to hang out with – and for inviting him to stay to fill a big gaping hole in my life. But at the same time, I can't make up a lie, because that's just not who I am.

At a loss, I gaze up at him mutely with sad, apologetic eyes and for the first time since I met him just a few days ago, I see frustration and borderline annoyance reflected back at me. To my disappointment, he drops his arm from around me.

'OK, I get it,' he says. 'You don't trust me, and I don't blame you. We've only known each other a few days, and perhaps you're regretting inviting me to stay. But the thing is, Lea, I haven't a bad bone in my body. I wish you got that.'

'I do. Honestly, I do.' I try my best to reassure him.

'Are you sure? Because everyone else I've met here seems to trust me more than you do. Kira certainly does.'

I take a faltering breath and avert my gaze. 'Of course she does.'

'What was that?'

'Nothing. Sorry.'

Shep exhales heavily, then seems to come to an agreement with himself. 'Look, I don't want to upset you, Lea, and I don't want you to feel uncomfortable in your own home. There's something going on with you – that's been evident from the first day we met – and while I don't have the right to ask you anything personal, I do have the right to make a judgement on this living situation. I'm clearly adding to your problems, so I think maybe it's best if I leave.'

'*What?*' My mouth drops open with disbelief. 'Where would you even go?'

He shrugs despondently. 'I don't know. Maybe Kira or one of the others might be able to help me out.'

I wince on hearing Kira's name, yet again.

'Anyway, I'm not helping here, so I'll leave you in peace. And I'll get myself packed up and out of your place by tomorrow morning.'

He shoots me what I interpret as a pitying look, then turns to walk out of the close, sending my mind spinning.

Is this what Shep's wanted all along? Has Kira already offered him a bed, and he's trying to find an excuse to go? If that's the case, then nothing I can say will make a difference. Maybe it's for the best. Maybe I've magicked up these romantic notions, because after finding someone to spend time with, I'm losing him so quickly.

But what if I haven't? What if I really do like him? If these feelings are real, then I have to at least test them out before it's too late.

'*Wait*,' I call after him, just as he's about to disappear out of sight.

He stops and turns back towards me, a weary expression on his face. 'What is it, Lea?'

This reaction nearly causes me to wimp out, but I force myself to ignore the anxious churning in my gut. I march right up to him and kiss him, with absolutely no idea how he's going to respond.

Chapter 13

The handful of seconds that pass while I essentially launch myself on Shep are a whirlwind of determination, terror, fear of rejection and then something almost magical. All this causes my limbic system to overload, shutting down my mental faculties, but I immediately tune back in when Shep pulls away from me suddenly.

'Lea, *what the feck was that*?' He takes a further step back, as if to keep me at a physical distance.

'Fuck, I'm sorry.' I rub my face with my hand, feeling a rising panic that I've just made the situation a whole lot worse.

'Seriously, what was that?'

'I don't know. I'm sorry. Can we just—'

'Forget about it?' He pierces me with an accusatory stare. 'Really? That's how you're gonna handle this? By shutting down on me... again.'

Humiliated that Shep didn't return my kiss, my eyes fall to the ground. With my moment of courage having passed, my instincts are screaming at me to do exactly as he's expecting. But I know that if he means something to me in the way I think he does, I need to own this, even if it's not going to lead to the outcome I think I want.

'No. No, I'm not going to do that. Because that would be a really shit thing to do. Shep, I'm... having some complicated feelings... about you.'

He seems taken aback by this. 'Complicated how?'

My face contorts from the agony of having to verbalise all this, when it's evident he doesn't feel the same way.

'Um… OK… this is going to sound really bad, but if I share, I have to share honestly. You're not what I'd usually go for.'

'That's an encouraging start.' He raises a comical eyebrow and I chuckle self-consciously, but at least it lifts the tension between us a little.

'I know. I told you it was going to sound bad, but what I mean by that is, I have a thing for hot, rugby-playing wankers who treat me like shit.'

'You mean the bloke you got dumped by on Saturday.'

'I'm not sure he dumped me. Technically, I'd say I dumped him…' I shake my head to force myself back on track. 'Anyway, that's not the point. The point I'm making is that I have a faulty picker, so I didn't even consider you in that way when we first met—'

'Well, let's not forget that I called you a "weird loner chick".' His mouth twitches at the corners, and I'm so grateful for his sense of humour.

'There is that, too.' I bite my lip in anticipation of sharing the part that will make me feel most vulnerable. 'I thought… no, I assumed that there was nothing between us, and that I was just warming to you as a person… a friend maybe… until I began to realise that maybe there was more to it than that. Oh, and you started dropping Kira's name into every other sentence.'

'You're jealous of Kira?' His face turns incredulous.

'Oh, come on. She's a bloody goddess and you know it. You have eyes.' I fold my arms and can't help a light smirk.

'I'm not saying she's not. She's an out-and-out stunner, and she's great craic.'

'See?' My lip wobbles, as hearing this confirmed out loud makes it ten times worse.

'She's also not into me.'

'How… how do you know that? It certainly sounds as if she is – and like you'd want her to be.'

Shep covers his mouth in what looks like an attempt to hide an amused smile. 'Kira's happily coupled up. With a woman. Her name's Alaija and she seems just as awesome as Kira.'

'Oh.' I flush at this unexpected revelation.

'So, now you know that Kira's not a threat, and you have no one to be jealous of, how do you feel about me? I'll admit that I was wondering for a moment there if that kiss was a stunt to stop me from moving out, or something crazy like that. But that would make no sense.'

On hearing this, guilt sweeps through me and I'm momentarily thrown by how perceptive Shep really is. I'm almost certain that's not why I did it, but I'm starting to wonder if he can read me better than I can read myself. How *do* I feel about him? I need to be sure and not mess him about.

Meeting his gaze, I have a momentary flashback to how good it felt when I kissed him – albeit only for a couple of seconds – and how I saw him differently when he hugged me. And suddenly I'm so clear that I have real feelings for him, I'm terrified I might start to cry again.

'I… uh… I like you. In that way. But I know you don't feel the same and that's fine.'

He narrows his eyes. 'What makes you think I don't feel the same?'

'Maybe because you didn't kiss me back, and then you pulled away from me in disgust?'

'Or... I did kiss you back at first – but you were too wired with adrenaline to tell – and then my brain kicked into gear and I realised I needed some answers.'

'Is that what happened?' I give a hopeful smile.

'What do you think?' He raises his eyebrows at me and I inhale shakily.

That's why I felt something amazing during that kiss. He was kissing me back.

Wetting my lips, I take a couple of tentative steps towards him, eyes locked on his, until he's so close I can feel his breath on my face. He lifts his hand and tilts my chin up towards him, kissing me tenderly at first, then more intensely, sending tingles of desire right through my body. I respond by pulling him into me hungrily, so I can feel every part of him pressing against me. This sends the temperature between us rocketing and leads to us getting friskier than we possibly should in a city-centre alleyway.

–

The next thirty-six(ish) hours are a bit of a blur. With Shep and I sharing a roof, our relationship instantly shifts from amicable landlady and lodger to *Love Island*-style shacking up – except we don't have a massive villa with a pool as our personal playground. We basically have the choice of four pokey high-ceilinged rooms to hang out in. I draw the line at the long narrow bathroom, which has all the practicality of stilettos in a snowstorm. Though I can't deny pondering whether a sexy shower in my tiny bathtub is entirely off the table. In theory it would work, but the reality would more likely see one of us in A&E

with a bruised spleen from an unpleasant encounter with the wall-mounted toiletries basket. Definitely not sexy or romantic.

Shep and I quite literally can't keep our hands off each other, and on Thursday, I'm actually counting down the hours until I can leave work. Just so I can go for street food with him before his 7:30 p.m. show. It's a dizzying experience going from thinking you don't see someone that way, to thinking they're the sexiest person on the planet, while also finding out you're a perfect match in every way – including in bed. So much so that I've had to keep checking in with myself to make sure what I'm feeling is real, and I'm not just using Shep as a convenient and temporary cure for my loneliness.

But it is real. It's like I've been a blinkered cart horse, trotting after all these blokes who met a narrow set of criteria, but who were ultimately poor choices for me.

Shep is fun and thoughtful – so thoughtful – and he seems to think I'm irresistible, which is quite a nice boost to my withered self-esteem. He also has an almost superhero-like ability to send waves of butterflies and naughty tingles through me with nothing more than a glance. The more I look into those gemstone-green eyes – especially when we're moving in perfect rhythm together – the more physically attracted to him I become. He's basically the human equivalent of catnip (to me, anyway).

–

Waking ahead of my alarm on Friday morning, after yet another late but incredible night together, I rub my bleary eyes, promising myself that I'll get some proper sleep this weekend. However, this resolve weakens the moment I roll over and see Shep beside me.

'Morning, sexy landlady.' He smiles at me sleepily. 'You're not getting up already, are you?'

'Soon.' Shifting across the bed, I snuggle into him while he wraps his arms around me tightly.

'You're a great teddy bear,' he murmurs contently, and I frown.

'I'm not sure how I feel about that. Makes me sound very unsexy.'

'OK, how about… you're an off-the-scale, smokin' hot teddy bear?'

'I'll take it.' I giggle, as he smothers my neck with butterfly kisses.

'When do you actually need to get up?'

'I could stretch it to twenty minutes at a push.'

'That's more than enough time.' He intensifies his kisses while his hands roam freely, causing me to gasp with pleasure, before I push him onto his back and straddle him.

Fifteen minutes later, after a brief but blissful morning workout, I get myself showered and changed – and, on joining Shep in the kitchen, I discover he's made me breakfast.

'Oh, thank you.' I kiss him on the lips, while he slips his arms around my waist.

'Anything for my sexy landlady.' He squeezes my bum and pulls me in for a full-on snog. 'You gonna come by the pub later, after my evening show?'

'No, I'm going to come before your early show and hand out some of your flyers on the street.'

'You are, are you?' He seems surprised, but also chuffed by this announcement.

'Yes.' I give a firm nod. 'I had some flex time built up at work, so I'm taking a half-day today. Normally, I don't bother taking any time back, but Tanya suggested I go and enjoy the festival.'

'So… you're gonna do that by handing out my flyers? I expect that's not quite what she had in mind.'

I shrug. 'It's up to me how I spend my free time, and this is how I want to do it. If you're going to make the big time, people need to know about you, so I'm going to do my bit to help that along.'

'You're quite the little diamond, aren't you?' He spins me round affectionately and I flutter my eyelashes.

'I have my uses.'

We share another lengthy smooch, then I dig into the toast and peanut butter he's made for me.

'I thought maybe we could grab some lunch together as well?' I suggest. 'You up for that?'

'Sounds great.' Shep puts the jar of peanut butter back in the cupboard. 'Maybe George Square Gardens? There's plenty of choice there.'

'Perfect, I'll message you when I leave work, then.'

'Looking forward to it. So, what's the plan for you and your muckers tomorrow night? Dinner first, maybe? Drinks after the show?'

I stop mid-chew. Crap, I forgot about that. I've still not heard back from Katie, which is an answer in itself. She won't be ignoring me, she'll just have forgotten to reply.

'I… um… I'm still working on it.'

'What does that mean?'

'It means what it means. I haven't quite nailed things down yet.'

'Right, sure.' He wipes some toast crumbs from the counter and dumps them in the bin. 'I was just thinking, maybe I could join you if you're doing something after? It would be nice to meet your mates.'

'Really?' I chuckle awkwardly, while squirming inside. 'You want to meet your landlady's friends?'

'No, I want to meet my sexy-landlady-who-I'm-sharing-a-bed-with's friends. You can find out a lot about a person from who they hang out with, and I'm keen to get a window into who you are.' He flashes me an appraising smile.

Shep obviously doesn't mean anything by this comment. How could he? He knows nothing of my life beyond what I've shared with him, but my shame-ridden hackles rise up all the same. What does it say about a person, then, if they have no friends to hang out with? If they spend most of their time alone, wishing they had? Does it mean they're a loser? A loner? A 'weird loner chick'? Shit, he's made me paranoid with that comment.

'So, what do you say?' Shep breaks through my torturous inner dialogue. 'Can I come play after the show?'

'We'll see.' I pull away from him and focus on my breakfast.

'Hey, what's eating at you?' He strokes the back of my neck in an attempt to soothe me.

'Nothing. I'm just… It feels a bit too soon to introduce you to anyone in my life. We've only been doing "this" since Wednesday – evening – so can we maybe have some time just us before we put ourselves out on show?'

'Aye, grand.'

Shep seems a bit baffled by my reaction, but I don't have the time or the inclination to start unpacking things with him right now. It's looking like it's going to be me 'plus none' for tomorrow's show, and I really don't want him to know that – or, more importantly, why that is. I did consider skipping it altogether, but he'll undoubtedly ask what I thought, and it was such a thoughtful gesture, I can't let the tickets go to waste.

'Look, don't take it to heart, yeah?' I swallow down the last of my breakfast and give him a peck on the lips. 'I don't mean it in a bad way. I'll see you at lunchtime. Make sure you have a stack of flyers ready for me for after.'

Chapter 14

Five hours later, it's become a beautiful, warm, sunny day, I've done half a day's work and I'm wading through the soup of festivalgoers as I approach George Square Gardens, which, in my opinion, is one of the best Fringe venues in the city. Entering the gardens through the narrow gate takes a few moments, due to the sheer number of people coming in and out, but once I'm inside, I'm greeted with a full-on festival atmosphere. The vast grassy area is jam-packed with people sitting at picnic tables or on the grass itself, eating, drinking, laughing and generally having a great time. It's so busy that it reminds me of a *Where's Wally?* illustration. It's also a very freeing sight and it immediately makes me smile. Looking around, I see a mouth-watering array of street-food stalls lining the perimeter of the gardens, churning out aromas of woodfired pizza, loaded fries and Asian spices.

I can see Shep standing off to the left, away from the steady stream of people, and the sight of him lifts my mood even further. That is, until I remember our conversation this morning.

I managed to get him off the idea of coming along to meet my non-existent friends, but my excuse was pretty weak. What if he asks again? I guess the best thing I can do is stay off the topic of my 'girls' night out' until after the fact. Then I can talk enthusiastically about the show, keeping the focus on that and his kindness in gifting me the tickets, while ensuring that the topic of my company is avoided completely. That will work, right? It kind of has to, because I'm not going to make up two imaginary friends and lie to his face.

'How was your morning?' I give him a quick kiss when I finally reach him.

I'm expecting to be greeted with his usual bright eyes and broad grin, but his characteristic bounce is distinctly absent.

'It was grand.' His tone is unmistakably flat. 'How was yours?'

I hesitate, thrown by his mood. 'Erm... it felt *really* long for a half-day. Probably because I was looking forward to getting away. Are you OK?'

'Yeah, I'm just tired.'

'Right. Shall we get some food?'

We do a lap of the food outlets to decide what we're having, but the conversation between us is somewhat stilted. It feels quite clear that Shep is not 'just tired', or at least he wasn't when we first got up this morning.

'Are you sure everything's OK, Shep? You seem a bit distant.'

'I'm grand.'

OK, that's been two 'grands' and not much more since we met up: there's obviously something wrong.

'Has something happened?' I probe gently. 'Maybe with your family? Or your show?'

'Nope. Nothing like that. Let's get some food in, then we can talk.'

'Um, sure.'

I feel like I've been knocked on my arse. What's going on with him and why do we need to talk? This is not the romantic al fresco lunch we had planned, it's more like... *oh, no*. He's about to ditch me. How can it be anything other than that? Dread settles over me, along with a slightly panicky sick feeling. I haven't given any thought to where this thing between us is or isn't going. It's too soon for that and I'm well aware that Shep's only here temporarily. However, judging by how my heart is racing, and not in a good way, one thing is clear: I must be developing feelings of some significance for him, because the idea that he's about to dump me is stirring up a wasps' nest of unpleasant sensations inside me.

We decide on pizza, as it's the nearest food stand, rather than because we've been enticed by the delicious aroma coming from the woodfired oven. Waiting for our food in silence, I attempt some further small talk, which Shep barely engages with. It's so painful, I almost walk off and leave him standing there, but I know that's not fair. If he's had second thoughts about us, and decided it's best if we take a step back, then I have to at least give him the chance to explain.

After what feels like an age, but in reality is only about ten minutes, our names are called and we seek out a patch of grass to sit on. Settling down on the ground, in among all the banter and laughter of the hundreds of people around us basking in the sunshine, I decide I can't take the silent treatment any longer. If this is over, then I don't want it strung out.

'Shep, what's going on?'

'Can we eat first?' He opens his pizza box and inspects the contents.

'No, we can't.' I reach across and close it back over again. 'I'm not good with being left hanging when I know there's something wrong.'

'But you're quite happy to leave others that way?'

His comment stings, but I can hardly contest its accuracy. I've been holding onto my own stuff in spades since I met him.

'That's fair,' I concede. 'The thing is, though, if you're going to break things off, then please make it quick.'

I'm hoping he's about to tell me not to be daft and ask where I got this paranoid notion from, but he doesn't. Instead, he looks pained, confirming my fears.

'Shep, please?' I prompt him.

He looks away for a moment, then his gaze lands on mine. 'Lea, I've spent too many years feeling inadequate because of what I want to do with my life.'

'Because of your family, I know.' I furrow my brow, wondering what he's getting at. 'What's that got to do with us?'

'When I asked you this morning if I could join you and your mates tomorrow night, I saw it. I saw your reaction.'

'Wh-what do you mean?' I stammer.

'I mean how horrified you seemed at the idea, then you covered it up by telling me it was too soon.'

'It is quite soon.' I attempt to defend my position.

'Maybe.' He gives a sceptical shrug. 'But that wasn't the real reason, was it? Be honest. You don't want your friends to know you're sleeping with your charity-case lodger. The shame was written all over your face. I can't be with someone – even in a casual way – if I feel like I'm their "dirty little secret".'

'That's what you think?' I rub my jaw, perplexed by what I've just heard.

'I know I'm not imagining this, Lea. Don't try to make out that I am.'

My head is full, Shep's accusation catapulting round my brain. He's tuned into my shame and embarrassment, but reached completely the wrong conclusion. And now he's breaking things off for a reason that isn't real. What do I even do with this? I don't ever want him to think I view him as some kind of lesser being, because I simply don't. I have nothing but admiration for him.

Anxiously tapping my fingers on my pizza box, I take a shaky breath, then look him straight in the eye. 'Shep, you're right, I do feel ashamed, but not in the way you think. I'm... I've...' I trail off, unable to say the words out loud.

'What, Lea?' His frustration with me is evident. 'If I've got this wrong then tell me what's really going on. I think, given what's happened between us the last few days, that I do have the right to ask.'

'You do.' Tears well in my eyes and I try to blink them away. 'Of course you do. Look, the thing is... I've got no friends, OK? I mean, I've got friends in the sense of people I grew up with and went to uni with, but they all live elsewhere, or have moved on with their lives. I don't have anyone to share those tickets you gave me with. That's why you can't come and meet me and my friends after the show. Because I don't have any.'

Hanging my head, my tears spill over, and I can't bear to look up and see the inevitable disbelief on Shep's face – along with the rushed judgement that this is the real reason I invited him to stay. His final confirmation that I'm a 'weird loner chick'.

In the following moments, Shep doesn't say or do anything – to the point that I wonder if he's got up and left. Daring a glance in his direction, I can see he's still there, but he looks taken aback and conflicted. My bets are on him wanting to do a bolt, but wondering how bad a person it will make him if he does.

'Say something, will you?' I eventually pipe up, unable to take the silence any longer. 'Or just leave, if that's what you want to do.'

'Shit, sorry, Lea,' he says as if he's suddenly remembered I'm there. 'I was so convinced I was right about your reaction this morning that it threw me when you said all that. And I'm not gonna lie, it's also made me wonder—'

'If I only invited you to stay so I wasn't on my own anymore?'

'Uh… yeah.' He winces and I'm unsure whether this is because he feels bad for asking this question or if he's worried he's right. He might also be wondering whether this 'thing' between us is even real.

'It wasn't my main reason. I did want to help you, but I'll admit it was an added bonus.' I press my hands against my burning cheeks, unable to look at him, and my deep-seated vulnerability seems to properly wake him up to the situation.

'Ah, hell, what am I even doing asking you that?'

'It's a fair question.'

'No, it's not.' He gives a determined shake of his head. 'After the kindness you've shown me, and the way we've… you know… connected… it's wrong of me to doubt you.'

'I don't think so.' I pick at a hangnail on my index finger, still finding it difficult to make eye contact with him. 'You may have jumped to the wrong conclusion, but you wouldn't have done that if I'd been open about my situation in the first place. This is my fault, Shep. I'm sorry, I completely understand you thinking I'm a loose cannon.'

'I don't think you're a loose cannon. I'm just trying to take all this in and catch up to the place you're at.'

My stomach emits a hungry grumble and my gaze shifts to my pizza box, but I know this has to be straightened out before I can eat. He's already nearly walked once, which means I need to share fully and completely this time or I will lose him.

'Let me help you with that then.' I shift my position so I'm sitting cross-legged and facing him. 'When I saw you looking so miserable last Saturday, I didn't approach you because I wanted company, I did it because I could feel your pain. I was in a similar place myself, but for different reasons.'

'You mean because you'd broken up with that rugby bloke?' Shep asks.

'Yes and no.' I bob my head side-to-side in a non-committal way. 'It was more than that. He'd used me, and that made me feel like shit, but also, I had no one to talk to about it. I'd tried to reach out to my oldest friends, but they were busy, and there was no way I was sharing all the gory details with my parents. I just felt really alone. More so than usual. I came out on my own because I couldn't bear sitting in my flat by myself when it felt like I was the only person in this city who wasn't out having fun.'

'I can see how it would feel a bit like that, living on the doorstep of all this.'

'Anyway, the God's honest truth is that I only really wanted to help you. You needed a place to stay and I had a spare room. It's as simple as that. Did I also like that I would have some company for a few weeks? Of course I did. I'm only human. But there were no ulterior motives, and there was nothing sinister about it. I didn't plan to lure you back to mine and then bed you. I genuinely didn't even fancy you—'

'You've mentioned that before. Let's not rehash the things we don't need to.' Shep runs what appears to be a self-conscious hand through his floppy brown hair, making me smile.

'OK, we'll not labour that point, but I suppose what I'm trying to say is that when I realised I might like you in that way, I almost didn't do anything about it. I wasn't entirely sure if those feelings were real, or if I was just enjoying having you around.'

'So that's what you meant when you said you'd been having "complicated feelings" about me. I thought that was an odd way of phrasing it.'

I nod. 'Yes, that's what I meant, but I didn't think it would help to go into detail at that particular moment.'

'You do fancy me, though, right? Don't tell me you're still not sure, because I've used my very best moves with you.' Shep obviously intends this as a joke, but by the looks of things, he's actually semi-serious.

'Do you still want me to? Or is that your ego talking?'

'Does a deer shit in the woods?'

'I thought it was a brown bear.'

'It's the UK version. Come on and catch up,' he deadpans, and I laugh.

'OK, but given I've just bared my soul to you, I could do with a straight answer.'

'Fair point. Of course I bloody want you to. I fancy the pants off you, especially those nice lacey blue ones you have.'

'They're teal,' I correct him.

'I don't give a shit what colour they are, it's what's in them that I'm interested in. Come over here, you.'

The remaining tension between us finally dissipates as delighted relief washes over me and I shuffle across the grass towards him. He pulls me in close, kissing me slowly and intensely, which I take as his way of showing me he's all in. My body responds by melting into him, enjoying the closeness and the feel of his lips on mine. There's also the citrusy scent of an eau de toilette I'm not sure I've smelled on him before, which lifts my senses further, making me even hotter for him.

When we break apart, I'm smiling but I'm not yet fully at ease, because there's one aspect of our conversation that's not yet been addressed.

'Lea, I'm sorry about your situation. I can understand why you felt uncomfortable about sharing, given the circumstances of how we met,' Shep says, as if reading my mind. 'Do you not have workmates you can go out with?'

'Not really.' I shake my head. 'They're all older than me. They have families. Tanya, our research fellow, has this idea in her head that I'm out every weekend with a pack of "gal pals". I never corrected her, and she just assumes I have this great social life.'

'What about activities or hobbies outside of work – sport even?'

'I did try a few meet-up groups and recreational classes, but I never clicked with anyone to the point we made plans to hang out, so I gave up. I'm just not the type to go out and manufacture friendships – it's really uncomfortable – and I guess I'm not someone who people are naturally drawn to either. It makes me feel like a bit of a loser if I'm honest.' My cheeks colour at this admission and I immediately regret sharing it.

'Hey, no it doesn't.' Shep gives me a squeezy hug. 'And for the record, I felt drawn to you last Saturday – once I got past myself.'

'Really?' I look at him with hopeful eyes.

'Really. You're fun – and you're also top-notch in bed.'

'*Oi.*' I bat him playfully on the shoulder. 'I thought you were actually saying something meaningful there.'

'I was. Then I made it smutty.' His eyes sparkle with mirth. 'It's an occupational hazard, but I meant it all. Honestly, you've nothing to be ashamed or embarrassed about. I've seen stuff in the news about loneliness being on the increase among young adults, so you're not alone in feeling alone. I'm lucky in that I have plenty of mates back home—'

'I knew you would.' I say this almost resentfully, then put my hand to my mouth apologetically.

'It's OK.' Shep takes it in his and kisses it. 'What I was saying is that I have a lot of mates back home, but within my family, I feel alone. When I found myself with nowhere to stay and facing having to go back, I felt really alone. Loneliness comes in many shapes and forms. It can also be about thinking no one understands or supports you.'

His words are like a cosy blanket, providing welcome and much needed reassurance.

'Gosh, Shep, I've never thought about it like that before. Thanks for making me feel less like the odd one out.'

'You're welcome.' He leans in and kisses me again. 'Now, shall we eat this pizza before the ants beat us to it?'

Chapter 15

After overindulging in our pizza picnic in George Square Gardens, Shep and I decide we need to walk some of it off, so we reluctantly leave our sun-kissed patch of grass and head across to the Old Town. Taking a slight left at Greyfriars Bobby, we wander down Candlemaker Row to the Grassmarket, with its historic marketplace and old tenement buildings, some of which date back to the seventeenth and eighteenth centuries. The place is brimming with wide-eyed tourists watching the street performers and taking selfies, and Shep insists we do the same.

One photo session and a performance by a rather talented magician later, we make our way along West Port and down Castle Terrace, where the castle itself strikes its most majestic pose for the city's visitors. I note that it looks particularly good today, framed as it is by the bright blue summer sky behind it. We then stroll along Princes Street, enjoying the visual contrast between the lusciousness of East and West Princes Street Gardens, and, behind them, the earthy volcanic crag and tail on which the castle and the Royal Mile are perched.

It's an amazing day to be out and about, and it's even better to be enjoying it with someone I can't get enough of. I feel almost smug, walking along the street holding Shep's hand, with him giving mine a little squeeze whenever he spots something interesting or entertaining, or even just as a show of affection. Those ones are the best, because they come with a look that makes me feel like I'm the only woman in the world.

Not that I need that validation, but after going out with one wanker after the next, it's just so lovely to be spending time with someone so thoughtful and 'un-self-indulgent'. Being out with Shep like this, it feels less like dating and more like being in the early stages of a meaningful relationship.

'You grand?' Shep glances at me as we're passing the iconic Jenners building on one side and the Scott Monument on the other.

'I'm good.' I chew my lip, self-conscious all of a sudden, as if he might read my mind and decide I'm getting too keen.

'Want an ice cream in the gardens before we head to The Canongate Tavern? I think we can justify it after all that walking.'

'Do I ever.'

'All right, then. My treat.' He pulls me into a hug, planting a kiss on the side of my head, while I giggle delightedly – and in one fell swoop, I'm a total goner.

-

An hour and half later, I've handed out almost all the flyers that Shep had ready for me at the pub. I'm not sure whether I'm actually allowed to give them out, not being one of the official Fringe staff, but I can't see how it would do any harm. It's not like I'm trying to fleece people or mislead them in any way. Shep's show is legit and it's free, plus he needs all the help he can get to put his name out there.

'You in the mood for a free comedy show?' I hold out my remaining two flyers to a small group of middle-aged tourists. 'It's a belter. Starts in ten minutes just down the street.'

'We're off to get sushi,' says a woman with an American accent and sunglasses that are so oversized, they almost look like those novelty ones. She takes the flyers from me, inspects them and hands one of them to a man in the group. 'Maybe tomorrow. Or Sunday.'

'He's not on tomorrow,' I clarify, in case they didn't read the flyer properly. 'But he is on Sunday. Hope to see you there.'

Waving them off with best wishes for their sushi experience, I leave my spot on the bustling junction between North Bridge and South Bridge, and make my way back down Canongate, crossing my fingers that Shep will finally have his full house. There have been only a few remaining seats at the last couple of performances, so hopefully this bit of extra promo will fill them.

On entering the pub and queuing for a drink, I note that the place is busier than usual, which pleases me – and will likely please the pub owner too. With it being out of range of the key Fringe locations, it doesn't do quite as well as other pubs further up the Royal Mile, which are constantly stowed out.

'You've done a great job,' Kira says when she comes to serve me. 'It's a full house. I'm not sure you'll even get through the door.'

'*What?*' I give her a disbelieving look and march through to the back room to check.

Sure enough, the place is full. Not just every seat taken, but there are also about ten people standing at the back, which may or may not be allowed, from a health and safety perspective. I really can't get through the door.

'*Fantastic.*' I clap my hands with delight and return to the bar, where Kira's now serving another customer.

'Sorry about disappearing like that,' I say when she comes to serve me again. 'It's proper packed out in there. You're right, I can't get in. I've seen it twice already, though, so it's no biggie. I'll just sit here and wait for him to finish.'

'As I said, great job.' Kira offers me a sparkly wink with one of her immaculately made-up eyes. 'What can I get you? This is on the house, by the way, for all the extra business you've brought in.'

'Wow, thank you.' I'm touched by this gesture. 'I'll have a lime and soda, please.'

'You don't want a real drink? I don't think I've ever seen a person opt for a soft drink as a freebie. Obviously, if you're teetotal or something, that's totally fine, though,' she adds, I'm guessing to avoid offending me.

'Oh, why not, then. I was just being polite. I'll have a G&T, thanks.'

'That's more like it. Take a seat, I'll bring it over.'

Grabbing one of the two remaining tables in the bar, I smile to myself while I wait. It feels great to have helped Shep out. He really deserves this opportunity, so I need to do more of that.

'Here you are.' Kira sets my drink down in front of me. 'There's another with your name on it if you want one – that's by order of the owner.'

She nods in the direction of the bar, where there's now an older man standing behind it. He gives me a friendly wave, which I return, mouthing, 'Thank you,' at the same time.

'You and Shep make a cute couple.' Kira hugs the now-empty tray she's holding.

'Thanks.' I blush. 'He's really sweet and fun… and totally addictive. I'm so glad we've met.'

'So is he.' She gives me a knowing smile, making me wonder what he's said to her. 'Anyway, I'd better get back to work. Enjoy your drink and let me know when you want another.'

Taking a long sip, I sit back with a satisfied sigh. I can hear Shep's audience laughing and whooping over the noise in the main bar, and it fills me with joy knowing he's being discovered by all these new people. It's a huge step forward for him, building a fan base outside his home city. I'm also pleased at how well I'm getting on with Kira since Shep introduced me to her after our first kiss. Funny how people always seem much nicer and more approachable when you don't consider them a threat. I cringe, feeling silly about how I got myself so tied in knots over her, and as I do, she looks across and gives me a thumbs up, which I return somewhat sheepishly.

–

When Shep's show is over, he bounds across to me, shaking his donations bucket.

'Um… it's not making any noise.' I straighten up, trying to peek over the edge. 'Is there nothing in it?'

'It's all notes.' He all but shoves it in my face, forcing me to draw back a little.

'What? No coins at all?'

'Not one. Not even euro cents. No bloody super-market shopping-trolley tokens—'

'Someone donated a shopping-trolley token?' I look at him in amazement.

'I've had several. Think some tight-arsed people use them to make it sound like they've made a proper donation.'

'That's so cheeky.'

'And not the half of it.' He scoops up the notes, shoves them in his pocket and puts the bucket down on the floor. 'Have I not told you about the half-pack of chewing gum, the empty nasal-spray bottle and the strawberry-flavoured condom I received?'

I snort with amusement. 'Adoring fan making a hint?'

'I dunno.' He shrugs. 'Never saw who threw it in the bucket. Anyway, you know what this means, don't you?'

'That you'll have lighter pockets walking home?'

'No. It means I'm worth paying for. If people are putting notes in, it means they've really enjoyed my show.'

I'm delighted by this and by his supersized grin. 'That's brilliant, Shep. Though I never doubted for a second that you're worth paying for.'

'Sometimes I have.' He looks into his bucket solemnly and I can almost see the wind dropping from his sails.

'Aww, come here.' I beckon him to come sit and he settles down beside me. 'That's because of your family and their bloody great superiority complexes. If they could get over themselves and come and see you perform, they'd get that this is your path in life, and see how much you're in your element when you're doing your thing.'

'Cheers, Lea. I'm glad you believe in me.' He places a limp hand on my thigh and I grasp it tightly.

'It's not just me who does. It's all the people who just rewarded you for a job well done. Focus on that. Not on jumped-up family members who can't see beyond the end of their stethoscopes.'

'I see what you did there.' His mouth twitches at the corners, but he's obviously still troubled. 'You're right. I should focus on the positives – they're what keeps me going. Thanks for the perspective.'

'Attaboy.' I squeeze his hand even more tightly in a show of solidarity and as he kisses me softly, my whole body lifts, making me feel like I'm floating on air.

'Want to get a drink here to celebrate your success?' I ask when we break apart.

'Damn right.' He glances across to the bar where Kira's standing, waiting for her next customer, then turns back to me. 'Actually, shall we go next door for a change of scenery?'

'Oh, you don't need to do that, Shep. I'm totally over the Kira thing.'

'I should hope so, given I'm about as attractive to her as a dose of scabies.'

I snicker. 'All right, I obviously didn't need to voice that one, but… isn't going next door a bit like cheating on this place? They just gave me free drinks for bringing in extra business.'

'I'm sure they'll live. Much as I like the place, it's a bit like being at work. I like to experience other places, you know.'

'And going next door is really branching out.' I raise a cheeky eyebrow.

'Watch it, you.' He tickles me, making me squeal, and almost everyone in the pub turns to stare at us.

'OK, let's go. *Now*.' I get up and walk out of the bar, hot with embarrassment.

A little over thirty seconds later, we're pushing open the door to the Old Town Inn, which is a traditional Scottish boozer – it's smaller and cosier, with a real cast-iron fireplace, natural wooden floorboards and tartan uphol-stery. It's also quieter, almost peaceful, with the people inside talking in hushed tones. I instantly love it and I can see the appeal for Shep. While The Canongate Tavern is nice, with its modern laminate floors, leather seating and upbeat background music, it's less 'leisurely pint' and more 'let's chase our Guinness with tequila shots' – which is probably exactly what the owner is aiming for with the amount of stag and hen dos that descend on the city year on year.

'What would you like?' I pull out my purse, ready to make our order.

'No way, this one's on me.' He takes it from me, shoving it straight back in my bag.

'Shep, no, let me buy you a drink to celebrate. You just had your first full house and it was a roaring success.'

'Lea, my show was only bursting at the seams because you literally went up the road and got me my audience.'

'That's not true.' I wave his statement away. 'You were only a few seats away from a full house before that. All I did was help to fill them.'

'And the ten-person space at the back.' He gives me a pointed look. 'You turbo-charged my audience so I want to buy you a drink as a thank you. Just like the folks next door did, and which I will point out – before you start to protest – you happily accepted.'

'OK, sure, buy me a drink, then.' I beam at him, already plotting to buy the next round. 'Though, to warn you, I'm going to keep handing out your flyers and I don't want you to buy me a drink every time. I'm doing it because I want to support you, so let me.'

'Fine by me. I'll happily take the bigger audiences… and I'll find other, naughtier ways to thank you.' His face spreads into an impish grin and I swear I nearly drag him straight back outside for a rerun of our frisky antics from the other day.

Chapter 16

Forty-five minutes later, we're on our second drink and I'm nicely chilled out, except for one thing: I made the age-old mistake of 'breaking the seal' too early.

'I need to pee again,' I announce to Shep, getting up from my seat.

'Again? You only went fifteen minutes ago.'

'And I'll be going a lot more before the night is out.' I nuzzle my face against his, stealing a kiss before tottering off contently to the ladies.

After doing my business and touching up my eye makeup, I return to our table to find Shep at the bar, chatting to two women who must have just walked in.

'Well, what do we have here?' I murmur to myself.

I'm getting used to Shep bantering with anyone and everyone, but it feels a little weird when he does it with women my age. I'm not jealous as such; perhaps insecure is a better word. I worry that he might click with someone else better than he does with me and, before I know it, I'll be alone again with only Netflix for company.

Feeling like I've walked in on a gathering I wasn't invited to, I slip back into my seat while sending a smile in their direction to avoid giving away that I'm intimidated by these goings-on.

'Lea, what you doing over there?' Shep spots me and throws me a quizzical look. 'Come and meet my oldest lady friends in Edinburgh.'

'I'll "old lady" you.' The taller of the two women pretends to whack him with her clutch. She's a sleek and perfectly polished Elizabeth Debicki lookalike, with a mane of wavy long blonde hair, the longest eyelashes I've ever seen (probably false, but good ones) and sparkly pink eye makeup.

'Think you need your hearing checked.' He raises an eyebrow in response to her twisting his words, this time earning himself an actual biff.

'I didn't know you had friends in Edinburgh, Shep.' I nod a 'hello' at the two women, who mirror me in return.

'He means we were the first people he met when he arrived in the city,' says the second woman, who has a more natural look than the first. Her beautiful hazel eyes need nothing to make them pop, and her black afro hair is pulled into a sleek bun, enhancing a bone structure to rival Naomi Campbell's.

'Ah. That makes more sense.'

'I'm Becca, by the way.' She offers me a warm smile that immediately puts me at ease. 'And this is Sal.'

'Nice to meet you both. I'm Lea. I assume this place is your local, if you've got to know this one.' I gesture towards Shep.

'It is for now,' says Sal and I must look confused, because Becca jumps in to explain.

'We've set ourselves a Fringe challenge.'

'Fringe challenge?' I glance back and forth between the two of them.

'A show each night of the festival.' Sal inspects her perfectly manicured nails, her tone matter-of-fact.

'Every night? Gosh, that sounds like fun – and a bit of a commitment. Is it a thing? Like a social media challenge or something?'

'We dreamed it up ourselves after one too many proseccos.' Becca fills in the blanks for me. 'It's our attempt at doing something different. Normally, we spend our hard-earned cash on a girls' holiday and fly somewhere sunny to lie on a beach for a week.'

'The jury's still out on whether that was a mistake.' Sal gives me a look of you-must-get-what-I-mean, and I respond with a knowing smile, despite having never had the pleasure of a trip away with friends. When I was at uni, I couldn't afford such luxuries and now that I can stretch to a week in the sun once a year, I have no one to go with.

'Well, regardless, I think your Fringe challenge sounds fab,' I say. 'Is it just the two of you?'

'No, there's a third musketeer,' says Becca. 'Tess. She's running late, but she'll be here soon.'

'Right, wow.' I'm a little envious of their girly threesome. 'So, when you say this is your local "for now", is this where you meet before you head to your scheduled show each night?'

'Full marks.' Sal flicks her hair behind her shoulder. 'Tess used to live in a flat just over the road.'

'We sometimes came here before,' says Becca. 'So we thought we'd make it our meeting point, as you can't always rely on the weather for the outdoor bars… And here's Tess herself.' She gives a little wave to the freckled redhead coming through the door, then the three of them greet each other like they haven't been together in weeks.

Watching this rigmarole, which I assume is repeated daily, further increases my envy. It's lovely that they have such a tight friendship – I just wish I had some of that in my life too. It reminds me of my uni days, when I had my own group of close friends. I remember at the time thinking it would last forever, which I later realised was naïve of me. I'd kill to just have some good(ish) friends I could meet up with semi-regularly, or call during a moment of emotional pain or indecision and know they would answer. The idea of having girlfriends I could go on holiday with each year is almost too exciting to contemplate. It also seems like such an alien concept to me.

'Hey, Shep.' Tess more or less wraps herself around him, setting off my threat radar. 'How are the shows going? Are you killing it? I bet you're killing it.'

'I'd say... as of tonight, I am officially "killing it".' He puffs up his chest, hammering on it with his fists, while his 'admirers' whoop and clap with delight. 'And it's partly thanks to this gorgeous lady here.'

The cheering stops and three sets of glimmering eyes fall on me, making me feel instantly uncomfortable.

'Tess, this is Leona,' Sal attempts to introduce us.

'Oh, it's Lea, actually,' I correct her.

'My mistake.' She narrows her eyes at me, making me wish I'd gone with 'Leona'.

'It's so lovely to meet you, Lea.' Tess lunges forward and envelops me in a hug, making me realise that's just her way and she's no threat. 'Are you and Shep... you know?'

'Sleeping together? Yes, we are,' Shep proudly announces and I turn scarlet. 'She's also my landlady and my saviour.'

'Oh, so *you're* the one who took him in when he was about to pack it all in.' Sal raises an appraising eyebrow, and I'm unsure whether she's judging me or congratulating me on bagging myself a 'boyfriend' on top of a temporary lodger – though, judging by her previous reaction, I'd put my money on the former.

'Um… yes, that was me.' I look to Shep, and he must sense my insecurity, because he reaches for my hand and clasps it tightly.

'Lea is one special woman, and I'm lucky to have met her.'

'*Aww…*' Tess and Becca put their hands on their chests in perfect synchrony, making us laugh. I then catch Sal rolling her eyes and I neutralise my expression, clearing my throat awkwardly.

Shep and I return to our seats while Becca, Tess and Sal order their drinks. Then their gaze lingers on the empty table next to ours, as if trying to work out whether they're expected to sit there or to leave us in peace.

'Come on and sit over here.' Shep gestures to the table. 'Lea and I aren't the hiding-in-dark-corners type, are we?'

He looks to me for confirmation and I nod, though I have to admit that there's a part of me that would happily stay lost in him, and him only, for the rest of the night.

'Of course, please join us.' I smile brightly at them, equally happy to have some rare female company, even if one of them isn't quite so friendly.

They slide into their seats and the light-hearted chat from before immediately starts up again – with Shep very much at the heart of it. I don't get the impression that any of them are keen on him in a romantic sense, but they certainly seem drawn to him like so many people are. Sitting back and allowing them the freedom to banter in the way they're used to, I'm able to get more of a gauge on each of them.

Tess appears to be the firecracker of the group. Nothing to do with her having red hair; she's just fun and sparky and high-energy. I find myself warming to her quickly, despite the fact she can't seem to keep her hands off Shep. She's clearly the touchy-feely type, meaning there are plenty of hand grabs, nudges and cuddles with her girlfriends as well – which I've noticed Sal doesn't receive quite as naturally as Becca.

Having already earned herself the label of 'the intimidating one', Sal is what I would call the 'cool cat' of the group. It's clear she takes pride in her appearance – she's so glam that she literally looks like she's stepped off the cover of a magazine. She seems to prefer to sit back and take things in, while throwing in her tuppence where it can achieve maximum impact. If I were being cynical, I'd possibly also badge her as the 'shit-stirrer' of the group, but as I don't know her, I'll reserve judgement.

Finally, Becca comes across as the kind and caring one. She listens intently, overflows with empathy and seems to be one of those all-round salt-of-the-earth types. The kind of person who, if you're lucky enough to have her as your friend, you should treat like the gem she is and never ever let her go. She'd be the ultimate BFF.

'Lea, what do you think?' Tess bulldozes through my moment of reflection.

I pull an apologetic face. 'Sorry, I got distracted. What do I think of what?'

'Shep wants us to go see his show. Is it worth it? You must have watched it about eight times by now.'

'You haven't been yet?' I'm surprised by this.

'We haven't had a chance,' says Becca. 'Between work, life stuff and trying to keep to our commitment of a show a night – all of which we pre-booked – there's not been any time. If I'm honest, I'm semi-regretting taking this whole thing on.' She covers the side of her mouth and play-whispers this last part to me.

'You're letting the side down, Becca,' Sal tuts at her, while sipping at her wine, the rim of her glass bright pink from the transfer of her lipstick.

Though this is positioned as a throwaway comment, it feels more cutting than that, and I find Sal's judgement of Becca a little unfair, given her previous comment about the jury still being out on not going abroad.

'I can imagine it sounds easier than it is,' I offer to Becca, earning myself a grateful smile from her and a frosty look of 'don't encourage her' from Sal. 'If you don't mind me asking, how do you all know each other?'

The three of them share a look, then Shep and I share our own look as a reflex reaction.

'I'm guessing you're not childhood buddies.' Shep sits forward, intrigued.

'No, we're not,' Tess admits. 'We're basically—'

'*Don't* say it.' Becca looks mortified all of a sudden.

'Oh, who cares!' Tess throws her hands up. 'They're not going to judge us, are you?'

'Definitely not,' I confirm at exactly the same time Shep says: 'It depends.'

'Actually, you might want to watch him.' I jab my thumb in his direction. 'Whatever you do say may be used as material in his show. I've already had a few red-faced moments in that room.'

'It's a sign of affection.' Shep blows me a kiss.

'It's a sign that anything is fair game, with you. Good thing I'm not someone who takes things personally. Or who seeks revenge in the middle of the night.' I throw him a faux-menacing look and he plays along, acting fearful.

'Well, what does it matter if I add it to the show, if you lot are never gonna come along? So, come on, let's hear it.'

Tess glances at Becca as if seeking permission, and Becca nods, though she still looks uncomfortable.

'Have you heard of *The First Wives Club*?' Tess asks us.

'Isn't that a film? A pretty old one, I think...' I search my memory. 'Ah, yes... about three divorced women who are friends. They take revenge on their husbands for leaving them for much younger women, right?'

'That's the one.'

'Are you saying you're friends for the same reason?' I'm puzzled by this.

Shep looks equally baffled. 'I'm thinking if your blokes left you for much younger women, they'd be getting into questionable territory.'

'It's not exactly the same,' says Tess. 'But we're basically best friends because of our shithead exes.'

'For real?' I'm riveted to hear more.

'Yup. They're all in a band together—'

'And they're a bunch of deadbeats,' Sal finishes Tess's sentence.

'It just took us a while to realise it.' Becca sighs, making me wonder if she's actually fully over her lost love.

'What revenge did you take on them?' Shep's face is shining with wicked interest.

'Uh-uh.' Sal shakes her head. 'That is a secret we'll be taking to the grave.'

'Spoilsport.' Shep's replacement phone buzzes on the table, signalling a notification, and he lifts it to see what it is. 'Ah, shite. The owner from next door is looking for me, and from the looks of it, it's not gonna be quick. I'd better go speak to him.'

He gets up from the table and I follow his lead, but he puts a hand out, signalling for me to stop.

'Lea, why don't you stay here? This is me about to get a telling-off. I don't really want you to witness it.'

'Oh, OK.' I glance uncertainly at our drinking companions. 'I'll maybe just head home, actually.'

The last thing I want right now is to return to my empty flat alone, but leaving Becca, Tess and Sal to their evening together is the polite thing to do. As I resume getting up from my seat, I catch some eye contact happening between them. I automatically assume this is relief at not having to play babysitter, but to my surprise, that doesn't seem to be the case.

'Why don't you stay and have another drink with us?' Becca gently touches my arm. 'We'll be here for another half hour.'

I look to Shep, who gives me an encouraging nod. 'Why don't you do that? Then you can come and give me a kiss before my next performance.'

This comment triggers another 'aww' from Tess and Becca.

'Um… only if you're sure?' I give the three women a tentative smile and receive big, warm ones in return. Well, Sal's isn't so welcoming, but two out of three is still a majority.

'Of course, we're sure, silly.' Tess reaches across and enthusiastically pats my arm. 'Come on, sit back down and we'll get another round in.'

'OK, sure.' I do as she says, then look up at Shep with a surprised shrug.

'Good stuff.' Shep leans over and pecks me on the lips. 'Have fun, ladies. Lea, I'll see you in a bit.'

Chapter 17

'Right, spill,' Sal commands, the moment the door closes behind Shep.

'Spill what?' I blink rapidly under her scrutiny.

'She means give us the goss on you and Shep.' Tess grabs both my hands, squeezing them excitedly. 'It's such a cool story. We want to hear all the deets.'

'Oh.' I take a sip from my drink in a bid to stall for time and hide my discomfort at this ambush from two women I've literally just met – especially when I'm already uncomfortable in the presence of one of them.

'Stop it, you two,' Becca reprimands her friends. 'Poor Lea's only known us five minutes and you're acting like a pair of gossip-starved paparazzi. Lea, you absolutely don't have to share if you don't want to.'

'No, you don't.' Tess pulls an apologetic, but equally disappointed, face. 'Sorry, Lea.'

The two of them shift their focus to Sal.

'Oh, for God's sake.' She raises her eyes to the ceiling, then folds her arms and sits back in her seat. 'Does she need wrapping up in cotton wool?'

Feeling awkward for having created a minor rift within their tight-knit group, I decide I need to give a little. Though I'm unsure about Sal, Becca and Tess are obviously genuinely nice people and I've had no one to share the whole Shep thing with. I am kind of dying to talk about it with someone, so why not these ladies, who have very kindly offered to keep me company? I can give them the redacted version, just in case.

'Tell you what.' I bolster my courage and take a breath. 'How about we get that drink in and I'll give you the PG version?'

'That works for us.' Becca nudges Sal in what I assume is a request for her to play nice, while Tess races to the bar to get our order in.

Fifteen minutes later, I've given them enough dirt to satisfy their curiosity and provide the 'ooh', 'aww' and 'you're shitting me!' moments they're so thirsty for. It's actually been fun sharing with them, and they've even offered me some welcome moral support. Because as much as I'm now far more at ease with Shep, I'm someone who always has a low level of self-doubt simmering away in the background, and I'm still a bit insecure over our set-up – basically, I'm worried I now need Shep more than he needs me.

'It's all so dreamy.' Tess leans forward, elbows on the table, her chin perched on her hands. 'Imagine the two of you get married and he becomes a massive globally recognised comedian. You'd have the ultimate love story to share with the world.'

'Eh… slow down.' I give a nervous chuckle. 'It's only been a week.'

'But you're hoping it's the start of something, right?' Becca asks. 'I mean, you sound quite smitten already.'

I give her question some proper thought, not least because I haven't actually been there in my own head yet. 'I don't know. It's certainly been an intense week, living in the same flat and with all the ups and downs. Feels like we've known each other a lot longer.'

'Kind of like *Love Island* or one of those shows where people are thrown into living together really quickly?' suggests Tess.

'That's exactly how it feels.'

'Well, good luck with that.' Sal scoffs dismissively, and we all look at her like she's the party assassin.

'What do you mean by that?' Tess asks. 'There are people who get married from these shows.'

'Yeah, and many more who end up hating each other's guts.'

My face falls at the idea that Shep and I could ever hate each other. I also can't help wondering why Sal felt the need to bring that up – and in such an unpleasant way.

'Sal, you're ruining this for Lea.' Becca puts her hand on mine reassuringly. It's such a simple gesture, but it tells me she's there for me.

'I was only stating a fact,' Sal jumps to her own defence.

'It's fine,' I reassure her, trying not to let her see that her behaviour is getting to me. 'You're right. That's exactly how it could go. I haven't given any thought to how things might pan out. I've just been enjoying spending time with him. My experience of meeting guys in this city is that they never seem to be sticking around – and they're not always upfront about that. At least I know from the outset that Shep is only here for the month, and the chances are it will just be a short-lived summer romance. I expect we'll go our separate ways once the festival is over.'

As soon as these words leave my mouth, the reality of our situation hits me, and my gut churns uncomfortably and a lump forms in my throat. I do my best to hide this, though, because I don't want to look like a sad idiot to my companions. I definitely don't want them telling him I looked devasted at the idea that we weren't destined for wedding bells and the patter of tiny feet. Particularly when that's not true. All I know right now is that I don't feel good about the idea of him leaving in a few weeks' time. And it could well be that Shep sees our current set-up as nothing more than a brief but intense fling to enhance the big fame-seeking moment in his life.

We chat a bit longer, with me steering us on to lighter topics so I don't have to deal with whatever that was, and so I can keep my moment of weakness fully off their radar. I'm not sure I fancy having any more grenades lobbed at me by Sal either. They tell me about the shows they've seen so far, and seem to enjoy playing back their experiences, especially their front-row ones where they've been picked on by the comedians. The remaining time before they have to leave seems to pass in an instant.

'Girls, we'd better go.' Becca points to her watch. 'We're going to be late.'

They scramble to get their things together, quickly downing the last mouthfuls of their drinks, while my mind drifts to Shep and his conversation with the pub owner. I hope it isn't going badly. If he's got involved in some kind of spat, I can imagine it won't help him get in the 'funny man' mindset.

'Bye, Lea.' Tess lunges at me for another overly familiar hug, which I have to admit, I kind of enjoy.

'Come and join us whenever you like,' says Becca on her way out the door. 'We're normally here around the same time every evening, and sometimes for longer if the show is later. There's no pressure to drink either, we're mainly on softies on school nights.'

'OK, sure.' I beam at her. 'As long as I'm not intruding.' My eyes involuntarily flit to Sal, who's thankfully got her nose in her phone.

'You're not. It's nice to have another friendly face in the mix.' Becca flashes me one of her kind-hearted smiles, then gives me a little wave and disappears from sight.

Feeling a bit weird about being suddenly alone, I sink the last mouthful of my own drink and shuffle out of the pub to find Shep.

On entering The Canongate Tavern, I look around but I can't see him. It's only fifteen minutes until his next performance, so chances are he's getting in the zone or whatever it is he does immediately ahead of his shows.

'He's already gone through.' Kira spots me from behind the bar and gestures towards the back room. 'Looks like it's going to be packed out again – I expect with some of the people you handed out flyers to earlier.'

'Oh, great. I said I'd see him before he went on, but maybe I'll leave it. Don't want to throw him off if he's already in there preparing himself mentally.' I step forward and lower my voice. 'He didn't get too much of a rollocking from your boss before, did he? I was concerned it might affect his performance.'

Kira's perfect eyebrows knit together in confusion. 'What are you talking about? He spent the last half hour or so sitting over there, relaxing with a pint. He couldn't have been more chilled. Also, Dave went home over an hour ago.'

'Really?' I try and fail to comprehend what she's just said. 'You mean he hasn't even spoken to him?'

'Not unless they talked on the phone, but I didn't see him doing anything except scrolling on his phone and sipping at his pint.'

My insecurities rear up like spooked horses, immediately wanting to know why Shep lied to me. Did he want rid of me? No, it can't be that. That makes no sense. It has to be something more innocent than that. Did he want quiet time ahead of going on stage, and he didn't want to offend me by telling me this? I can't really see that either. It's not his style. Shep is more upfront than that, which means he was up to something... *Oh, my God*, I know exactly what he was doing. How did I not suss that before?

'Right, I'm going to kill him,' I announce to a perplexed Kira, then march through to the back room, all thoughts of not wanting to throw off his performance forgotten.

Chapter 18

Politely but determinedly squeezing my way through the group of people standing at the back of the venue, I pound down the aisle between the rows of occupied seats, walk straight past the microphone stand and dart behind the curtain.

'Hey, there you are.' Shep greets me with a smile. 'I was starting to think I wasn't gonna get my pre-show kiss.'

He steps forward to slip his arms around me and I take a step back, putting my hands on my hips.

'There's still a strong likelihood you won't. How was your conversation with Dave?'

He puffs out his cheeks. 'It went on a bit. He's a real stickler for leaving things how you found them, almost to the point—'

'Shep, cut the bullshit. I know you've been sitting in the bar enjoying a leisurely pint.'

'Ah, shit… you caught me. Well, you know, I like to take some quiet time ahead of my performances, go over my set in my head—'

'Also total bullshit.' I fold my arms and stare him out. 'How could you do that?'

'Do what?' He tries for a look of wide-eyed innocence.

'Don't pull that look with me.' I keep my voice low, careful not to share our altercation with Shep's audience.

'You know exactly what I'm talking about. You set me up… on a bloody playdate!'

'Mmm… that's not quite how I would put it. In my head, a playdate with you and three other women would play out quite differently—'

'*Shep.*'

'Yep?'

'What the hell were you thinking?' I hiss at him.

He frowns, his voice rising as he lays out his defence. 'What do you think I was thinking? You told me you don't have any mates to hang out with—'

'*Shhh*… keep your voice down, would you?' I put my finger to my lips, still giving him the evil eye. 'I don't need the added humiliation of the whole audience hearing. It's bad enough that you told Becca, Tess and Sal, and now they feel obliged to let me hang out with them again.'

'They invited you to join them again?' Shep looks delighted to hear this.

'Yeah, but only because you told them I'm a Norma-no-mates.'

'No, I didn't. I admit, I did set that intro up, but only I knew what was really going on.'

'So you didn't tell them?'

'I did not.' He shrugs. 'I made no mention of Norma-no-mates, pals-free-Paula… not even buddyless-Babs.'

'One derogatory term to describe my situation is more than enough, thank you very much,' I scold him, but I'm now finding it difficult not to smile.

'You're the one who started it. That's not at all how I see you.' He steps forward and gently takes me by the shoulders. 'Look, all I wanted to do was help you in the same way you helped me. You told me you find it difficult to make new friends, so I created an opportunity for you.'

'Yeah, well, I never asked you to.' My eyes fall to the floor, the lightness I briefly felt already fading away.

'Hey, come on.' Shep lifts my chin with his finger. 'I can see you're uncomfortable about this, but there's no need to be.'

'Surely you'd feel the same if someone tried to manufacture a group of friends for you, because you couldn't find your own.'

'I guess. Or maybe I'd feel that way if someone had to take pity on me and offer me a room for free because I couldn't afford to pay.'

I look up and into Shep's shining green eyes, which are telling me something very specific.

'Lea, we all have moments of vulnerability in life. Do you think I felt good about you taking me in?'

I shrug. 'You seemed happy enough about it.'

'Because I was desperate, and it meant I could stay here. But inside I was ashamed and felt inadequate – in the same way you do over your own situation. I wondered what you really thought of me and I was relieved when we got on so well. But then I made the mistake of thinking you liked me as much as I liked you, and—'

'So you *were* going to kiss me that night in The Meadows!' I'm almost triumphant in my declaration of this.

He gives me a puzzled look. 'Um, yeah, but that's not the point I was making. What I was gonna say was: when I felt like you hated the idea of me kissing you, because I was your charity-case lodger, I plummeted straight back to shame and inadequacy, just like you feel now.'

'But you know now that wasn't it at all, it was—'

'That you just didn't find me attractive, I know. I can't hear that enough.' He adopts a wounded expression, but in a way that lets me know he's fine.

'Sorry.' I giggle. 'I guess you were only trying to help, as you say.'

Shep rubs the backs of my hands tenderly with his thumbs then makes a show of seeking out eye contact with me.

'Let me ask you two things: did you have fun with them? And do you think you would do so again?'

I nod. 'Well, yeah, they seem like great girls. Though I'm not too sure about Sal.'

'Yes, she's more of an acquired taste, but Becca and Tess are dead on.'

'I really liked them.'

'Grand.' He smiles at me. 'Then ditch your pride and meet up with them again. And don't let Sal put you off. I can be there with you to begin with if you like, until you're comfortable going to meet them yourself.'

Digesting Shep's words and the good intentions behind them, I realise he's right. He's doing nothing really that different to what I did for him, and I need to get over the embarrassment of it all. As he says, he's created an opportunity for me, and now it's up to me whether I make the most of it.

'Thanks, Shep. You're one thoughtful bugger and I'm lucky to have you around.' I squeeze his hands and he draws me in for a make-up kiss of sorts (though we hadn't really fallen out).

'You're welcome, sexy landlady. Now – and I mean this in the nicest way possible – can you get the hell out of my dressing room so I can start my show?'

After Shep's show, we're both on a bit of a high – especially with it being packed out again and the audience clearly loving it – so we decide to have a couple of drinks at the bar, while chatting to Kira and the other bar staff. It's so lovely and companionable, sitting there enjoying the banter, like I'm part of the 'in crowd'. That might sound a bit sad, but when you've been starved of social contact to the extent I have, an experience like this – especially on the back of meeting Becca, Tess and Sal earlier – makes me feel like I've won the friendship lottery. Not that I could call any of the people involved friends... other than Shep, who's soared past the friend zone and secured himself a guaranteed spot in my bed every night. I mean it more symbolically than anything.

Unsurprisingly, Shep is the focus of everyone's attention. Pumped up from yet another successful performance, he keeps everyone laughing with his quick-witted responses and his ability to rib them to the point they're uncomfortable, but at the same time still craving his attention. Watching him in his element like that, I find him so attractive and I feel myself melt every time he gives me a look or squeezes my hand. We may be drinking, which obviously heightens everything, but one thing is becoming very clear to me: I definitely don't want this to be a short-lived summer fling. I'm developing real feelings for him, which means I'm in danger of getting hurt – again.

'You all right?' Shep scrutinises my expression all of a sudden and I realise I've been staring at him while lost in my thoughts.

'Fine.' My cheeks colour in embarrassment. 'Just... enjoying being here.'

'I'm glad to hear it.' He smiles at me, his cute dimples giving me all the feels, then takes my hand in his and gives it another of his affectionate squeezes. 'I am too.'

Feeling the warmth of his skin against mine and those amazing eyes on me, I sense my mind being pulled in two different directions: caught between enjoying the intimacy of the moment, and thinking about how soon that hand will be gone, along with its owner. And how painful I already know it will be to say goodbye. But is that really where my focus should be? Giving myself an internal shake, I decide that the here and now is what I should be paying most attention to. If all I'm going to have are a few more weeks with Shep, then I need to make the most of them.

Chapter 19

When I wake up on Saturday morning, I'm greeted by an empty spot beside me in bed. Rubbing my bleary eyes, I'm about to throw back the duvet and go to find Shep, when the bedroom door is literally kicked open and he bursts through it, brandishing a tray laden with what I'm guessing is breakfast.

'Good morning, sexy landlady.' He grins at me, barely giving me enough time to sit up before plonking the tray in my lap.

'Are you really going to keep calling me that?' I look up at him with a drowsy grimace.

'You don't like me calling you sexy?'

'No, I don't like you calling me a landlady. It makes me feel like I'm seventy-five. And frumpy.'

He ponders this. 'OK, how about... sexy mistress of the house?'

'Now I sound like a dominatrix.'

'I could get on board with that.'

I narrow my eyes at him. 'Yeah... I couldn't.'

'Right, then. I'll give it some thought.'

'You do that.' I shoot him a good-natured but scathing look. 'So, what's all this?'

My eyes roam the delicious-looking spread in front of me, my stomach rumbling in response to the sight and smell of it. There's a small bowl of mixed berries, a yoghurt, a mug of steaming tea and a plate of freshly made scrambled eggs with smoked salmon.

He leans in and kisses me softly. 'It's for being you. I hope you like smoked salmon and scrambled eggs.'

'I do.' I pick up the fork from the tray, scoop some up and taste it. 'Mmm… that's good. Is that fried soda bread underneath it?'

'It is. It's fusion cuisine.'

'Would we say putting Scottish and Northern Irish fayre together is fusion?'

He frowns. 'Are you gonna eat that or do I need to take it off you for showing a blatant disregard for my culinary genius?'

'Sorry.' I sneak a cheeky glance at him before diving into my food. 'It is really tasty, thank you so much. Just what I need for my hangover.'

Shep climbs onto the other side of the bed, stretching himself out beside me, and I feed him mouthfuls while I'm eating. He's either intentionally served me a plate intended for two or his portion sizing is way off.

Sitting there, chewing contentedly while sipping at my tea, I can feel my drowsiness lingering. Not only have I been getting less sleep than usual, but I've also been out most nights in the last week, which I'm not used to anymore. And the truth is: I'm exhausted. As much as I'm loving hanging out with Shep, maybe I need a chilled night in to sort me out. Not sure I want to go into a second week at work with my eyes hanging out my head, especially when—

'So, I've been thinking,' Shep interrupts my thoughts. 'It's my night off. How about we go see Cath Armstrong together? We could go for dinner first. Like a meal out, not just fish and chips or something from a street-food truck. It could be our first proper date?'

My hand goes to my mouth. 'Oh, I completely forgot about the show.'

I'm also now realising that my idea of a night in is a non-starter. On digesting all this, discomfort creeps over me.

'Shep, you don't need to do that.'

He chews and swallows the latest mouthful I've fed him. 'What do you mean?'

'I mean you don't need to come with me because I don't have anyone else to go with.'

'Were you not listening there?' He cocks his head, giving me a questioning look. 'Why would I suggest dinner and a proper date if I was pulling a pity move? If that were the case, I'd have said, give me one of the tickets and have a pint waiting on my seat.'

'Oh.' I try to respond positively to his light-hearted teasing, but my self-consciousness persists.

'Lea, you do realise the only person making a big thing out of your stuff is you?'

'That's not true.' I immediately go on the defensive. 'You were weirded out when you thought I'd only invited you to stay because I was sad and desperate. You also called me a "weird loner chick" when we first met, remember?'

'Yeah, I did. I was a total dickhead for doing both those things and I deeply regret using those words.' He shakes his head in frustration. 'Now, are you gonna ruin the moment, or are you gonna put me out of my misery and agree to go on a date with me?'

Dialling back his obvious exasperation with me, he reaches across and playfully ruffles my hair, which has the instant effect of lightening the mood.

My face spreads into a smile, while my inner voice tells me I can sleep when I'm dead. 'OK, let's go on a proper date.'

–

Just before seven p.m., I gingerly step out of my bedroom into the hallway, my high heels click-clacking on the wooden floorboards as I do so. It's the first time in ages that I've got properly dressed up to go out. In fact, it's been so long, I almost don't recognise myself in the mirror. My hair is tonged into loose ringlets – I'm far from a pro, so it's a bit of an amateur job, but it makes my hair look thick and glossy. I've put on more makeup than usual, so my eyes are glittering with a tangerine sparkle and I've defined them with jet-black liquid eyeliner. It's my attempt at making them pop, inspired by Sal's killer eye makeup the evening before. I'm also wearing a green chiffon shift dress that's probably a bit too short – the expectation being that I'll spend the whole evening self-consciously pulling it down at the back.

Looking at my reflection, I wince, wondering if I've overdone it. I'm also wondering why I felt the need to get so glammed up. Was it because I wanted to look nice and it's a rare opportunity to do so? Or was it because of the conversation I had with Becca, Tess and Sal about Shep, and the impact it had on me? Until that point, I genuinely hadn't thought much about where things would go – or more likely not go – between us. But now that Pandora's box has been opened, I know these musings are going to hang over me like a cloud of relentless Scottish drizzle. And no surprises, there's a part of me that's blindly hoping this "first proper date" we're going on is a sign of something more significant developing between us.

'Come on now.' I give myself a quiet pep talk in the mirror to bring myself back to earth. 'You knew from the start what this was.'

'That you talking to yourself again?' Shep calls out.

'Um, no,' I call back. 'I'm just saying I'm ready.'

'At last. I was starting to think that—' He emerges from the living room and stops dead when he sees me. 'Oh, wow. Who's this stunner?' He follows this up with an appreciative whistle.

'Stop it.' I fold my arms across my chest, feeling like livestock being inspected at an auction.

'Stop what? Admiring the beautiful woman I'm lucky enough to be taking on a date tonight?'

'I mean stop taking the mick.'

'I'm not taking the mick. I just haven't seen you dressed up before. You look incredible.' He steps forward and coaxes me into a long, slow kiss that makes me shiver with desire.

'All right, let's go.' I wriggle out of his grasp before things go any further, and I have to do my makeup and hair all over again.

We spend the walk to the restaurant – a rustic and reasonably priced Italian place on Newington Road – arguing about who's paying for the meal, eventually agreeing that we'll split the bill. Shep's view is that he asked me on the date, so he should pay, but as he's already paid for the show tickets – and because he's not exactly flush, though I don't mention this part out loud – I'm of the view that I should cover it.

'Have you heard from your family at all since you've been here?' I ask him when we're finishing off our main course. 'I hope it's OK to ask. It's just that you haven't said.'

I pop my last forkful of king prawn risotto in my mouth and wait for his response.

'Not a word.' He sighs heavily and I immediately regret bringing this up when we've been having such a lovely evening together.

'I'm sorry. That must be upsetting for you.'

'They're making a point. It is what it is.' He listlessly stabs at the remains of the pizza on his plate.

I purse my lips, feeling his pain. 'I really do think if they were to watch you on stage, they'd see this all differently.'

'I'm not so sure, to be honest. They might be willing to accept that I'm good at it, but it'll never change their view that I should be following the family path. It's like some kind of prestige thing and I'm tarnishing our name.'

'It's not like you're a criminal.'

'No, but in their eyes, it probably is a crime of sorts.' He gives a hopeless shrug, and all I want to do in this moment is phone up his parents and bawl at them for being so shit.

Reaching across the table, I take his hand. 'Sorry, I shouldn't have brought it up. Let's change the subject. Unless you want to talk about it?'

'No, it's a waste of time.' He rubs my fingers with his thumb. 'Let's talk about you. We've been on me, and the highs and lows of my comedy career, for most of the meal.'

'That's because it's fascinating. OK, what do you want to know?'

'I don't know. Like, what's the focus of the research project you're working on?' Shep tops up my wine glass with the cheap, but perfectly acceptable, bottle of Pinot Grigio we've ordered. 'You've never told me anything about your job.'

I lift my glass to take a sip, and shrug. 'It's not exactly a riveting topic of conversation. Not like having a career as a comedian.'

'I suppose. Though it depends on what you see as interesting.'

'The project I'm working on is cardiac related.'

'You're in medicine too?' Shep facepalms. 'There was me thinking I'd escaped that world.'

'I'm not.' I laugh and shake my head. 'I did start my studies thinking I wanted to be a pharmacist, but in the end, I realised it wasn't for me and that the research side of medicine was what I was most interested in.'

'I guess I'll let you off. Especially as you're hot and you're giving me lots of sex.'

The young waitress who's appeared to clear our plates at the wrong moment clears her throat awkwardly and does a U-turn, as if she's suddenly needed elsewhere.

'Good timing.' I smirk into my wine. 'I thought you were a master of delivery.'

'How do you know I didn't do that on purpose?' He has a glint in his eye that almost makes me think he did. 'Anyway, back to you, tell me more about your research study.'

'You don't really want me to tell you about it, do you?'

'I do.' He balls up his napkin and discards it on the table, his gaze lingering on me. 'We're on our first real date and first dates are important. I want to know more about you, and your job is part of who you are. Stop avoiding the question, Miss Deflector.'

'I'm not deflecting. It's fairly complex and probably difficult to understand if you don't have a background in medical science.' I wince on saying this, concerned that Shep will take offence, given his dysfunctional relationship with medicine and medics. But he doesn't seem fazed by this comment.

'Try me.'

'OK, I'm working on a project to develop a new cancer drug. It's very close to my heart because my great-aunt Lizbeth – who I inherited my flat from – died from cancer. I stayed with her during my first two years of university, when I couldn't afford to rent a room in halls or a shared flat. She was really kind to me, so it's sort of my way of paying her back, if that makes any sense.'

'It makes a lot of sense.' He smiles at me with sympathetic eyes. 'I'm sorry to hear about your aunt.'

'It's fine. She was quite old, but it's still never easy.'

Shep nods and holds my gaze, and unless I'm imagining it, there's a moment of real emotional depth between us – one that makes me think he's also considering whether there might be an 'us' beyond the end of the month.

Forcing my focus away from this hopeful reflection and back to our conversation, I proceed to tell Shep a bit more about the project, but it's not long before I spot his eyes glazing over. 'See, I told you it wasn't Saturday-night chat.'

He seems to come to, pulling an apologetic face. 'Sorry, Lea. I was trying to listen, but you're right, I'm not following the lingo.'

'You don't need to apologise. It's clear that area's not for you, otherwise you'd have followed in the footsteps of your family.'

'True. I could have hidden it better, though.'

I shake my head. 'I disagree. I like that you're easy to read.'

A smile plays on the corners of his lips. 'If only I could say the same for you, Miss Deflector.'

'Hey, enough of that cheek. My skeletons are now glaringly on show, as you well know. And if that's your replacement nickname for me, then "veto". I definitely prefer sexy landlady over that.'

'See, sometimes all it takes to accept the status quo is to know there's nothing better.'

'You're an idiot.' I chuck my napkin at him and he expertly catches it.

'Yeah, but I'm your idiot.'

'For now.'

'Better to have had and lost an idiot than to never have had one at all. Means you'll appreciate who comes next all the more.' He grins across the table at me, and I stick my tongue out at him while my insides go into a tailspin.

If that's not clear evidence of his feelings about us, I don't know what is. This 'date' we're on is obviously nothing more than a prop to add some superficial shine to our steamy live-in situation. Perhaps even to make it feel more acceptable. I've been an idiot to think it was anything other than that.

'You all right?' Shep peers at me. 'You look a bit green all of a sudden.'

'I'm fine.' I rummage through my handbag as a way of avoiding eye contact. 'Probably just eaten a bit too much. Some fresh air will sort me out.'

'Shall we just get the bill, then? Show starts in half an hour, so we don't have time for dessert.'

I nod mutely, feeling a crushing disappointment, and watch as he signals to the server. How can I – after repeating the same pattern over and over – meet a guy I know isn't planning to stick around, and still think that somehow things will turn out differently? Is that blind faith or just stupidity?

'That was fantastic!' I'm practically bouncing along next to Shep as we exit the show venue at the Pleasance, Cath Armstrong's brilliantly wicked humour having cheered me up significantly since the end of our meal.

'I knew you'd enjoy it.' Shep slips his arm around my waist, giving me an affectionate squeeze as we follow the stream of fellow festivalgoers outside.

'She was hilarious. That bit about the banana in her handbag. Oh my God, I nearly wet myself.'

'I'm glad you didn't. That would have made it an awkward first date.'

'Do you think people actually do that?'

'What? Wet themselves at comedy shows?'

'Yeah.'

He seems to shake his head in amusement at my daft question. 'I've never really thought about it, but I guess it's possible. You could do a research study on it.'

'Can you imagine?' I snicker. 'Bringing people to a Cath Armstrong performance and asking who's still dry at the end of it.'

'Hey, why not my show?' Shep digs me playfully in the ribs. 'Are you saying I'm not funny enough to make people piss themselves?'

'Aww, of course you are. I bet the seats in your venue have been soiled many times over. I just said Cath Armstrong because we were talking about her show.' I glance across at him but he's no longer paying attention, having just received an alert on his phone, so I wait patiently for him to tend to whatever has come in.

'*Holy shit*,' he exclaims, his mouth forming a perfect 'O'. 'Check this out. A mate just sent it to me.'

I take his phone from him and read the headline on the screen out loud, while he watches me intently.

'"Dark horses of the Fringe – the top free shows in Edinburgh this summer". Are you in this or something?'

'Just read it,' Shep urges me.

I quickly scan the article before reading it properly. 'Oh my goodness, you are in it. You're number two. "Second on my list and making his debut at the Fringe is Northern Irish comedian Shep, with his stand-up show, Caught In The Act. When I took my seat at this one, I was hoping for some decent comedy, but what I got was a whole lot more. Shep hasn't just produced a hilarious and bone-gratingly honest stand-up routine, he's also weaved through a Michael McIntyre-style game show element that brings Fringe audience participation to a whole new level. No spoilers here, but if you're game for a laugh, get yourself along to see him." Oh wow, Shep, this is incredible.'

'Can you believe it? I'm a "dark horse" of the Fringe.' Shep's shaking his head like he's struggling to digest this fortunate turn of events.

'You know what? I can.' I hand him his phone back, then reach up and cup his face with my hands, before giving him a big smacker on the lips. 'Congratulations! You deserve this. The only thing I think is wrong with that article is that you should be number one.'

'Ah, you're biased.' He bats away my compliment. 'You haven't seen any of the other free shows on that list.'

'No, but I have just seen Cath Armstrong. I've also watched plenty of other stand-up comedians on TV and at the festival in the past, and I think you're as good as any of them.'

'You really think so?' Shep's expression changes to one I read as hope mixed with self-doubt.

'I know so. Don't let that family of yours get in your head. You've just been put on the map by...' I check the article again, having not yet looked at the publication. '...*Main Attraction*. Ooh, that's awesome! They're like the voice of all things entertainment.'

'I have been put on the map, haven't I?' Shep's face breaks into a full-on grin and he pumps the air triumphantly as we make our way out of the courtyard. 'This shit just got real.'

'Which means you need to be 100 per cent with every show from here on out – because now you never know who might be in your audience.'

'Bring it on.' He puffs himself up as if demonstrating he's ready for the challenge. 'This is exactly what I needed to get me fired up. I came here chasing a dream, but deep down I don't think I ever really expected to get lucky. I hoped for it, as everyone does, but the odds were stacked against me—'

'And now they've turned in your favour.' I beam at him.

'Bloody hell, Lea, I owe you so much. If I'd got on that flight home that night instead of bumping into you... If you hadn't offered me somewhere to stay, or I'd said no when you did, I'd have—'

'No, *stop*.' I bring us to a halt and take Shep's hands in mine. 'What might have been is irrelevant. That's one thing I've learned through my research work. Don't get lost in alternative scenarios where the data isn't offering anything meaningful. Focus on the facts and what the evidence is telling you in the here and now.'

Shep raises a tentative hand. 'You want to put that in plain English for the non-lab rat people here?'

'Very funny. In your case, that means forgetting what might have been if you'd made a different decision, or if things had played out differently. *Fact*: you decided to stay in Edinburgh and you just got your first big endorsement. This means you now have *evidence* that what you're doing is working, and all your focus should go into delivering a top-notch show. That's all that matters.'

'You're right. Totally.' He grabs me and kisses me hard on the lips. 'You're a bloody genius, Lea. How did I get so lucky as to bump into you?'

We resume our walk back to mine, Shep now the one with a significant bounce in his step, while I can't help poring over what the facts are telling me about us. We may have just been on our first proper date, but between Shep's comment at dinner and this glowing review, which could well lead to the big break he's been seeking, I really can't see an eventuality where we end up together – and that makes me very sad indeed.

Chapter 20

Over the next few days, Shep and I fall into an easy rhythm of eating, sleeping (together), working (in our vastly different careers), and hanging out at mine, The Canongate Tavern and the Old Town Inn. It's cosy and companionable, hot and steamy, engaging and enjoyable – and it's quite possibly the best month of my life so far. That obviously shows I'm way too into the guy who's soon going to pack up and leave, possibly for pastures rich and famous. But doesn't every 'holiday romance' feel like that? It's intense, it feels like everything, then it's over – and the monotony of real life resumes.

As long as I don't think about it all too deeply, I'm able to stay in the moment and just enjoy the experience.

I also enjoy getting to know Becca, Tess and Sal a bit better during another couple of visits to the Old Town Inn with Shep, between his shows. Well, I enjoy getting to know Becca and Tess, that is.

Sal's behaviour is pretty consistent with my first impression of her: catty and unpleasant, and when she's not centre of attention, she spends most of her time scrolling on her phone, as if nothing anyone else says is as important as her own input. It almost makes me wonder why Becca and Tess – who are both so lovely – are such close friends with her. But then they have a shared past and a connection that I'm not privy to, so perhaps it makes perfect sense to them – and as they are so solid, if I want to hang out with them then I have to accept that Sal is part of that package deal.

Though I don't like to pick favourites, Becca is the one I connect with most, probably because she's what I'd describe as the deeper member of the group. That's not to say that there's anything wrong with Tess. She's super bubbly and friendly and so welcoming. She just operates at a level that makes it that little bit trickier to develop a meaningful bond with her.

On Wednesday morning, I'm double-checking the patient information I've created for our next drug trial, when Tanya bustles in, looking harassed.

'Hi there, you OK?' I ask.

She looks at me and blinks. 'I'm unsure how to answer that, Lea. Not only am I here an hour later than planned, I also think I've left my phone at home.'

She yanks off her coat and hangs it up, then rummages through her bag frustratedly.

'I hope I've not left it on the kitchen counter. I wouldn't be surprised after the morning I've had with those little buggers.'

'You mean your darling children?'

'When you have teenagers, you'll understand.' She shoots me a knowing look. 'They were scrapping like stray cats. I swear I nearly dragged the two of them to the school bus stop by their ears.'

I chuckle, enjoying this mental image. 'Hopefully, they'll grow out of that phase soon.'

'I can only hope and pray. How are you? How have the last two days been?'

'Fine. The patient information for the next trial is nearly ready. How was the conference?'

She raises her eyes to the ceiling. 'Long. Dull. Bad conversation. Even worse food.'

'Sounds dreamy.'

'You know what would be dreamy? A coffee. Shall we?'

More than ready for a break, I get up and stretch, then chum Tanya along the corridor to the cafeteria.

'I've been meaning to ask, how are you getting on with your temporary lodger?' She regards me over the top of her spectacles while we wait in the queue.

'Fine.' I aim for a nonchalant nod, which Tanya immediately sees through.

'Oh my, you took my advice.'

'What advice?'

'I suggested you open your mind a bit with this one.'

'Ah, you mean your comment that Shep might be "everything I never knew I was looking for".' I waggle my eyebrows at her. 'Yep, that stuck in my head like a rusty nail and had me thoroughly confused – along with all the other nonsense my mind conjures up. I've certainly learned that romance isn't "one size fits all", so… thanks.'

'You're welcome.' She assumes a self-satisfied expression. 'How's the sex?'

I blanch. 'What?'

I can't believe she's asking me this in the middle of the university cafeteria – or at all.

'Lea, darling, it's basic biology. There's no need to get all tied up.' She leans in conspiratorially. 'Plus, when you've had as long a dry spell as I've had, you have to get your kicks elsewhere. That's the reality of having kids. They kill your sex life.'

'Right. Well, then…' I bluster. 'It's… fine. It's good… I mean, great. Really great.'

My pre-bedtime antics with Shep the night before flit through my mind and I redden, still uncomfortable talking about this with my senior colleague.

'Excellent. I thought you had a glow about you late last week. I hope you used your afternoon off well.' She winks at me and I realise she thinks I took the time off to spend it shagging.

'Oh no, it wasn't for that. We had lunch and a walk, then I handed out fliers for Shep's show. It was lovely.'

Tanya scrutinises me. 'That doesn't sound like a lodger-with-benefits arrangement. You care about this man… Ah, here we are… two large cappuccinos to go, please.' She puts in our order with the barista before turning back to me expectantly.

'I don't… Yeah, I do.' I give a wince of a smile.

'Well, that's marvellous. Does he feel the same about you?'

'No idea. Best way I can describe it is like a holiday romance. It's full-on, you know, but we're both aware that it's a time-limited thing.'

Tanya purses her lips thoughtfully. 'And you don't want it to be.'

'No,' I admit, suddenly feeling quite vulnerable beneath her sympathetic gaze. 'I'm falling for him. I can feel it, and I don't think he's in the same place.'

'The path to true love is a winding little bugger, isn't it?'

'It so is. Anyway, I guess I just need to keep myself in check and not let things get out of hand – emotionally, I mean.'

'That makes sense.' Tanya looks out the window wistfully. 'But it will be harder than you think.'

'I know.' I grimace.

We fall silent and our conversation prompts me to think back to the one holiday romance I had as a teenager, while on a campsite in France with my parents. I had to hide it from them, as they would never have been OK with it, which made it all the worse when the boy I'd met left to go home two days before we did. Because I couldn't tell them what was wrong, I had to pretend I was happy and having a great time, and then I'd go for these walks on my own and cry my heart out. That was bad enough and – despite the positive intentions I've just conveyed about not getting too involved – I expect the end of this month is going to feel a hundred times worse.

'Lea, your coffee?' Tanya's voice breaks through my inner turmoil.

'Sorry, I was—'

'Lost in your thoughts. I understand.' She hands me my drink and we exit the cafeteria, strolling back in the direction of the lab. 'I know this isn't particularly helpful, but the best thing you can do is try not to second-guess what might or might not happen in a couple of weeks' time. The more you overthink things, the less time you'll spend enjoying the moment. Your lodger… What's his name again?'

'Shep.'

'Which is short for?'

'Ciaran,' I say automatically, then clock her confused look. 'Sorry, Shepperd. His name is Ciaran Shepperd.'

'Right. Well, all I was going to say is that Ciaran needs to have this time with relaxed Lea, not Lea who's getting antsy about how and when things might end between you. Take it from me, I was a nightmare date in my twenties.'

'Really?' I'm unable to imagine this. 'In what way?'

'I was clingy and insecure.' She frowns, as if hating that she could ever have allowed herself to be that way. 'Could never keep a boyfriend, and I couldn't understand why, until some awful ex-public-school chap called Rupert told me I'd be as well to have "desperate" tattooed on my forehead.'

'What a horrible person.'

'He was, but the irony of it is that he was the one who helped me the most. Every time I told my girlfriends or my parents I'd been dumped – again – they were of the view that the offending blokes didn't deserve someone as wonderful as me. The only person who told me that I was the problem was Rupert. As unkind as his feedback was, it made me take a good look at myself.'

'And?'

'It turned out he was right. After that, I made sure I always had other things going on in my life than just dating, and it worked. My husband, John, was my first and only long-term relationship after Rupert.'

'Gosh, Rupert really did help you, then.'

We reach the lab and perch ourselves on a couple of stools.

'It was a far better parting gift than the one I gave him.' Tanya's eyes glint almost sinfully.

'Uh-oh?' I bite my lip expectantly.

'I sent him an anonymous parcel of fish guts.'

I nearly spit out my coffee. 'You didn't.'

'Still wish I could have seen his face when he opened it,' Tanya reminisces. 'Anyway, I guess what I'm trying to say is: don't be like young Tanya. Be relaxed, be yourself, and you never know. He might find it harder to say farewell than you think.'

'That's sound advice. Thanks, Tanya.'

We settle into our respective research-related tasks for the morning, working away in silence for a good hour-and-a-half, before Tanya plonks herself down beside me.

'I've been thinking... when can I meet him to suss him out?'

'Meet him?' I give a puzzled shake of my head while trying to digest Tanya's latest curveball.

'Yes, I want to scope him out. Get a feel for what's under the hood... not in a dirty way,' she adds quickly, catching my perplexed expression.

'I thought you said I should play it cool.'

'Of course. You must. Doesn't stop me having a little nose around, though, does it?' She rubs her hands together gleefully. 'Why don't the two of you take a break from the bedroom and have dinner with John and I at my place on Saturday?'

'You mean a dinner party?'

'Yes, if you can give that label to a gathering of four.'

I'm unsure how to respond to this unexpected invite. It's obviously very kind, and I like Tanya a lot. But she also has an ulterior motive, which she's had no shame in presenting upfront. That's the part that concerns me slightly.

'Come on,' Tanya cajoles me, picking up on my hesitation. 'Don't make me spend another Saturday night cleaning my bathrooms.'

'It does sound lovely,' I say. 'The dinner, not the bathrooms. And Shep has a day off on a Saturday, but—'

'Did we not just talk about you not overthinking things? Text him and see what he says. If that's all it takes to scare him off, he's not worth your time, no matter how good he is in bed.'

I puff out my cheeks, aware that I can't vocalise what's really holding me back. 'OK, I'll see what he says.'

Reaching across to my bag, I find my phone and tap out a message to Shep, careful to make it sound as casual as possible.

> Hi Shep, hope your day is going OK. My (lovely but slightly bonkers!) workmate is asking if we'd like to have dinner at hers on Saturday. Thoughts? xx

I hit send and try to conceal my agitation while waiting for his reply, which thankfully comes within a minute or so.

> Sounds good. Tell her I'm a whisky man. x

I look up at Tanya. 'He says he's in. And to let you know he drinks whisky.'

'Super.' Tanya looks delighted. 'We have a whole whisky cabinet he can explore. John's a fan too. Oh, I can't wait to play Cupid again.'

I narrow my eyes at her. 'You never said anything about playing matchmaker. That's not part of the agreement.'

'No, of course not. I'm just teasing.' Tanya beams at me in a way that makes me very suspicious and slightly nervous about what she might have in store for us.

Chapter 21

Shep has offered to help Kira move some heavy items at her flat during the gap between his performances, so in the evening – after a hearty pep talk in front of my hall mirror – I haul my big-girl pants on and rock up at the Old Town Inn to meet Becca, Tess and Sal by myself. This is a huge step for me. I haven't even told Shep, in case I wimp out. Though I've hung out with the girls twice since we first met, he was there both times, and it just felt like we were regulars in the same haunt. Tonight feels very different. I'd also be lying if I said the idea of being around Sal without him there doesn't terrify me a bit. So much so that, on approaching the pub, I get a bad case of the jitters, and nearly turn around and head straight home.

'Lea, it's so good to see you!' Tess jumps up, suffocating me with a hug the moment I tentatively make it through the door.

'How are you?' Becca reaches across and squeezes my hand as soon as I've slipped into one of the tartan upholstered chairs at their table.

Both of these actions really help to calm my nerves, allowing me to relax a little.

'I'm good, thanks.' I smile at them, still somewhat self-consciously. 'How are you all?'

'Great,' Becca answers for all of them. 'So pleased you've joined us again.'

'Shep not with you tonight?' asks Sal by way of a greeting.

'No.' I shake my head. 'He's helping out a friend – one of the staff from next door – so I thought I'd pop along and have a drink with you. Hope that's OK.'

'Of course it's OK,' says Becca. 'Isn't it, ladies?'

'Yah-huh.' Tess nods vigorously. 'The more the merrier, right, Sal?'

'Always.' Sal shoots me a smile that doesn't quite reach her eyes.

After offering to get everyone another drink – which they decline due to having half-full glasses – I nip up to the bar to get myself one, then return to my seat.

'So, what's tonight's show, then?' I take a satisfying slug of my G&T.

'One of the greats,' says Tess. 'Jimmy Carr, the master of one-liners.'

'Oh fab. Isn't his show across at the EICC? I saw a poster advertising it. That's a bit of a trek from here.'

'Tell me about it,' Sal complains. 'I have to "trek" all the way there in these.' She sticks a slim, tanned leg out from under the table to show me her stylish but wholly unsuitable skyscraper sandals. 'I thought tonight's show was a few doors along from here. Turns out that's next week.'

'Uber?' I suggest.

'We'll see if we can get one,' says Becca. 'Though it's difficult during festival time. If not, we can get a bus. We won't leave Sal to struggle.'

'Pray for me.' Sal adopts a martyred expression, making me laugh, and unless I'm imagining things, she seems to shoot me a dirty look.

Caught off guard by this, I shrink back in my seat, confused. Was that not intended as a joke? Or is it that I'm not allowed to enjoy her jokes?

'Oh, stop being such a princess.' Tess flicks Sal's hair, earning herself an acidic response.

Note to self: never ever touch Sal's hair. Not that I would dare to, anyway.

We continue to chat – with me picking my way across a metaphorical minefield to avoid any further snide looks or remarks from Sal – and it's not long before the conversation moves on to dating and matters of the heart. This is an area we haven't previously covered together, other than the grilling I got about Shep last week. I guess it isn't a topic that Becca, Tess and Sal would necessarily cover in his presence. As it turns out, they're all single, which surprises me, though it probably shouldn't. If any of them were in a long-term relationship, it's unlikely they'd have committed to three weeks plus of nights out on the trot. That is some undertaking and I expect most other halves would feel a bit miffed by it.

They are also all active on the dating scene – outside of this Fringe festival challenge – though Becca seems a far less enthusiastic participant than Tess and Sal. In fact, I can't help thinking, from the way she talks, that this month off is something of a relief for her. This seems to confirm my previous impression that Becca's not really over her ex, and I decide I want to ask her about it, if I ever have the opportunity to talk to her on her own.

'So are you going to see him again?' Tess is quizzing Sal on whether there will be a second date with the guy she had lunch with on Sunday.

It seems Sal is the only one out of the three of them who's still trying to keep that side of her life going during the festival, and daytime dates obviously need to be a part of that equation.

'Nah, he was hot and all but he's moving to Australia. Not going to waste my time if I already know it's not going to go anywhere.'

My curiosity is piqued on hearing this. 'He isn't a rugby player called Paul by any chance, is he?' I ask, before thinking through the possible repercussions of posing this question.

'Yeah, he is.' Sal frowns. 'How did you know that?'

I swallow, now regretting my ill-thought-through decision to pipe up. 'Because… I was recently seeing him. Only, I wasn't fortunate enough to get the truth from him to make that decision myself.'

'You're kidding.' Tess looks appalled. 'You mean he led you on and used you for sex? What a prick.'

'That's pretty much it, in a nutshell. So, lucky escape I'd say.' I direct this last statement at Sal with a sympathetic smile, hoping this will spare me from being in the firing line.

'See, that's the problem with this city.' She throws her perfectly manicured hands up in the air and I can't help breathing a sigh of relief that she's directing her anger elsewhere. 'The dating pool is ridiculously small. We're all just recycling each other's waste.'

'I'm sorry that happened to you, Lea,' Becca says across the table to me. 'He sounds like a real jerk.'

'And what about me?' Sal swirls the ice in her glass, shooting me a stare that's icier than her drink. Guess I didn't get off scott-free after all.

Tess scoffs. 'You only went out with him once and you got the truth.'

I'm not sure why – especially given her behaviour towards me – but I feel the need to defend Sal on this one. Perhaps I'm also hoping it might win me some much-needed points.

'To be fair, he was probably only upfront because he'd boasted all over social media about moving. Sal would have found out very quickly.' I focus my attention on her. 'Seriously, you've dodged a bullet on that one, Sal. He doesn't deserve someone like you.'

Sal lifts her chin in what appears to be an attempt to regain her composure, and despite myself, I do actually feel for her. Dating is a tiring and endlessly disappointing task. It's so hard to find someone as great as Shep.

'What about you, Lea?' Tess prods me in the ribs. 'Now we finally have you on your own again, how are things with comedy loverboy?'

Having not yet been the subject of the chat, I'm expecting this question and I've decided to be open with the girls.

'Things are great. Or as great as they can be when you know your relationship has an expiry date.' I wrinkle my nose, giving away my position.

'Oh, hon.' Becca takes my hand in hers.

'You can't tell him any of this, though,' I quickly add.

'Of course not.'

'That's part of our pact – not a word outside our three-some.' Tess draws her fingers across her mouth in a zipping motion. 'Now our foursome, obviously.'

'Thanks.' I give her a grateful look. 'It's been on my mind since you asked me about it last Friday. We're getting on so well and I've honestly never met anyone like him – probably because I've been distracted by self-obsessed wankers like Paul.'

I involuntarily glance across at Sal, who has checked out of the conversation – probably because it's no longer focused on her – and is now on her phone.

'Anyway,' I continue. 'I'm trying to live in the moment and make the best of things, but it's always at the back of my mind. The big goodbye. The clock is counting down to my heart getting broken, and there's nothing I can do to change it.' A heavy sigh escapes me.

'Are you sure?' Tess asks, ever the optimist. 'How do you know he's not thinking the same?'

My head is shaking in rejection of this suggestion before Tess has even finished speaking. 'He's not. I can feel it. It's also there in the way he talks. He's laid-back about everything… everything but his stand-up career. That's what he's chasing. Not me.'

'Aww, Lea.' Becca sounds genuinely gutted for me.

'It's fine.' I feel a rush of raw emotion, tears threatening, which I blink away before anyone notices. 'I knew what this was from the start. But having now identified what a decent guy is, hopefully it will stand me in good stead for my next relationship. Right?'

'Absolutely.' She smiles at me warmly. 'And we're here anytime you need to talk. We'll help you through it. Won't we?' She glances at Tess and Sal.

'Damn right,' Tess practically yells. 'We know exactly how to sort out a broken heart: it involves French Martinis and a fake dating profile.'

I suck my teeth. 'That sounds a bit… dodgy.'

'Trust me, it does the trick.' Tess gives me a mischievous wink, while Becca rolls her eyes to the ceiling, clearly not as bought into this 'alternative remedy'.

It's at this point that we realise that Sal hasn't said anything, probably because she's been scrolling on her phone through the entire exchange. She must feel our eyes on her, because she glances up. 'What? OK, yes to whatever I missed.'

'Thank you.' I look round them gratefully. Despite Sal's obnoxiousness, I am starting to feel part of their little group. And, who knows, maybe one day she and I will become friends – perhaps she just needs time to warm to newcomers.

We're not far into another topic of conversation when Sal lets out a snarl of frustration.

'Everything all right?' Becca asks her.

'Um… yeah.' She rubs her face, then stops as she seems to become aware that she's messing up her makeup. 'My sister just messaged, asking if I can babysit – Friday night into Saturday afternoon. I said no, because… well, I'm not free any night this month. She knows that. Not sure why… Oh, she's messaged back.'

Sal reads the message and makes another loud huffing noise.

'What is it?' asks Tess. 'Has something happened?'

'She and my brother-in-law have booked an overnight stay in Glasgow for their tenth wedding anniversary, and my parents have had to pull out from babysitting because my dad's ill.'

'Oh no, that's rubbish.' Becca pets her bottom lip. 'But also, your poor dad.'

'He'll be fine, it's just a weird summer flu thing,' says Sal. 'It does suck for my sister and Rob, though. Guess they'll just need to cancel and try again another time.'

This comment is followed by a stunned silence, which prompts Sal to pause midway through responding to her sister and look up from her phone. 'What?'

'You're not seriously going to let them miss out on their tenth wedding anniversary celebration because you have your umpteenth comedy show to go to, are you?' Tess's tone is incredulous.

'Uh, yeah.' Sal looks at her as if she's stupid. 'We're doing the Fringe challenge.'

'Which isn't a real thing.'

'It is now. If I've sacrificed a beach holiday for this, I'm damn well going to see it through.'

Becca's eyes narrow, homing in with laser-like focus on her friend. 'Sal, what is this really about?'

'I don't know what you're talking about.' Sal pouts, returning her attention to her phone.

'Are you concerned about missing out?'

'No, it's… I'm… fine. I had arranged to meet someone after the show on Friday, all right? He's hot. Look.' She holds her phone out, showing us a profile picture of the guy in question.

'Ahh…' Becca, Tess and I respond in unison as we admire the unquestionably sexy specimen, but faced with our lack of real enthusiasm, Sal quickly caves.

'Argh, fine, I'll do it. Mister hot-piece-of-ass here will have to wait.'

'I'm sure he'll be willing to reschedule.' Tess shifts to the wall-mounted bench on the other side of the table and puts her arm around Sal in an attempt to make her feel better. Unfortunately, all this achieves is Sal looking deeply uncomfortable while revising her reply to her sister.

'Hey, Lea, how about you join Becca and I on Friday night?' Tess says suddenly. 'You can have Sal's ticket.'

Sal's head shoots up. 'Would you steal my grave as quick, Tess?'

'Huh? What did I do?' Tess sounds genuinely perplexed.

'Do you not think maybe it's for Sal to decide what happens with her ticket?' Becca prompts her.

'Sorry, I was just trying to be practical. No point in the ticket going to waste.'

'Whatever.' Sal shakes her head in irritation, her focus already back on her phone. 'Lea, take the ticket.'

'Erm… I never said…' I stammer, feeling somehow like I'm now in the bad books, despite not having said a word. 'Could you not sell it online, Sal? Or give it to a friend?'

'I can't think of anyone who'd take it and I don't "sell things online".'

'OK, well, how about I give you the money for it, then? So you don't lose out.'

'Look, just take the ticket, will you, Lea?' Sal shoots me a scathing look, making me flinch. 'Let's not turn this into a drama.'

'Erm, OK.' I sense my face reddening from the awkwardness of this interaction. 'Thank you. That's very kind.'

My eyes dart to Becca, who gives me a reassuring smile and a slight shake of the head, which I interpret as 'don't think anything of it'.

'Great, that's sorted then,' Tess declares with a little too much oomph for my liking, given what's just gone down. 'Lea, meet us here on Friday at six p.m. for pre-show drinks and we'll show you a good night out.'

She grins at me and I'm pleased to feel such a warm welcome into the fold. However, it would have been a more comfortable experience if it hadn't been at Sal's expense. That said, I'm delighted to be able to tell Shep

175

later that, not only did I come here by myself, but I've also now got social plans for both Friday and Saturday nights this weekend. That's quite a turn of events – and a turn of fortune – from where I was less than two weeks ago.

Chapter 22

On Thursday after work, I head for home instead of The Canongate Tavern, and I'm not expecting to see Shep until later – that is, if he even comes back before I head to bed. Because having finally waved the white flag the night before, after my meet-up with the girls (which he was delighted to hear about), I've agreed with him that I'm going to have a relaxing night in with just my book and Netflix for company. It seems funny that, after so desperately wanting to have a social life, I'm now craving some time alone to rest and recharge. But I guess it's all about balance. Regardless of how good a social life a person has, surely everyone needs to power down at times. We are humans after all, not robots.

Moments after I've dumped my handbag on the floor and kicked off my shoes, Shep appears through the door.

'What are you doing here?' I cock my head in surprise.

'Don't sound too pleased to see me.' He pecks me on the lips with a grin.

'I am. You know I am. I wasn't expecting you, though, as you know. And it's a pain for you to come all the way back here between shows.'

'Maybe I couldn't wait until later to see you.'

'OK, now I know you're talking bull.' I push him play- fully and he grabs my hand, pulling me into him. Then he nuzzles my neck with his stubble, knowing fine well I find that really tickly and unbearable. 'Argh, stop it!'

'That's what you get for doubting the sincerity of my gesture.' His eyes twinkle mischievously, then he stops his antics but keeps a hold of me. 'Your spare main-door key is a dud after all, by the way. I almost couldn't get in just now. You don't have another, do you? I wouldn't want to have to wake you later.'

'Nope, afraid not. Why don't you take my keys for now and get a new one cut for yourself tomorrow? They're in my handbag. I can meet you after work to get mine back from you.'

'Good plan.' He finally lets go of me.

'So, why are you really here?' I ask.

'I couldn't face fish and chips again. Or anything from a food truck. There's only so much of that you can eat before you start craving a salad.'

'You're craving a salad?' I give a sceptical laugh.

'Not as such, but something like pasta and sauce – with some of that green stuff in a bowl on the side. That would hit the spot.'

'Well, you're in luck, because I was about to make a pot of spag bol. I make it with bottled sauce, so it'll only take twenty minutes. That work for you?'

His eyes light up. 'Damn right it does. In my mind I'm already licking the plate.'

'Saucy.' I waggle my eyebrows at him and he guffaws.

'You'd do a good one-liner routine.'

'Yeah, if it were three-jokes long.' I head into the kitchen and start piling the ingredients I need onto the counter. 'Not sure anyone would turn up for that. I certainly wouldn't be getting glowing write-ups from the local media.'

Taking a sneaky glance at him while locating a spatula to stir the sauce, I see Shep inflate with pride. It's the kind of disbelieving pride that's born out of self-doubt and an unexpectedly amazing happening, not out of arrogance, and I can't help but feel all warm and fuzzy for him. He more than deserves this chance at something incredible – especially given what he's had to put up with to achieve it.

We work as a team, getting the food ready while chatting away companionably. He prepares the 'green stuff', grates some cheese, and sorts drinks and cutlery, while I man the sauce and the pasta on the cooker. It's one of life's unremarkable moments, yet it feels wonderful beavering away side by side like this – like I'm part of a real couple – and it makes me yearn for something more committed. Something longer term. This predictably sends my brain in the direction of where things are really headed: the sad fact that Shep and I have a shorter expiry date than some of the food items we're handling.

'You've gone quiet.' He picks up on my change of mood.

'Oh, sorry.' I smile at him. 'I'm a thinker. Get lost in my brain sometimes.'

'I'm sure you do, with that analytical mind of yours. Work stuff?'

'Something like that. Just mulling over a problem.' I don't elaborate and Shep doesn't enquire further, probably because he's assuming it's a research-study issue and he won't be able to follow it, nor will he be interested enough to try.

'Hope you manage to solve it,' he simply says.

Yeah, me too, I reflect wistfully, feeling a disconsolate tug at my heart.

My estimation of serving dinner within twenty minutes is pretty accurate, and for some unknown reason – perhaps because Shep is on the clock – we don't even bother going to the table in the living room. We just serve up and stand at the counter, eating our food while chatting away. Well, I eat, and Shep shovels the pasta and sauce into his mouth like he's been told it's his last meal.

'This is great,' he says when he finally stops for a breath. 'You're a mean cook.'

'I didn't do much.' I twirl spaghetti onto my fork with a smile. 'You should be sending your compliments to the conglomerate that manufactures the sauce.'

'I don't know. I've seen a few car-crash meals come out of a jar. The hand that makes it is still important.'

When we've finished eating, I put our dirty plates and glasses in the dishwasher, and tell Shep to leave the rest of the clearing up to me. Then I wander through to my room to get changed out of my work clothes and he follows me, as he usually does.

'I enjoyed that,' I remark. 'Out of a jar or not, spag bol is proper comfort food.'

'Do you know what my comfort food is?' Shep asks.

'What?' I step out of my trousers and pull my top over my head.

'You.' He saunters up behind me, slipping his arms around my waist and planting butterfly kisses on my neck that explode into a tingling longing. This, and the feel of his hands on my bare skin, wipes out any urge to call him on that ridiculously cheesy line.

'I'm not sure you have time for this,' I murmur.

'I'll take my chances.' He turns me around, kissing me passionately while pulling off his own jeans and T-shirt, and we sink onto the bed, becoming quickly tangled up in each other.

Within minutes, we're locked in the throes of passion, moving rhythmically together while moaning with pleasure, when my flat buzzer echoes deafeningly through the hallway.

Shep's head jerks up, like a gazelle braced for danger. 'Who the hell is that?'

'It's probably just someone wanting into the building,' I say. 'Ignore it.'

He seems satisfied with this response, quickly getting back in the mood, but moments later the buzzer goes again.

'Oh, bugger off and get someone else to let you in,' I yell. 'Can't you tell we're busy?'

We share a giggle and as we once again fall back into our rhythm, I can hear footsteps on the stairs, which confirm what I thought: it was someone I don't know, looking to be let in.

That is, until I hear a knock on my flat door and a familiar voice.

'Oh fuck. That's my dad.'

'*Holy shit.*' Shep leaps off me and we both dart around in a panic, locating and pulling on our clothes at lightning speed.

Chapter 23

'He-llo-o?' my dad's voice echoes through the hallway. 'Lea, are you here?'

He's clearly heard Shep and I scuttling around in my room.

'I'll go out and distract him,' I hiss to Shep. 'Once we're in the kitchen, you can sneak out, yeah?'

'All right.' He gulps. 'You'd better hope I make a good Ethan Hunt.'

'What?'

'*Mission: Impossible.*'

'Helpful.' I adopt a sarcastic tone. 'I hope your escape tactics are better than your current banter.'

'I thought it was funny.' Shep looks a bit miffed. 'Seems someone's lost their sense of humour.'

'Really? Would you prefer we saunter out of here together and I introduce you as the guy who's boning me for the month?' I eyeball him and he holds up his hands in apology. 'OK, good. Follow the plan and we'll be fine. Oh, and break a leg today,' I add as an afterthought, giving him a brief squeeze of a hug and a kiss on the lips.

'Lea? Is that you?' my dad calls out again in an uncertain voice.

'I'm here.' I emerge into the hallway fully clothed, trying my damnedest not to look flustered. 'I was having a catnap, so I had to make sure I was decent.'

'Oh, sorry, love.' He pulls an apologetic face and removes his spectacles. 'You didn't answer your buzzer, so I assumed you were out and let myself in. I was going to leave something here for you.'

'Is that you just back from your trip?' I can't help but notice that he looks a bit weary. His piercing blue eyes aren't shining as brightly as usual, and I might be wrong, but his thinning brown hair seems more streaked with grey than the last time I saw him.

'Yes, I was flying out and back through Edinburgh rather than Glasgow this time, so I thought I'd nip round and see if you were here.'

'You should have called,' I chastise him to discourage any further unannounced drop-ins. 'What if I hadn't been in?'

'Well, then I was just going to drop something off for you… as I said.' He gives me an odd look, which I return with a bright smile, while inwardly kicking myself for such an ill-considered comment. 'I got you a small gift from Germany.'

'Ah, yes, you did say. That's so lovely of you. Would you like a cup of tea?' I usher him towards the kitchen, without waiting for an answer.

'So, how have you been?' My dad surveys the dirty pots on the cooker top, while I thank my lucky stars I already put the dinner plates and glasses in the dishwasher.

'Fine.' I fill the kettle and switch it on. 'You know, the usual. Things are good at work. I'm really enjoying the project I'm on.' I realise I need to deflect and take the focus off me so that I don't give anything away about my current set-up. This, of course, is supremely difficult with a parent. 'How was your trip?'

'Eh… it felt long this time. I was only away a week, but after a few days I was longing for my own bed. I must be getting old.'

'Never.' I dismiss this comment outright. 'You're still a spring chicken.'

'You're a terrible liar, Lea.' He reaches out and touches my cheek affectionately. 'Always have been.'

'I know. It didn't serve me well as a teenager. Always the one getting caught when everyone was up to no good.'

He chuckles. 'Well, it certainly served your mum and I well.'

Taking two mugs out of the cupboard, I add a teabag to each and pour in the steaming water.

'Can you get the milk out of the fridge for me?' I ask this for the sole purpose of getting my dad to the other end of the kitchen, while I do a quick check on Shep.

Peeking my head out of the kitchen door, I see that he is indeed on his way out of my bedroom, embarking on his mission to make it out of the flat undetected. He winces and I give him an encouraging thumbs up, then duck my head back inside the kitchen.

'Thanks.' I take the milk from my dad and discard the used teabags, my mind focused on Shep, willing him to achieve a Houdini-style getaway. 'Where were you in Germany, then?'

'The North,' he says. 'Hamburg.'

'I don't know Hamburg. Is it nice?'

'Nice enough. It's a large port city – known for being "Germany's gateway to the world". Has a river running through it – the Elbe – and it has a couple of lakes too.'

'That does sound nice.'

Squeak.

'What was that?' My dad's ears prick up like a blood-hound.

'What was what?' I pretend I didn't hear the almighty great creak that just came from one of the dodgy floor-boards I forgot to warn Shep about.

Ignoring my lame attempt at putting him off the scent, my dad strides out of the kitchen, with me at his heels.

'What the—' He stops abruptly on spotting Shep, who's balancing on one leg, clutching my handbag and looking incredibly suspect – with the flat door wide open behind him.

It takes me all of two seconds to realise what's going on. He must have remembered at the last moment that he was to take my keys tonight; however, to the uninformed eye, it looks as if he's an opportunist thief who's tried my front door and got lucky.

'Lea, call 999.' My dad backs up, steering me into the living room. 'Young man, I don't know what you're after, but I suggest you disappear before the police arrive. Do not force me into a citizen's arrest.'

'Dad…' I try to get his attention, realising this has got way out of hand.

'Just do as I say, Lea.' He reaches out to the shelving just inside the living-room door and picks up a heavy vase, which he's obviously intending to use for self-defence if it comes to it.

Though my dad is shielding me and obscuring my view, I can still see Shep's eyes grow wide with alarm.

'Dad, no. *Stop*.' This time I assert myself properly. 'He's not an intruder. His name is Shep.'

'Shep?' My dad turns to me and it's clear that he's struggling to process what I've just said. 'You mean you know this man?'

'I do.'

'Well, how do you know him? And what kind of a name is Shep?'

'Uh… it's a nickname,' Shep offers from the hallway. 'Ciaran Shepperd. Good to meet you, sir.'

My dad puts the vase back down on the shelf and looks at me helplessly. I rub my jaw regretfully.

'Sorry, Dad. Shep is my…' I suddenly realise I don't know how to finish my sentence.

'Boyfriend.' Shep does it for me, offering my dad a weak grin. 'Probably not the best way for us to meet for the first time.'

He approaches my dad, who still looks utterly shell-shocked, and extends his hand. 'I apologise, sir. It really is good to meet you.'

He takes Shep's hand and shakes it. 'You too. I think. Though, may I ask, why is my daughter hiding the boyfriend I didn't know she had away from me?' His appraising eyes land back on me.

I can almost see the cogs whirling in his brain, putting everything together – the unanswered buzzer and the scuffling in my room – and his jaw drops in realisation.

He clears his throat, his cheeks pinkening. 'Right, well, perhaps we won't dwell on that. Shep, rather than you making a run for it, how about you join us for a cup of tea?'

Shep shifts on the spot and I can tell he's uncomfortable about declining my dad's offer, given how the last few minutes have panned out.

'Oh, he can't, Dad.' I step in to save him. 'Shep's due at a festival show shortly.'

'I see. No problem.' My dad eyes Shep warily, making it clear it is in fact something of a problem. 'Then we must do it another time.'

'Of course.' Shep and I nod in unison.

'Dinner on Saturday evening? Lea, I can speak to your mum and we can have a proper family get-together. I'm sure she'll be keen to meet Shep, assuming she hasn't already.'

'Nope. She hasn't. Doesn't know anything either,' I quickly reassure him. 'But I'm afraid we can't do Saturday evening. We're going to my colleague's house for dinner.'

'Fair enough. We'll do Sunday lunch then.' This is a statement rather than a question, and it fills me with dread.

Because I know my dad, and when it comes to keeping me safe, he makes an overprotective mamma bear seem like a puppy barking at a dandelion. If he'd met Shep through a normal: 'Dad, this is my new boyfriend, isn't he wonderful?' type of introduction, he would have been curt but polite, so as not to upset me. Then when my back was turned, he'd have bared his teeth (in a symbolic sense) to make sure Shep knew not to mess with me or him. It would have taken Shep quite some time to win him over – if he were to manage that at all. However, given that only moments ago my dad was brandishing a vase and threatening to go full Jackie Chan on Shep, even I can understand why, right now, he's not just leaning towards a 'no' but a 'hell, no'. And in the midst of all this ridiculousness is the fact that Shep is not even my boyfriend.

'Erm… Dad, maybe leave it with us to—'

'Sunday lunch would be great, sir,' Shep interjects and I stare at him as if he's out of his mind. 'My show doesn't start until four thirty in the afternoon, so that will work perfectly. I'll look forward to it. And to meeting Lea's ma. She's told me such great things about you both.'

'Has she now?' My dad's appraising eye shifts to me once again and I plaster on an innocent smile.

'Of course, Dad. Why would I say otherwise. You and Mum are totally awesome.'

'OK, we'll see you on Sunday, then, Shep.' My dad shakes Shep's hand again, this time with what looks like an iron grip, which is clearly his way of asserting his authority. 'I'll let Lea know the where and the when.'

'Great stuff.' Shep spreads his arms in what I interpret to be a gesture of I-really-have-nothing-to-hide. 'Well, I must fly on, or I'll miss the start of my own show. See you Sunday, Mr... Lea's da,' he finishes off pathetically.

I cringe. Poor Shep doesn't even know my surname, because he's never asked and it's never come up in conversation. I only know his because of the whole nickname thing.

My dad frowns. 'You can call me David. I'm not keen on "sir" and I'm not sure "Mr Lea's da" works either.'

'Right you are, David.' Shep grins at my dad while backing away towards the door. 'Lea, I'll see... um... Call you later?'

'Sounds good.' I wrinkle my nose at his indiscreet cover-up. 'See you.'

Shep transfers something metallic to his pocket, which I realise is the set of keys he was getting from my bag, then makes his exit. The moment the door closes behind him, I pat my troubled-looking dad on the arm.

'Let's re-boil the kettle and you can tell me all about Hamburg.'

Chapter 24

'Oh, that's freakin' hilarious!' Tess bangs the table with her fist. 'I can't believe your dad thought Shep was a burglar.'

It's the following day and I'm in the Old Town Inn with Becca and Tess for drinks ahead of our Friday night show together.

'You must have been mortified.' Becca's face is brimming with sympathy, though she's laughing at the same time.

'That's not even close.' I shake my head, my cheeks burning from re-living the experience. 'I'm not sure there is a word to describe how I felt. How I still feel now, just thinking about it.'

'Sal's going to love this story,' says Tess. 'You'll need to tell her next time we're all together.'

'OK, sure.' I'm not as convinced of this, but I am pleased that my unfortunate parental encounter is providing some great bonding material with my new 'gal pals', as Tanya would call them. Apparently, that is what we are now – Tess made this abundantly clear the last time we were together.

'Sal must be really bummed about missing tonight's show.' I sip at my glass of white wine reflectively. 'It looks like it's going to be a good one.'

'She'll live.' Tess casually pushes her long bouncy red hair behind her shoulders. 'Let's get back to your daddy–daughter–sexy–lodger triangle. What happened after Shep left? And how is he after nearly getting his arse kicked by your dad? Quite literally.' She chortles at her own joke.

'Well, needless to say, my dad wasn't for telling me about his trip to Hamburg after that. I basically had to offer up enough to satisfy his curious-slash-suspicious mind, without giving away the bits that would result in me – a grown woman – being lectured and told off by my father. I was just so relieved he didn't bring up the whole interrupting us during sex thing. I really couldn't have coped with a "birds, bees and STDs" talk on top of all that.'

'Ah, that's priceless!' Tess claps her hands delightedly.

'And Shep?' Becca prompts me to answer Tess's second question.

'Was surprisingly cool about the whole thing. After he knew the cops weren't about to blue-light in and cart him away. And get this… To save face… both our faces…' I furrow my brow at my ineloquence. 'And to avoid any awkward questions or my dad finding out about our shacked-up situation, Shep introduced himself to my dad as my boyfriend.'

'Good move.' Tess gives what appears to be an impressed nod.

'That's not all. My dad then asked Shep and I to have lunch with him and my mum on Sunday, and while I was in the middle of making an excuse for us, Shep bulldozed in and accepted the invite.'

'Ooh, what do you think that means?' Becca leans in, her and Tess sharing a look of intrigue.

'I think it means he's an idiot,' I declare. 'I mean, who likes meeting the parents at the best of times, never mind when you've more or less been caught red-handed shagging their daughter?'

Becca looks thoughtful for a moment. 'I'm guessing it's one of two things. Either he's falling for you as much as you are for him…' She sees my face light up with hope and holds up a hand to slow me down. 'Or—'

'He has a death wish,' Tess jumps in.

'Not actually what I was about to say.' Becca affectionately shushes her. 'What I was thinking, and I'm sorry for this, Lea, but—'

'As a comedian, Shep might like to put himself in situations that have the potential to provide him with new material.' I rub my suddenly weary forehead, the lightness of the moment now eclipsed by this unwelcome reality check.

'Yes. That's exactly what I was going to say.'

On hearing this confirmation, a swell of emotion overcomes me, and my eyes brim with tears, as my previous fear of becoming nothing more than the inspiration behind some of Shep's stand-up material is resurrected.

'That doesn't mean I'm right,' Becca rushes to add, taking one of my hands in hers across the table. 'It's just something to consider. And if it is why he agreed to lunch, it doesn't mean he doesn't care about you, nor does it even mean it was a conscious decision. It might just be his way.'

Tess grabs my other hand and squeezes it hard. 'Best you go into it with your eyes open, as Becca says, so there's less chance of you having regrets later down the line.'

I nod, wiping away a rogue tear. 'What the hell have I got myself into? All I wanted was to help him out of a tight spot and maybe enjoy a bit of company at the same time.'

'How do you mean?' Becca cocks her head curiously.

'Oh, you know, he was going to have to go home if I hadn't—'

'I don't think that's what Becca was referring to,' says Tess. 'You said you wanted company.'

It's only as she says this that I realise I've overshared. Looking away from them, I weigh up whether to spin a story or tell the truth and risk the same reaction I first got from Shep.

'Lea, you're in safe company with us.' Becca encourages me to open up. 'Isn't she, Tess?'

'Of course.' Tess plonks a hand on her chest as if to signify her trustworthiness. 'As I said before, nothing goes outside our foursome.'

Taking in their genuine concern (at least that's how I read it), I decide I need to put my faith in these girls, because if their offer of friendship is real, once Shep's gone, they'll be all I have. Plus, I'd never be brave enough to share this with Sal around, so it might be my only opportunity.

'OK, but can we keep this just between us?' They nod, while I screw up my face in embarrassment at the thought of vocalising my predicament, then I take a courage-inducing slug from my glass. 'I've sort of been a bit lonely… well, very lonely…' I fill them in on my situation, without bothering to sugar-coat anything to make myself look better – why would I, when I'm already showing such a level of vulnerability?

To say Becca and Tess are understanding and supportive is an understatement. They rally around me, pledging 'unconditional life-long friendship' (no surprise that those high-drama words came from Tess) and to never allow me to be in that situation again, regardless of whether they or I were in long-term relationships. They make me feel safe and – like Shep, after his initial blip – they're adamant that I have nothing to feel ashamed of. It's so much more than I could have expected, and such a weight off, knowing that when Shep leaves, I won't be right back to where I started.

We then have a brilliant evening out at the show together, grabbing dinner from a street-food truck beforehand, and enjoying a 'debrief' over a cocktail afterwards. It's a perfect night, and I find myself kind of wishing I could join in with their Fringe challenge. That said, what I don't want to do is overstay my welcome and leave them regretting their decision to recruit me as one of their own. So, I'll take things gently and earn my place with them, as I've always done with everything else in my life.

Chapter 25

On Saturday evening, after a lazy morning in bed and an afternoon on the sofa, guffawing at back-to-back episodes of *Superstore*, Shep and I get ready to go to Tanya's place. Having never been invited to dinner at a proper grown-up's house before (my parents don't count), I'm a bit lost on what to wear. After pretty much emptying and trying on my whole wardrobe, I eventually decide on an outfit similar to the one I wore on my 'first date' with Shep – though I opt for a dress that won't give Tanya or her husband an eyeful of my arse if I bend the wrong way. I also tong my hair again, pleased to note that I do a slightly better job than last time. And with my makeup, I stick to nude shades, my aim being to look like I fit in with a more mature demographic.

Click-clacking my way across the creaky floorboards to the living room, where Shep's glued to the TV, having spent all of five minutes getting ready himself, I do a little pirouette.

'Does this say first-dinner-party-at-older-and-slightly-inappropriate-colleague's-house?'

'To the letter.' He gives a chef's kiss to punctuate this, then switches off the TV, gets up from the sofa and puts his arms around me. 'It also says: "Shep, I want you."'

'No, it doesn't.' I wriggle out of his grasp. 'Not when we're already going to be late.'

'And whose fault is that?' He grins at me while I stick my tongue out at him.

'Come on, funny guy. Let's go.'

Thirty-five minutes and two buses later, we approach a stylish new-build apartment block in the Roseburn area of the city. It's one of those complexes that seem to be made mainly from glass, with endless – and immensely sturdy-looking – floor-to-ceiling windows positioned next to roomy balconies and terraces, which are framed by (yet more) glass balustrades. My assumption is that this is to provide its occupiers with panoramic views and optimise the light for an exclusive city-living experience; however, I've seen enough of them streaked with nausea-inducing amounts of bird crap to think that maybe they're not quite living up to those intentions. Though that is perhaps a small price to pay, and one I could definitely bear if I ever had the chance of living somewhere like this.

'This is nice.' I raise my eyebrows at Shep. 'Tanya must be on good money to be living here.'

I locate and press the buzzer to her apartment, then we wait patiently until someone answers.

'Hello?' It sounds like it might be one of Tanya's teenage kids.

'Oh, hi. It's Lea and Shep. Your mum's expecting us.'

There's no response other than the click of the door being unlocked, followed by the intercom handset being dumped clumsily back in its cradle.

'Thank you,' I call into the intercom, despite knowing I won't be heard.

Shrugging at Shep, I push the main door open and we enter the building foyer, which is a damned sight more inviting than the claustrophobic musty-smelling stairwell where I live.

'I am so jealous that they have a lift,' I practically moan as I hit the button to call it.

'Lifts are for lazy people,' says Shep. 'And people who need them, obviously. Your stairs will keep you fit and healthy.'

'Yeah, let's see if you feel the same after several years of climbing mine.'

The moment this comment is out of my mouth, I instantly regret it. It was intended as off the cuff and light-hearted, but it was also carelessly shared, and its insinuations (i.e. that I'm starting to hope for something longer term) are clear. I can tell that Shep is trying to pretend he hasn't noticed, but his expression and body language leave me in little doubt he's interpreted it in the way I'm fearing.

We take the lift to the fifth floor in silence, me stewing over my cock-up, and Shep... well, who knows what he's thinking. Maybe I'm just being paranoid. When the lift doors ping open, we step out into a small corridor with just three doors, one of which is wide open, allowing us to see a long spacious hallway with expensive-looking laminate flooring.

Approaching the open doorway, I double-check the apartment number, then I hesitate and look uncertainly at Shep.

He raises an eyebrow. 'Hope we've got the right place, or someone's about to get one hell of a surprise.'

Suddenly, the door at the very end of the hallway is yanked open and Tanya bustles through it, wearing a floaty pastel-coloured summer dress.

'*Jacob*, I thought I told you to let our guests in,' she hollers to what seems like no one in particular as she strides along the hallway towards us.

'I did let them in,' the same voice we heard through the intercom yells from behind one of the doors.

'I meant greet them at the door and bring them through to the sitting room,' she barks back, then turns her attention to us. 'I'm so sorry, you two. Honestly, you would have thought they were raised by wolves. Come on in. I've got the fizz – and the whisky – ready.' Her gaze lands on Shep. 'It's lovely to meet you…'

'Ciaran,' he quickly supplies, which is helpful as Tanya clearly doesn't want to address him by his nickname, and it seems she's forgotten his real one.

'Ah, of course. Ciaran.' Tanya gives him a sparkling smile. 'Lea's told me such wonderful things about you.'

'Has she now?' He obediently plays up to Tanya's effusiveness, but doesn't look at me, which I take as another bad sign.

'Oh, yes.' Tanya's totally oblivious to the unfortunate dynamics at play. 'And I'm hoping you'll be telling me equally wonderful things about her tonight.'

I wince at this remark, while Tanya beckons for us to follow her into the living room, which is huge, with the biggest corner sofa I've ever seen and the same floor-to-ceiling windows I was admiring from outside. There's also a set of French doors that open onto a sizeable garden terrace, complete with elegant outdoor furniture and planters bursting with a kaleidoscope of colourful summer flowers.

My jaw drops in astonishment. 'Wow, Tanya. Your apartment is incredible.'

'It is a lovely aspect.' She hands me a glass of fizz and Shep a whisky, and we thank her. 'Ciaran, my husband, John, suggested you start with a Ballavulin. I'm supposed to give you some story about it being the malt he cut his teeth on, but I suspect it's his way of testing if you're a real whisky drinker. As far as I'm concerned, any peaty malt tastes like I've landed face down in a bog.'

'So not a fan, then?' Shep grins at her and I can tell he's filing all this away as inspiration for future show material.

Still stuck on how amazing the apartment is, I wander across to the window to get a proper look at the view.

'Oh gosh, you're overlooking the Water of Leith. Tanya, this place is stunning. It's like something out of a luxury lifestyle magazine.'

'It certainly didn't come from a paltry university salary, before you get ideas.' She winks at me. 'John used to work in academia, like me, before he went through an early midlife crisis and sold his soul to the finance industry. Not that I'm complaining. It means I get to live here, and I hardly see him due to the ridiculous hours he works. That's what I call win-win. Ah, here he is, the apple of my eye...'

Shep and I share a look roughly translated as 'did she actually just say that?', as Tanya's husband, John, enters the room, and I have to look away to avoid laughing out loud and giving the poor man a complex.

'Evening.' He nods politely at us, then Tanya does the introductions, and we respond with the usual pleasantries and chit-chat.

John is exactly what I'd imagined as a partner for Tanya. He's tall, slim and balding, with glasses and crinkly eyes that put you at ease with one look. And he's wearing jeans, a plaid shirt and a tweed jacket.

'Why don't the two of you head out to the terrace with your drinks while John helps me with the starters,' suggests Tanya. 'There are some nibbles on the table, provided those ruddy seagulls haven't already eaten them or shat on them.'

She all but shoos us through the French doors while dragging her protesting husband, who'd clearly rather be relaxing with a malt, off to the kitchen.

Stepping out onto the terrace and into the warm(ish) evening air, I breathe deeply and give a laboured sigh. 'Isn't this the life?'

'It's not bad at all,' says Shep, but rather than joining me where I'm leaning on the balustrade, he makes a beeline for the snacks on the table, which fortunately seem to have escaped the attention of the gulls.

I try to stay in the moment, enjoying my fizz while taking in the view, but of course, my brain won't let me. Not when there's a lingering awkwardness between us. Though the last thing I want to do is make things worse, I also can't bear the idea of this becoming a thing. Turning away from the view, I join him at the table.

'That comment I made before… about how you'd feel after climbing the stairs in my building for some time. It was just banter, you know? I didn't mean anything by it.'

'I know.' He pops a couple of cashew nuts in his mouth and parks himself on the cream outdoor sofa.

'You know?' I frown. 'Then why did you go all weird when I said it?'

Shep looks like he's contemplating how to answer this, perhaps trying to decide how to respond in a way that gets him in the least bother. Just as it seems he might be about to say something, Tanya and John appear through the French doors.

'How are you two getting on?' She beams at us expectantly.

She obviously isn't asking this with any deliberate intent, but with my unanswered question still hanging in the air, her words have the effect of reigniting the stiltedness between us. Thankfully, Tanya and John appear oblivious to this, and she seems to read our tight smiles as genuine.

'It's not a patch on the Med.' Tanya waves her arm theatrically. 'But it's our little paradise spot, isn't it, John?'

'So you keep telling everyone who visits.' John winks at us, while Tanya pulls a bored face.

'Don't mind him. You'll eventually forget he's there.'

Stifling a giggle, I steal a glance at Shep, who seems to be doing the same.

'The starters won't be long,' says Tanya. 'Jacob is going to keep an eye on them. In the meantime, Ciaran, we're fascinated to hear about your experience at the Fringe. I've never met a comedian before.'

From the way she's watching him, you'd think Tanya had discovered a novel fragment of genetic material – and from the way Shep responds, it seems he's also picked up on this.

'We're a fairly unremarkable species, really,' he says. 'We eat, sleep and shit the same as everyone else.'

I blanch at this remark, my panicked eyes darting to Tanya and John, who thankfully seem quite amused by it.

'No, it's great being a comedian in many ways, but it's tough too. Like it is for so many creatives – actors, writers, artists. We're all chasing the dream, hoping for that big break, but the reality is: for most of us it's a penniless life in pursuit of the Holy Grail.'

'Uh-huh.' Tanya nods. 'We don't value our creatives enough in this country.'

'But you're doing well with your show, aren't you?' I'm keen to throw in some supportive words.

Shep nods, taking my cue. 'Aye, it's going OK. It's a free show, in case Lea hasn't mentioned it.'

'Everyone's got to start somewhere.' John sips at his whisky reflectively. 'How's the Ballavulin?'

'Rich and peaty. Just how I like it.'

'Good man.' John tips his head in approval. 'So, your show is being received well, it seems.' He says this as a statement rather than a question, which catches my attention.

'It is,' says Shep. 'I've had a full house for several days now. I'm chuffed about that.'

'And he got a positive write-up in the media,' I can't help pitching in.

'I saw that,' says John. 'In one of the broadsheets. Tanya had mentioned your stage name, so it jumped out at me.'

I furrow my brow. 'No, that was online. On the *Main Attraction* site.'

Tanya and John scoff in unison and I give them a bewildered look.

'Apologies.' Tanya reaches out and touches my forearm. 'It's just that there's no way John has been on the *Main Attraction* website. He's a literature snob in the same way that I am an intolerant mother. Darling, why don't you see if you can find the paper you saw it in?'

'Yes, ma'am.' He playfully salutes her and disappears inside, returning a minute or so later holding a newspaper folded open at the Culture section. 'Here we are, Ciaran. Your name in lights.'

Shep and I huddle over the short article, which mentions 'razor-sharp wit', 'a refreshing approach to stand-up' and Shep doubtlessly returning in the future as a paid act.

'Shep, this is amazing!' I beam at him. 'You've been endorsed by a broadsheet now too. That's a big deal.'

I can see he's trying to play it cool because of the company we're in, but from the twinkle I can see in Shep's eye, he's clearly buzzing.

'Thanks a million for sharing this, John.' He passes the paper back and John holds up his hand to stop him.

'Keep it as a souvenir. It would only end up in the recycling.'

'Well, I think this calls for a celebratory toast,' declares Tanya.

She plucks the bottle of fizz from the cooler on the table, quickly tops up her glass as well as mine, then pours some fizz for Shep and John, handing them each a flute.

'To a bright future in the funny industry.' Tanya holds out her glass and we obediently follow her lead, clinking and saying 'cheers'.

Just as we're leaning back in our seats with contented expressions, a deafening beeping from inside the apartment rips through the pleasant ambience.

'*Oh, for goodness' sake*, that child of ours can't be trusted to wipe his own backside.' Tanya thrusts her flute in John's free hand and dashes indoors to deal with what are probably now very burnt starters.

Chapter 26

After a slight delay while the living room is aired, and a second batch of starters are whipped up and put in the oven, we sit down to eat at Tanya and John's huge rustic oak dining table. John pours a 'Pouilly-Fumé with notes of citrus, exotic fruits and white flowers' – that's white wine to the rest of us – which is delicious and evidently not a cheap bottle, so I have to concede that it does deserve the pretentious introduction. Our starters of Stilton, pear and walnut soufflé are equally mouth-watering – not something I've had before, and I decide I'd like to have a shot at making them myself at some point.

The conversation at the table is light, humorous and enjoyable, with Tanya and John bickering good-naturedly throughout. It seems clear that, while they publicly rib and goad each other, they're a solid couple who are still very much in love, despite Tanya's occasional comments to the contrary. Their childlike behaviour aside, it feels like a very grown-up experience and I really quite like it. It's different to going to the pub or on a night out – very much a 'coupley' experience. I actually feel a bit sad when I realise it's not something that's likely to be repeated when Shep moves on, and I'm living the single life again.

We're just starting on our main course of venison wellington with potato dauphinoise and steamed vegetables – another culinary triumph (who would have guessed

Tanya was a chef extraordinaire!) – when the conversation comes back round to Shep and his comedy career. Or rather, how I helped to save his comedy career.

'So, Ciaran…' Tanya has a glint in her eye that puts me on edge. 'It seems, with these gushing write-ups, that the only way is up for you now.'

'That's certainly what I'm hoping.' Shep saws through his venison wellington with his steak knife and pops a piece in his mouth.

'I think it's wonderful that things have worked out so well for you. And to think, if you and Lea hadn't bumped into each other that day, it might have been a different story altogether.'

'I've had that thought many times myself.' He nods, while I try to catch Tanya's eye to signal to her not to take this topic of conversation any further.

She either doesn't notice me or – more likely – she purposefully avoids my stare.

'It's almost as if there was a little bit of fate going on there, don't you think?' She proceeds to wander into conversational territory I really don't want her in.

'I honestly can't thank Lea enough.' He reaches across and pats my back affectionately, while I force a smile in return. 'I'm not sure I believe in that hocus–pocus stuff, though.'

'Of course.' Tanya seems to reflect for a moment, while I attempt to burn a hole through her face with my retinas. 'Being a scientist, I probably don't either. I guess I'm just a hopeful romantic – love a bit of serendipity. And the two of you make such a lovely couple.'

Oh God. She did not just do that. If Tanya weren't my senior colleague, she'd be getting a kick under the table right about now. Well, if I could actually reach her under this gigantic oak tree. Unfortunately, all I can do is look on helplessly as this cringeworthy exchange continues to unfold. As this rate, poor Shep will be thinking we cooked this evening up together to try and move things on between him and I – especially after my unfortunate comment earlier on.

Having taken another mouthful of venison at the wrong moment, Shep does that hand gesture thing that indicates he'll respond as soon as he's swallowed. I suppose I should consider it a relief that he hasn't choked on his food. Unable to look at him, I play with my own meal, waiting with bated breath for his reply. I'm desperate to hear something to reassure me that he's not freaked out by Tanya's blatant attempts at playing Cupid. Even better would be a glimmer of something positive – any indication that Shep sees a future for us beyond the end of the festival.

In the end, I get neither.

'I think we all know I'm punching above my weight. Right, Lea?' He says eventually, giving me a comical nudge while I wither in my seat. 'She wasn't even attracted to me to begin with.'

'At least you know your place in the pecking order. Always best to know who's boss,' John quips, earning himself a look from Tanya that ironically confirms his statement.

'At my ripe age, Ciaran, I have plenty of wisdom stored up that I like to impart on you young ones,' Tanya proclaims, as if there are several decades between us, when in fact it can't be any more than twenty years. 'I also have much more useful advice than my husband, and I guarantee you that a relationship built on a true connection, trust and mutual respect will last longer and be far more fulfilling than one based on animalistic sexual attraction.'

She pauses briefly to sip from her wine glass, and I sneak an anxious look at Shep. He appears somewhat bemused by this 'speech', which has seemingly come from nowhere.

'That's not to say that great sex isn't something to aim for,' she continues, making me wish I could tape over her mouth. 'John and I made a hobby out of it before our little darlings came along. Now the best I can hope for is some fun with the shower head of a morning.'

This final comment is met with stunned silence – even from John. I shrink down in my seat, mortified that I've willingly brought Shep into this situation, knowing full well that Tanya has boundary issues. I'm now thinking this whole dinner-party idea was a very bad one indeed.

–

On Sunday morning, I wake up groggy and hungover from too much booze. Our evening with Tanya and John continued to be an equally eye-opening and butt-clenching experience, right through dessert, coffee and liqueurs. Before last night, the closest I'd come to having an after-dinner digestif had been opening a pack of McVitie's to satisfy my sweet tooth. While I might ordinarily have enjoyed this novel experience, it was difficult to focus on anything other than my excruciating discomfort, as Tanya continued to drop the most unsubtle hints ever at Shep.

She obviously thought she was playing a masterful role as matchmaker. Breaking news: she was not – and this propelled me to drink more and more to drown it all out.

Our night then came to a close with us making a collective vow to do it again before the end of the month. I had my fingers firmly crossed behind my back at that particular moment. Then Shep and I took a taxi back to mine, fell into bed and were out cold within moments of our heads hitting our respective pillows.

As I roll over and see Shep lying asleep beside me, I feel a bit sick thinking about what must have been going through his head the evening before. He was a perfect dinner guest and played along with the banter to an exceptional level, but how could he not have felt uncomfortable with Tanya attempting to steer our relationship like that. While she had, to some extent, given away her intentions in advance, I had expected her to assume a more covert role. Instead, she made it so obvious what she was up to, she may as well have scrawled: 'Ciaran, will you make an honest woman out of Lea?' across the French windows in marker pen. As it turns out, Tanya's even more of a character outside of work than in, which I guess makes sense. She does need to have some air of professionalism at work.

Under normal circumstances, I'd happily hang out with her, because she's great fun, but there's no question that last night was a mistake. I'm very concerned that she has unintentionally bulldozed any chance Shep and I might have had at a real relationship – no matter how minuscule that was. He also never answered my question about why he went all weird when I made that joke about climbing my stairs – not even when it was just the two of us on our way home – and I couldn't bring myself to ask again. Through personal experience, I've learned that men can be flighty at the best of times, so when faced with the spectacle that was last night, us going our separate ways in a week or so's time (both physically and emotionally) now feels like a foregone conclusion.

Unable to take any more of these burdensome thoughts, I silently climb out of bed, gather some clean clothes and head for the shower in the hope it will shift my thinking and maybe even my hangover. Then, once I'm dressed, I head to the kitchen to make us some breakfast.

'Morning, any chance of a cup of tea?' Shep appears in the doorway as I'm getting the breakfast cereal out of the cupboard.

He's all dozy and bleary-eyed, which makes him look utterly adorable. My heart skips then sinks, all in a single moment, as my worry about last night and the dread of the clock unapologetically counting down our time together pile upon me like earth being dumped off the back of a truck.

'Morning, yes of course.' I smile at him, keeping this inner turmoil firmly locked away. 'Why don't you take a seat at the table and I'll bring it through?'

He slopes off to the other room, while I slump against the kitchen counter and take a long contemplative breath. I really never expected this to be how things would go when I offered Shep my spare room two weeks ago. Through my own lack of foresight, I'm now feeling extremely vulnerable and staring down the barrel of sure-fire heartbreak. And the worst thing about it is that the connection I have with Shep – even after only a couple of weeks – trumps any feelings I ever had for Paul the wanker, or the series of similarly self-obsessed idiots I dated before him. In fact, it tells me that I never scratched the surface with any of them. Our relationships were shallow and superficial, and I honestly couldn't say I knew any part of them – other than the part that comes out to play under the bedsheets, that is.

I don't know whether it's the situation Shep and I have found ourselves in, living in such close quarters, or whether he's so different to those other guys. Perhaps it's a combination of both. But it's forced us to communicate and interact on an entirely different level. It really is like things are moving in fast forward, and in terms of getting to know each other, we're already months ahead of where we would ordinarily be. I've watched people on reality TV dating shows talk about this type of thing when they're interviewed, and I've cynically always thought it was just a ploy to suck the viewers in. However, I can honestly say that I now understand exactly what they're talking about. And unfortunately, I can also understand how things can go to shit so quickly when their cosy bubble bursts and real life resumes.

'You still alive in there?' Shep calls from next door, snapping me back to reality.

'Um… yep. Be there in a sec.'

I quickly scrabble around, getting the tea made and everything we need out of the cupboards and drawers, then I ferry the cereal boxes, crockery and milk through to the table.

'I could have helped. You didn't need to do that all yourself.' Shep picks up the box of cornflakes and pours himself a generous portion.

'It's fine.' I dismiss his comment. 'Distracts me from my hangover.'

And from my pre-heartbreak woes.

Once I've brought everything through, I take a seat opposite Shep and sip gingerly at my steaming mug of tea.

'That was quite a sigh.' Shep's spoon pauses halfway to his mouth.

'Was it?' I'm not even aware that I let out a sigh at all.

'I'd say an eight.'

'Out of ten?'

'Out of five.' He raises a curious eyebrow.

'Oh.' I stiffen, and immediately try to think of a plausible excuse, because I know he'll ask.

'What's with you? Anything I can help with?'

Drawing a blank, I say nothing and simply give a pained shake of my head.

He puts down his spoon and sits forward. 'OK, now I know there's something wrong. That's what you do when something's eating at you. Come on, spit it out.'

His intense green eyes are fixed on mine, stirring up a flurry of emotions that are so overwhelming, I have to look away. I desperately want to ask him if I ruined things with my clumsy comment last night, or if Tanya did with hers. If there was even anything to ruin in the first place, or if these deep terrifying feelings I've developed are just one-sided. Instead, I add sugar to my tea, despite having never done so before and purely to stall for time. Then, as my brain finally kicks in and offers me what I need, I meet his gaze, sincerely hoping that my face isn't giving everything away.

'I'm just... um... a bit worried about today.'

'You mean the lunchtime grilling I'm in for?' He grins, seemingly convinced by my answer. 'Should it not be me who's nervous? I'm the one who nearly got my head caved in the other day.'

'That is true.' I pause, trying to form a convincing enough response. 'The thing is: I know my parents.

They're amazing people, don't get me wrong, but they can be full-on. My concern is that—'

'They'll scare me off?'

I'm thrown by this interjection, which was not at all what I was expecting from him. Is Shep indicating that there is something to scare him off from? Like the possibility of a longer-term relationship? Or is this just another one of his endless quips?

'Well, no.' I opt for the safest response. 'We both know that this meet-the-parents situation is a sham to avoid me having to admit to "picking up a stray", taking him home and shagging him for the month – no offence intended. If they knew the truth, I'd get an absolute roasting.'

'With me facing a grilling and you potentially a roasting, it's starting to feel like *we're* lunch.'

'Ha, yeah.' I laugh, then my expression turns serious again. 'I guess I'm nervous that either the truth will accidentally come out or they'll put you through a really awful experience.'

Obviously, what I really want to say is far more than this, but it's all I can share and it is the truth. Well, *a* truth – a much tamer one than the one I feel too vulnerable to share.

'Hey, Lea.' Shep reaches across the table and rubs the back of my hand with his thumb. 'You don't need to worry about me. If I can deal with hecklers hurling nonsense at me when I'm on stage, I can handle your folks. They might even give me some inspiration for a future show...'

His words sting so sharply that I have to work hard to keep my face neutral while my insides go into meltdown. Becca's previous comment about this being a possible motive for Shep agreeing to the lunch reverberates like a pinball in my mind. She was right. He might think he's placating me, but there's no smoke without fire, as the saying goes. Which means that we really are on the road to goodbye in around ten days' time.

Blissfully unaware that I'm no longer listening to a word he's saying, Shep carries on talking for a good thirty seconds before I finally re-engage with the conversation.

'Anyway, let's try and enjoy the lunch as best we can, yeah?' He gives my hand a reassuring squeeze.

'Sure, let's do that,' is all I can manage by way of a reply, while I try very hard not to burst into tears.

Chapter 27

At 12:30 p.m., Shep and I are standing outside the entrance to Melville's, a quaint Scottish restaurant on William Street, in the West End. It's a place that's been around so long – having built its solid reputation through the use of local seasonal produce – I'd say it's become a bit of an Edinburgh institution.

'Ready?' he asks me.

'Are *you* ready?' I pull a pained face.

'Lea, I was born ready.'

'I don't know what that means, but I'm glad you're going in with fighting spirit. Just try and remember what that feels like, yeah?'

The confident smile on Shep's face falters slightly, and though I'm ashamed to admit it, I get a little satisfaction out of this. Because I'm still smarting over his earlier comment about using my family dynamics for stand-up material – though probably more from what that insinuates about his reasons for being here. If my parents act like I think they will, though, they'll deserve all they get. I mean that in an affectionate sense, of course.

'All right. Let's do it.' Shep pulls open the door and strides inside, with me at his heels.

'There they are,' I hear my dad exclaim at a volume that lets everyone in the minimalist, but tastefully decorated, restaurant know we've arrived, causing me to colour with embarrassment.

'Hi, you two.' I swoop in and hug my mum, then trot around the other side of the table to give my dad a kiss on the cheek. 'Dad, you've already met—'

'Indeed, I have.' He gets up from his seat to shake Shep's hand in what is clearly a 'power move', because my dad is at least three inches taller than him.

'And, Mum, this is Shep. Obviously.' I give a helpless shrug that betrays my discomfort, then I melt into the background while she follows my dad's lead and gets to her feet as Shep steps forward to greet her.

'It's great to meet you—'

'Karen,' I quickly supply from behind, before Shep can resort to 'Mrs Lea's ma' in the same way he did with my dad.

'Karen,' he parrots me. 'Really great.'

'It's a pleasure to meet you too, Ciaran.' She's clearly been filled in on the whole name thing.

With the introductions done, we all stand awkwardly until my dad invites us to sit.

'This seems like a nice place,' says Shep as he slips into his seat.

'Oh, it is.' My mum's perfectly styled blonde bob bounces on her shoulders as she nods enthusiastically. 'Lea, David and I have been a few times.'

'It's really popular,' I add, then look at my dad. 'Which makes me wonder how you got a reservation at such short notice *and* during the festival.'

My dad smiles almost smugly. 'I called and asked them to let me know if they got a cancellation – said there would be a generous tip in it for them. The woman I spoke to said she remembered me from our previous visits.'

'I'd "remember" you too if there was the offer of a generous tip.' I nudge Shep and he obediently chuckles, then immediately straightens his face when my dad's appraising eyes land on him.

'So, shall we cut to the chase and see if you're a good match for our daughter?' says my dad, in what can only be described as a 'dick move', undoubtedly designed to punish us for that shared joke.

I wince in anticipation of Shep's response, but he doesn't flinch.

'What would you like to know, David?' he asks. 'I have nothing to hide.'

'That wasn't the case a few days ago.' My dad raises a patronising eyebrow. 'I distinctly remember you trying to hide your existence from me entirely.'

'That was my fault,' I rush to explain. 'I panicked and told him to sneak out. You already know that.'

We're temporarily spared from further scrutiny by the server, who has come to take our drinks order. My dad makes a show of choosing a 'good' bottle of wine, as he always does when we eat out, despite the fact I know that, at home, he drinks pretty much anything that's been on offer at Tesco. Then as soon as the drinks order is in, we're approached by another member of staff about our food choices. By the time that's seen to, the wine has arrived and is being poured, and my hope is that this elongated distraction will allow for a natural shift to a more relaxed and amicable tone.

More fool me.

'So, back to you, Ciaran…' The moment we're left in peace, my dad's focus is back on Shep like flies on horse-shit. 'What do you do, aside from dabbling in comedy, which I assume is more of a hobby?'

I close my eyes tightly in despair. This is literally the worst question my dad could have kicked off with. I'm desperate to leap in and save Shep from having to answer, but I realise that's not the right thing to do. Re-opening my eyes, I expect to see Shep's face radiating annoyance, layered with the perpetual hurt his family have so unfairly bestowed upon him, but if he's feeling it, he hides it very well.

'Actually, stand-up comedy is more than a hobby,' he says. 'I'm trying to build a career out of it.'

'Right.' My dad does a really bad job of hiding his surprise. 'You think you can make a living out of it?'

'I do.' Shep nods. 'I am already making money from it. I'm no investment banker, granted, but at least I can go to sleep at night knowing that the only person I'm at risk of bankrupting is myself.'

I laugh at this. 'See, he's a natural, Dad.'

'You certainly seem to be able to joke your way through an awkward moment.' My dad's face is impassive.

'It's an essential part of the job,' says Shep. 'That and being able to self-deprecate.'

'I see. And if you don't mind me asking, at the point when you're at risk of bankrupting my daughter as well as yourself, what will you do?'

'Oh, my God, please stop,' I can't help but butt in this time. 'Dad, I realise your nose is out of joint because of how you found out about us… um… being involved, but that doesn't make it OK to interrogate Shep like this.'

'His name is Ciaran, darling,' my mum pitches in rather unhelpfully, her blue-grey eyes seeking out mine. 'Is it not a bit odd to call your boyfriend by his nickname?'

'Sure, whatever,' I mumble. 'More importantly, can you pull him into line?'

I jerk my head towards my dad, who's wearing such a pompous expression, I'd quite like to take a handful of butter from the dish on the table and smear it all over his face. That would wipe the smile off it, for sure.

Mum thankfully answers my plea for help. 'David, for the sake of our daughter and our ability to show our faces here again, would you tone it down a bit? I'm sure Lea and Ciaran are miles away from being financially intertwined, and quite frankly, you're giving me a headache.'

For a second, my dad looks like he's about to backchat her in the way I've seen him do so many times – and which was possibly one of the reasons they got divorced in the first place – but then he seems to think better of it and visibly powers down.

'Ciaran, perhaps we should focus on something lighter.' He stops short of an apology, but at least seems to acknowledge that a change of conversational direction may be wise. 'How about we start with the basics: how did you two meet and how long have you been in a relationship?'

Though I'm relieved my dad has stopped figuratively throwing his faeces at Shep in a misguided attempt to show he's the alpha, these two perfectly reasonable questions fill me with dread, as I realise the mistake Shep and I have made. Our off-the-wall experience at Tanya's place and our foggy heads from drinking too much have caused us to overlook something very important: getting our story straight.

Gnawing anxiously on my bottom lip, I glance at Shep, who gives me an almost imperceptible nod that I understand to mean 'follow my lead'. After a moment of nervous contemplation, I swallow thickly and return the gesture, giving him the go-ahead.

After another short pause while our delicious-looking starters are served, Shep pulls off such a masterful interpretation of how we met and got together that I have to hold myself back from giving him a standing ovation. Instead of fabricating a completely different story, which is what I probably would have done – and which would have surely unravelled the moment we were put to the test on any part of it – Shep basically tells my parents everything that did happen, including the fact that I didn't initially see him as a possible partner. However, he doesn't mention his lack of accommodation at the time and our current living arrangements, nor the intensity of the spats between us that led to our first kiss. He paints it so well, it almost comes across as a fairy tale of him winning my love after I saved him.

'Oh, isn't that lovely, David?' Thankfully, my mum appears to have been won over by Shep's recounting of our 'love story'. 'Lea was the kind stranger who offered Ciaran some moral support in his hour of need and helped him get back on his feet.'

My dad licks his lips like a lion preparing to devour its prey, and I'm pretty sure I see Shep gulp.

'Sure,' he says. 'If your definition of "lovely" is our daughter being romantically pursued by a man she so selflessly helped. And him continuing to hang around, despite her having made it clear upfront that she wasn't interested in him. I have another word to describe that. It's called—'

'OK, that's enough of that,' I interject in a singsong voice laced with panic. 'Dad, I think you've completely misinterpreted that chain of events. Shep wasn't "pursuing" me, and I wasn't "not interested" in the sense that you're imagining. I was very much enjoying spending time with him. I just took a bit longer to catch up on that front, and now I'm so glad I did.'

I give Shep a doe-eyed look that's only part theatre and he mirrors it perfectly, making my insides dance with joy, despite the fact I know that this is all for show.

'Look, David...' Shep adopts a conciliatory tone. 'I know we got off to a shaky start and I am genuinely sorry about that. I get how protective you are of Lea, and while I'm not a father myself, I can understand why. She's a wonderful person, and the last thing I would want to do is hurt her...'

While Shep continues to appeal to my dad's human side – which to this point has been completely absent – I watch and listen with a mix of deep longing and sadness. Because what I'm getting right now is a window into how things could be if Shep and I were to take our relationship to the next level. Given the chance, he's the kind of man I would proudly have as my boyfriend: caring, protective and respectful.

Yes, yes and yes, please.

Only, none of this part is real. Our 'relationship' is essentially built on raw animalistic attraction and favours of the non-sexual kind. I gave him somewhere to stay and supported him to get his numbers up at his show. In return, he helped me build some friendships and now he's doing this favour for me here, to keep me out of hot water, while probably at the same time crafting a hilarious new show called: *I'm Meeting the Parents, Get Me Out of Here*. If I weren't so saddened by the impending loss of Shep from my life, I'd probably find it quite funny myself.

'…I guess all I'm saying, David, is that I may not have known Lea long, but she's already important to me. I just want to make sure you know this.'

Shep takes my hand and squeezes it, and I know exactly what that squeeze is attempting to convey. He means every word – but purely in relation to our current context, which my parents are not privy to. It feels clear to me that, in the nicest possible way, he's making sure I don't misread anything that's happening here, which feels lousy, but at the same time, it's more than I could ordinarily expect. As much as I feel deflated by it, I am grateful to Shep for all of this.

We all look to my dad, whose face is giving nothing away. He appears to be reflecting on Shep's words, and he's taking way too much time over it. This, I consider to be another power move, and I decide I've had enough of his nonsense.

'Dad?' I seek out eye contact with him, making it clear I'm expecting him to respond positively, or he and I will have a problem.

'Ahem… right.' He clears his throat in a very dad-like way. 'Well, thank you for that, Ciaran. I suppose we can let bygones be bygones and start afresh.'

'Thank you, David.' Shep bows his head a little, still playing up the subservient role.

'Yeah, thanks, Dad.' I grin at Shep, who seems relieved at having turned things around – and I'm not sure whether this part is for show or not.

With the tension between us having finally eased, we dive into our respective starters, and spend the next couple of minutes positively critiquing them, remarking on how the restaurant never fails to deliver top quality food.

'Did you not mention that you have a show this afternoon, Ciaran?' My dad swirls the wine in his glass and sticks his nose in it like he's some kind of connoisseur.

'I do, yes.' Shep rests his fork and knife on his plate. 'I still have plenty of time, though. It doesn't start until half-four.'

'You don't have to be anywhere after this, do you, Karen?' my dad asks.

My mum, who has been caught mid-chew, quickly swallows her food and looks delighted by this question. 'I most certainly do not.'

'Great, then we'll come along. It will be good to see you in action, Ciaran.'

I choke on my water and quickly turn to see Shep's reaction. He's smiling, and I know he tells me he's unflappable on stage, but I'm certain I detect the slightest hint of discomfort. What the hell is my dad playing at? That's not 'letting bygones be bygones', that's essentially putting Shep under surveillance. The last thing he needs when he's trying to build his dream career is his pretend-girlfriend's dad sitting in the audience, giving him the evil eye and (oh God, please, no) maybe even heckling him. I really wouldn't put it past my dad at this point.

'Dad, I'm not sure that's such a good idea,' I attempt to rescue Shep from this preposterousness.

'Why not?' My dad holds up his hands in a show of bafflement. 'Ciaran's a professional comedian. If he's going to make the big time, he'll have to put up with worse than having his girlfriend's mum and dad in the audience. Isn't that right, Ciaran?'

'That's 100 per cent right.' Shep locks eyes with my dad and there's no mistaking what's passing between them: this game is on.

So much for their fresh start, I think to myself, as they continue to stare each other out, and it takes everything I have not to put my head in my hands and wail with frustration.

Chapter 28

After our lunch, which thankfully became less of a stag fight once the time and place for the world's most inappropriate duel had been set, we head across town and I usher my parents into the Old Town Inn to give Shep some much needed space ahead of his performance.

'Shep, I'm so sorry about my dad.' We're standing on the pavement outside the pub, away from my parents' line of sight. 'He's always been super protective, but this is the worst I've ever seen him.'

'Lea, it's grand.' Shep draws me into a reassuring embrace. 'I'll forget he's even there.'

'Are you just saying that to make me feel better?'

'I'm not. Your da is right. If I want to play with the big boys and girls of the comedy world, I have to be able to deal with whatever is thrown at me.'

'I guess.' I furrow my brow and look up at him with apologetic eyes. 'But he should still know better.'

Shep chuckles and touches my cheek affectionately. 'Remember, he isn't actually my girlfriend's dad or a potential future in-law of mine, so really he's just another member of the audience.'

'Of course,' I murmur, while doing my best to hide the hurt I shouldn't be feeling from this statement. 'I guess that does make things easier, though it's never pleasant to have someone butting heads with you, regardless of who they are.'

'That is true. But I can also see the funny side of this, can't you?'

'It is pretty ridiculous,' I admit with a scoff.

'See, there you go. Now, go and entertain your folks, and I'll see you after the show.'

'OK. I'll buy him a large whisky in the hope that chills him out a bit.'

'Great thinking.' Shep plants a kiss on the top of my head then disappears into The Canongate Tavern, while I embark on my challenge to tame the beast that is my dad.

Pushing open the door to the Old Town Inn, I notice the place is busier than usual. All the tables are occupied by tourists eating generous platefuls of pub grub. Perhaps it's better known for a good lunch, and a welcome rest from roaming the narrow closes of Edinburgh's Old Town, than an evening drinking den.

My parents are sitting at the back, by the toilets, so I head in that direction, and as I do, my hand is grabbed by someone at one of the tables I pass.

'Lea, there you are! We were trying to get hold of you.'

'Oh, hi.' I'm surprised and delighted to see Becca, Tess and Sal sitting together, smiling at me (well, Becca and Tess are smiling; Sal is looking at her phone, as usual). 'Is it not a bit early for you to be here?'

'That's why we were trying to reach you,' says Tess, who was the one who grabbed my hand. 'We decided to go to Shep's show this afternoon. Becca messaged you to see if you wanted to join us.'

'Sorry, I've been… managing a bit of a situation. Those people over there…' I signal towards my mum and dad, who are looking in our direction, obviously wondering who I'm talking to, '…are my parents.'

'Gosh, of course.' Becca's face lights up with recognition. 'Today was the lunch with your mum and dad. Was it that bad?' She winces in anticipation of my answer.

'I'll fill you in properly when they're gone, but right now, all I'll say is that my dad's in sniper mode and we're having a pre-show drink.'

'You mean your parents are going to Shep's show?' Becca looks horrified. 'If your dad hasn't taken to Shep, that's hardly going to improve his opinion of him.'

'Wait a minute,' barks Sal, who seems pissed that she's not in the know. 'Why was he meeting your parents? I thought you got that this thing between you and him is just a month-long shagathon. What have I missed here?'

'Nothing,' I reassure her, while feeling intimidated by her abrasiveness. 'What they all think of each other is not what I'm most worried about. I'm concerned my dad's going to put Shep off his game and that it will create an issue between us.'

'For God's sake,' she scoffs, giving me a withering look. 'Shep's a big boy. He can look after himself.'

'I know that. I'm just… Never mind.' I look across at my parents again, and see that my dad's out of his seat and heading in our direction. 'Shit, here he comes. Please do not say anything about Shep living with me. They don't know about that, and they'll kill me if they find out.'

'Pinky promise.' Tess locks her little finger on mine.

Quickly glancing at the others, I see Becca giving an affirmative nod, while Sal simply rolls her eyes, which I have no time to interpret as anything other than agreement.

'Thank you,' I mouth at them and turn to my dad. 'Dad, sorry, I got waylaid. These are my friends, Becca, Tess and Sal. I didn't know they were going to be here this afternoon.'

'What are the chances?' My dad goes into full charm offensive – the total opposite to how he's been with Shep. 'Good to meet you, ladies. We're about to go and see Lea's new boyfriend's show. We're hoping he's got some talent, so this one doesn't spend the rest of her life skint if it works out between them.'

'*Dad.*' I scold him.

'Apologies. Can't blame a dad for wanting to look out for his daughter, though, eh?' He winks at my friends, and I shake my head in irritation. 'Anyway, can I get you ladies another drink?'

'I'll get them, Dad,' I jump in quickly. 'You paid for lunch, so please let me.'

'Would you look at that,' he continues to charm the knickers off my new friends. 'That's when you know you've done a good job – when your daughter insists on getting a round in. Nice to see you all. I'll leave you in peace.'

They smile and say goodbye, then their attention returns to me.

'He seems lovely,' says Becca as soon as he's out of earshot. 'It's a shame Shep isn't seeing that side of him.'

'Isn't it just.' I grimace.

'I assume your plan is to get him a bit pissed so he enjoys the show and leaves Shep alone?' says Tess.

'That's exactly the idea.' I pluck my purse out of my handbag and back away from them with a pained expression. 'Wish me luck.'

Forty-five minutes later, we take our seats in the venue at the back of The Canongate Tavern. Unfortunately, despite me pleading with my dad not to make this an unbearable experience for everyone involved, he insists on sitting in the front row and invites Becca, Tess and Sal to do the same. So, the six of us end up within spitting distance of where Shep will be doing his thing. I'm basically mortified by this, but all I can do is sit there and pray that this won't go the way I'm fearing it will.

Having arrived early to make sure we got seats – which I'm obviously now wishing we hadn't – we chat among ourselves for the best part of twenty minutes, before the lights go down and Shep's disguised voice booms through the speakers.

'Ladies and gentlemen, can I please ask you to give a warm Edinburgh welcome to… Shep!'

Everyone in the room claps, while my dad mutters, 'Was that Ciaran doing his own intro?' in my ear, and I shush him to discourage him from any further commentary. Shep bounds out from behind the curtain – in the exact same way as every other time – plucks the microphone out of its cradle and does his pacing thing to check out who's in the room.

'Good afternoon, how're you all doing? It's great to see you.' He clocks the line-up in the front row. 'Some of you more than others.'

He grins at the six of us, then his gaze lands solidly on my dad, and I start babbling, 'Oh, God, oh God, oh God,' under my breath. The two of them appear to stare each other out for several moments, then Shep gives a sly chuckle and scans the audience again.

'Tell me, how many of you are here today with your other half?'

We all look around as some hands go up.

'All right, I'm counting fifteen hands, which means one of you has brought both your other halves – that's awkward – we have a throuple in the room, or... someone's not fessin' up.'

The smiling audience continue to look around curiously, until another hand is slowly raised through what seems to be a bit of a tussle.

'Ah, there we are.' Shep zones in on the bloke whose hand has just been dragged up by his girlfriend, and who looks like he wants to crawl into a hole and die. 'How long have the two of you been together?'

'Three months,' the man mumbles.

'What was that?'

'Three months.'

'Ah, that explains it.' Shep clicks his fingers in recognition. 'You're still to learn that free will is a luxury enjoyed only by the single people.'

There's a ripple of amusement as the poor guy tries very hard to disappear into his seat, though I note that he is at least laughing. Shep gives him a comical nod, then returns his attention to the wider room.

'OK, now keep your hand up if you've *met the folks*.'

Only eight hands stay up.

'Where did you meet each other's?' Shep asks one of the four remaining couples.

'At my husband's art exhibition,' says the woman. 'We met each other's parents on the same night.'

'Ah, you're an artist. Well done, my man.' Shep nods at the woman's husband approvingly. 'Always good to meet a fellow creative. So, you say you met each other's parents on the same night, and they also met each other? Oof… risky. What was that like?'

'It was great,' says the woman at the same time as the man says, 'Like facing a firing squad,' and the whole room erupts with laughter.

'Are you two sure you were at the same event?' Shep gives them a cheeky grin. 'No, the reason I ask is that I just *met the folks*…'

There's a collective 'ooh'.

'I mean I literally just met them four hours ago… and now they're sitting right here in the front row, willing me to fuck up.'

Laughter breaks out again as I glance around in embarrassment, now in the spotlight alongside my parents.

'No, I'm being unfair. The meet-the-folks lunch was great – the food was great, I mean. The experience itself was like being watched by a very hungry bear, and it left me wondering if I'd misunderstood the invite. Like maybe rather than asking me to lunch, my girlfriend's da meant he was gonna *have me* for lunch.'

To my surprise, my dad guffaws, while I clap my hands together with delight on realising this joke came from our earlier conversation. I'm also super relieved to see that my dad seems to be taking Shep's 'revenge' on him in good faith.

Leaning forward slightly, I look in the direction of Becca, Tess and Sal. Sal isn't paying attention to me – or to Shep, for that matter – so I'm unable to catch her eye, but Becca and Tess both look across and wave. Subtly pointing to my dad, I give them a covert thumbs up before play-wiping my forehead with the back of my hand. Becca beams at me while Tess responds with a super-enthusiastic double thumbs up.

Having clearly decided he's inflicted enough of a counterblow on my dad, Shep moves seamlessly onto the main content of his show, with which I'm now very familiar. What I'm also very familiar with is the amused groans from the audience when Shep unveils his massive bingo card. The pride that I've felt each time I've watched him perform balloons as I revel in seeing my parents, as well as Becca and Tess – though unfortunately not Sal, who doesn't seem to be paying Shep the slightest bit of attention – falling about with laughter at his jokes.

About halfway through, he reaches a particularly funny story about generational differences, and I smile in anticipation of the reaction he'll get when he shares the punchline.

'…So there I am,' he says, 'on the back seat of the bus, sandwiched between these two wee grannies, basically getting told off on behalf of my whole generation for being too lazy and entitled… for being rude… not respecting my elders…' Shep plays this out as if they're right there on either side of him and he's nodding down at them, which creates a ripple of giggles. 'For inventing the evil that is social media – I think that one in particular was quite unfair. Then, I kid you not, when they've finished giving me the lecture of the century, the one on my left lets out a ripper of a fart—'

The place explodes with laughter, causing Shep to have to pause, as he always does at this point. He nods vigorously as he looks around the audience with disbelieving eyes.

'It was something you'd expect a cow to produce… not a human… never mind a frail old lady. Then, as the bus slowed down for the next stop, the two of them get up and the farter says to me, "We'll leave you to stew on that, young man."'

The hilarity in the room rises even further, as the audience members look at each other with incredulity.

'I'll never know whether she was referring to the telling-off or the fart.' Shep snickers. 'But there's a small part of me that likes to think the two of them sit at home together, eating beans and onions and Brussel sprouts, and then one of them says to the other: "Right, Nora, shall we go get some craic on the bus with those fresh-faced wee buggers?"'

The room breaks into applause, while Shep throws his hands up dramatically, and as it's petering out, a guy in the second row behind Becca, Tess and Sal shouts, 'On her phone. *She's on her phone!*'

I realise he's pointing to Sal, who's lost in her device to the point she has zero awareness she's just been singled out.

'I'll handle this.' Shep puts a finger to his lips and makes a show of creeping across towards Sal while she remains none the wiser.

'*Boo!*' He shouts at her good-naturedly, giving her the fright of her life, while everyone else whoops with satisfied delight.

Shep then goes to the huge bingo card and puts a cross through 'On their phone, the rude bastard'.

'There you are. Proof that Nora and her pal were right about us "youngsters" – and about social media being the root of all evil. Ah well, better to be lazy and rude and miss one of the best comedy shows of the Fringe...' he pauses for a reaction and gets a couple of cheers, '...than be guilty of unashamedly gassing Generation Z on public transport.'

Everyone laughs, while Sal simply looks around in confusion, having evidently missed the story about the bus farter.

At the end of the show, Shep gets his usual rip-roaring applause, and afterwards my mum, dad, Tess, Sal, Becca and I file out of the room behind the rest of the audience.

'Well done. Again!' I beam at Shep as we reach him, while dropping a tenner in his bucket.

He gives me a look. 'Lea, I've told you before, you don't need to—'

'I know, but I want to.' I refuse the note he's trying to return to me. 'So, what did you all think?' I ask my parents and Becca, Tess and Sal, who are also putting their monetary contributions in Shep's bucket.

'It was brill!' Tess flings herself at Shep like a bouncy ball, giving him a congratulatory hug. 'You're so funny. Isn't he funny?' She turns to the rest of us.

'It really was great.' Becca smiles warmly at Shep. 'You're a natural.'

Sal is still glued to her phone, so I turn to my parents. 'Well?'

My mum looks to my dad, obviously keen to hear his view on things first, and we all follow suit. My dad clears his throat.

'Ciaran, I'll be honest, I really wasn't sure about you to start with—'

'No, really?' I pull a sarcastic face and everyone chuckles.

'All right, daughter. Rein it back in.' He tweaks my nose while giving me a jokey warning look. 'What I'm trying to say is that you're clearly a very talented comedian and I now think I understand you a bit more.'

'Are those words of acceptance, David?' Shep asks with a cheeky half-smile.

'You know they are. Don't push it.'

'Right you are.'

'Also, take note. If you hurt my daughter, even once, that acceptance will be withdrawn – permanently.'

'Got it.' Shep nods, then looks to my mum. 'How about you, Karen? I need to know I've got your seal of approval as well.'

'Oh, you had it from the moment you gave that speech about Lea in the restaurant.' My mum waves her hand casually. 'I'm also protective of my daughter, but not in the same caveman way as this one. Just look after her, please. And like David says, don't hurt her.'

'So that's another successful show, and parental approval – all in one afternoon.' Shep shakes his bucket, which doesn't make much noise, as it's filled mainly with notes again. 'This deserves a drink on me.'

Chapter 29

After our drink together – which was a far more pleasant experience than our lunchtime ruckus – Shep heads through to the back room to get prepped for his next performance and my parents head home. As it's just us girls left, Tess suggests we go for a bite to eat before they head off to their scheduled evening show. She also has the idea to check if there are any tickets left for me to join them. It seems that luck is on my side, because I do manage to get what is literally the last available ticket at one of the pop-up booking offices.

Once that's sorted, we head up the hill in search of somewhere to eat. The cobbled High Street is crammed to bursting point with street acts and meandering tourists taking up almost every square foot. In stark contrast to the heavily overcast sky, the atmosphere is vibrant – filled with laughter and smiles and whoops of joy. All this accompanied by the faint sound of bagpipes filtering through the air, no doubt coming from one of the city's many buskers. Soaking it all in, I experience a sense of immense pride that this is where I live, alongside what I recognise to be a true sense of contentment. Being here like this, hanging out with three awesome girls, it's a wonderful feeling. I've found my 'crowd' and now I feel at home in my own city again.

'You good?' Becca, who's walking beside me, behind Tess and Sal, must have sensed my euphoric mood.

'I'm… great.' I smile at her, a bit overwhelmed all of a sudden. 'Thank you so much for inviting me into your friendship group, Becca. You have no idea how much it means to me.'

'You don't need to thank us.' Becca chummily links her arm through mine. 'You've slotted right in. Almost as if it were fate.'

'Oh, that's sweet of you.' I scrunch my nose, touched by this remark, while at the same time knowing full well that fate had nothing to do with it.

'It's almost as if you and Shep meeting was fate too,' she says. 'You're such a sweet couple.'

'Yeah, but for how long?' I sigh and look to the sky, then a thought pops into my head and I lower my voice. 'I hope you don't mind me mentioning this, but whenever your collective exes are mentioned, you seem almost wistful… maybe even regretful? Your reaction is different to Tess's and Sal's.'

'You've noticed that, huh?' She touches her hair in what seems like a self-conscious way. 'I guess I'm not as good at hiding it as I thought.'

'Hiding what? You don't have to tell me, but I'm a good listener. And I would never share with anyone else.'

'I know you wouldn't.' She smiles at me and a warmth grows inside of me, as if a long-extinguished candle has been lit in my heart on finding a kindred spirit.

'So, what's your pain about, then?' I ask. 'You've listened to my man-related woes, now you need someone to listen to yours.'

'There's not much to say. Things were fine and then they got messy. The guys didn't behave well, and we were right to end things with them. It's just that Byron wasn't the same as the other two. He got drawn into stuff he wasn't comfortable with, and he only went along with them because he didn't want to be cast out of the band. Sal has it all sewn up in her mind that they were as bad as each other, and she was the driver of our agreement never to go back, but…' Becca tails off and it appears that she's holding back from voicing what's on her mind.

'But you wanted to,' I fill in for her. 'You wanted to, but you went along with the pact, because you didn't want to be alienated from your own friendship group. Just like Byron, really.'

'Yes.'

I take her arm and guide her to a stop. 'Becca, you should never feel pressured into doing anything you're not comfortable with. That's not how friendship works.'

'I know. But nobody "pressured" me.'

'I'd argue that they did, but in a more insidious way. Was Tess as into this idea as Sal?'

Becca shakes her head. 'No, but she did seem happy enough to go along with it. She was so hurt by Kevin, I couldn't stir up all that pain again. Plus, she and Sal are pretty tight, so I would have been the one left out in the cold, if you get what—'

'There you both are.' Tess appears out of nowhere and unwittingly steamrollers through our conversation. 'This place is bonkers busy. Feels like we need a safety rope so we don't lose each other.'

'Are we eating or what?' Sal appears behind Tess, looking hangry.

'Yes, let's eat,' says Becca, and she mouths, 'thank you,' as the four of us set off again.

It's a bit of a chore trying to find somewhere, but after a few unsuccessful tries, we manage to get a table in an American-style pizza place in the Grassmarket.

We enjoy some further chat about Shep's show and I'm pleased to hear that both Tess and Becca rate it among the best they've been to. They also reassure me that Sal hasn't had the best attention span during the other shows either, with the distraction generally being a hot guy sliding into her dating app DMs.

'So, sue me,' Sal responds, with a defensive shrug.

After we've munched our way through two shared portions of chicken wings, our pizzas are served. Tess and I waste no time in diving into our loaded cheesy slices with our fingers, while Sal and Becca opt to use a knife and fork.

'I've been dying to ask, what happened when Shep *met the folks*?' Tess imitates Shep's angle on this from his show.

'No, hold on…' Sal raises a commanding hand. 'I need caught up first. No one's bothered to fill me in on what I missed the other night.'

What's so irritating about this is that Sal doesn't give two hoots about me or my situation with Shep. She's just making this about her and how she perceives she's been 'wronged' by not being kept in the loop.

'Of course, sorry.' I offer Tess an apologetic look and she waves me on. 'On Thursday, Shep and I were in my flat… um…'

'Getting it on,' Tess supplies with a wink and what I consider to be unnecessary humping gestures with her arms.

'Thank you, Tess.' I colour and Becca giggles.

'Anyway, we were… doing that, when the buzzer to my flat unexpectedly went…'

I fill Sal in on the whole story, including the agreement that my dad, mum, Shep and I would have lunch together today. Despite making a song and dance about being left out, Sal doesn't seem amused or even that interested. This makes me feel quite uncomfortable, particularly as her eyes continually flit to her phone while I'm talking.

'Isn't that the funniest thing you've ever heard?' Tess pounds the table in much the same way she did when I first told her, seemingly oblivious to Sal's indifference. 'So, tell us about the lunch, then. How did that go down?'

'Only if you want to.' Becca gives me a meaningful look.

'Obviously she wants to,' says Tess.

'Perhaps, but Lea still gets to decide that herself.'

'It's OK, I'm happy to share.' I reach across and clasp Becca's hand appreciatively, catching Sal narrowing her eyes as I do, but not allowing her to put me off. 'I'm feeling the need to get things off my chest, so I'm grateful to you ladies for letting me do that.'

I take a sip of my drink, then launch into an animated playback of our lunch, including how it didn't feel like Shep was acting the whole time. Recounting it back, I'm tugged in all different directions emotionally. It's a funny story, but it's also super confusing for me. I do know that it was all a charade, I'm not kidding myself in that respect, but the way Shep looked at me and the way he talked to my parents about me really did seem to be at least partly genuine. I mean, unless he's a seasoned actor as well as a comedian, surely there's no way he could have played things up to the level he did – and so convincingly. If I'm right about that, could it mean that he's feeling the same way about me as I do about him?

The girls listen with patience and interest (well, Sal appears to half-listen, which is as much as I can expect), and it's clear they understand that I'm still working this through in my own head while I'm telling them about it.

'…And that's when I walked into the Old Town Inn and bumped into you,' I eventually say with an air of finality. 'That's you all caught up.'

Unsurprisingly, Tess is first to jump in with her thoughts. 'Your life seems to be one long comedy show, Lea.'

'Tell me about it.' I roll my eyes. 'Though prior to Shep crash-landing in it, it was pretty empty and dull, so I'm not complaining.'

'Oh, totally. You wanna know what I think?'

I nod a little too earnestly.

'I think he's smitten. There's no way he could have pulled that off if he wasn't totally into you.'

I am, of course, elated to hear this.

'What do you think, Becca? She's got a great read on people.' Tess nods vehemently, as if agreeing with herself.

Becca looks thoughtful for a moment. 'I think there's no doubt Shep has real feelings for you. It's even possible he's falling for you – though I can't say for sure, as you know, and I wouldn't want to raise your hopes.'

'I understand.' I'm grateful for her openness and realistic outlook.

'The things that keep floating through my mind are that he's not from here and he's pursuing a career in comedy. If he's dead set on living his dream, which I'm sure you'd want him to, it could be that the timing just isn't right for you both. I'm sorry, Lea, I know that's not at all where you wanted me to go with this.'

'It's fine, Becca. I'm already hyper-aware of these issues myself. I guess the question for me is: do I put myself out there and tell him how I feel? Because if he feels the same and neither of us says anything, then this all ends when it needn't have. But equally, if he's not in the same place I am, it ends with my heart being broken, and probably any chance of us remaining friends – albeit at a distance – being lost.'

'That is a tough one.' Becca taps her fingernails on the table while giving me a sympathetic look. 'I guess only you can decide. I suppose another question to ask yourself is: if you don't say anything before he leaves, will you always regret it? Because regardless of which way things go, you'd at least have your answer.'

I rest my elbows on the table and puff out my cheeks. 'That's actually the biggest question, isn't it? I expect the answer is that I would regret it.'

My mouth has become dry all of a sudden, so I take a good glug from my Sprite and my eyes land on Sal. Being brutally honest, I'm not sure I want her input, but if I don't invite her to share her thoughts, there's no question that she'll make an issue of it.

'What do you think, Sal?'

'I'm not sure I should share what I think,' she says to my surprise.

'Oh, why's that?'

'Because I'm the one who's going to tell you what you don't want to hear.'

I blanch, then try to cover up this reaction. 'OK, well, either way, I'd like to hear your opinion. I need to deal with this with my eyes wide open, so maybe that's a good thing.'

I catch Becca and Tess sharing a look, but with my focus on Sal and my heart already in my mouth, I don't give it too much thought.

'Go on, hit me with it,' I prompt her.

Sal puts down her knife and fork, and finishes chewing the piece of pizza she's just popped in her mouth.

'I think you should back the hell off.'

'*What?*' Becca, Tess and I all say in unison.

Sal lifts her chin defiantly. 'The guy wants to make it big in comedy. If you put this on him, at the very least you'll mess with his head and throw him off when his focus needs to be on his career. And worst case: you'll distract him to the point he takes his eye off the ball and never makes it big. Do you want that on your conscience?'

There's a stunned silence, while we all digest this.

'Why… why do they all have to be negative outcomes?' I ask eventually. 'Why is there not a best case where I become his biggest fan and help him achieve his dream? I've already done that to some extent.'

'Yeah, she has,' Tess chips in to support me.

'*Seriously?*' Sal practically snorts with derision. 'With the travel and the hours Shep will have to put in, that's a pathetic fantasy that belongs in a Hollywood movie, but if you want to believe it's a possibility then by all means.' She gives a pompous wave of her hand as if she's talking to a bunch of idiots.

'Sal, come on.' Becca's now the one coming to my aid. 'That seems a bit harsh.'

'Harsh but true?' Sal looks back at us with an obnoxious smirk.

'Way harsh, regardless of whether there's any truth to it.' Tess stares at her, clearly appalled, as a deep discomfort rises within me.

'Hey, it's all right.' I wave my hands in a bid to calm everyone down. 'I did ask Sal for her opinion and she's entitled to share that, even if it doesn't feel good to hear it.'

'Exactly.' Sal shoots a scornful look at Tess and Becca rather than acknowledging me having her back, which she doesn't at all deserve. 'And I'm sorry, Lea, but if Shep wanted a long-term relationship with you, would he not just come out and say it? He's not exactly shy. Also, from the sounds of things, he seems to have made it clear that him having lunch with your parents was just his way of returning a favour. Anything you read from it is likely to be out of your own desperation for a happy ending, not because it's how things really are.'

This is the most I've ever heard from Sal in one go, and while I did defend her right to speak up, it really stings. So much so, that I can feel a lump of raw hurt gathering in my throat.

'Sal, I know you're entitled to your opinion, but there are some things you just don't say out loud,' Tess wades in once more. 'And definitely not in the way you've said them.'

'Maybe we should change the subject,' I suggest, trying to keep my voice even. 'You've all given me really helpful insights, so thank you. I don't want to use up any more airtime on this.'

Glancing around my new friends' stony faces with an appeasing smile, I feel horribly guilty that my personal drama has driven a wedge between them, so I move us onto a lighter topic and work hard to get the conversation going again. Despite what they've said about me now being one of their group – and the fact that Sal is the one in the wrong – I'm still the outsider here, and I don't want to be the one to come between them.

Thankfully, they come around one by one and the conversation begins to flow again, meaning I'm eventually able to sit back and think over what was said. Between them, Tess and Becca pretty much gave me what I needed: positivity and reasons to be optimistic, but with a dollop of realism. If that was all that had been said, I probably would have gone home tonight ready to speak to Shep and accept whichever way things went. But Sal's cruel words are echoing round my head, drowning out everything else. Because, much as they were delivered in a heartless way, there was some validity to her points.

Naturally, I've been looking at this from my own perspective. But is that what I should be doing? Shep hasn't given any indication he's looking for more, so what possible reason do I have to think he is? The weight of these questions is hard to bear, because it seems I've been trying to write our story in the way I'm hoping it will turn out, despite the fact that all the evidence is pointing in another direction entirely.

Chapter 30

After the show, I say goodbye to the girls then head in the direction of George IV Bridge. I battle my way through the relentless flow of tourists and locals out for the evening – all of whom seem to be going in the opposite direction – and it's only when I reach The Meadows that I get a sense of space around me, allowing me to think and breathe again.

The show was great, but I'd say – and I realise I might be biased – that Shep's is better. What it did do, though, was provide a welcome temporary distraction after the brutal reality check that Sal unapologetically offered up. Now, making my way home alone, my body feels fit to burst from all the raw and conflicting emotions. I had considered messaging Shep – who, I expect, is perched at the bar, chatting to the staff in The Canongate Tavern – and maybe joining him. However, as soon as the claggy evening air hit my nostrils, I felt a nauseating churning in my gut, so I decided to head home and give us some space from each other. With only a week until the festival ends, it's time I got used to being on my own again anyway.

I don't know if it's more psychological than anything else, but when I step through the main door to my building, the three flights of stairs feel steeper and more of a challenge than usual. Trudging up them, a sense of impending loss sets in further with every step; an emptiness that feels far greater than that of the weeks and months before Shep came into my life.

On reaching my flat, I kick off my sandals, and as I put my keys down on the hall table, I catch a glimpse of my troubled reflection in the mirror and sigh heavily.

'I guess it'll just be you and me again soon,' I say to it with mournful eyes. 'God, I'm going to miss him so much. What do I do? Do I tell him how I feel, or do I let him go?'

Turning away from the mirror, I almost jump out of my skin as the bathroom door suddenly opens and a smiling Shep emerges through it, with just a towel round his waist.

'Does it ever talk back to you?' he asks in place of a greeting.

'*Oh my God*, Shep. You scared the life out of me. I thought you'd still be at The Canongate Tavern. You didn't... You weren't... um... listening, were you?' My cheeks are blazing at the possibility he heard what I said.

'Nah, your secrets are safe. All I heard was some incoherent mumbling. I was too busy thinking about what happened after my show.'

'Oh?' I cock my head with interest. 'What happened after your show?'

'Guess.' His eyes flash mischievously.

'Why do I have to guess? Can you not just tell me.'

'Where's the fun in that? Come on, take a guess.'

'OK...' I look to the ceiling in search of inspiration, really not wanting to play this game right now. 'You got a huge donation in your bucket.'

'Nope.'

'You... found out you got another great review?'

'Close. Guess again.'

'Aww come on, just tell me.' I suddenly feel utterly depleted.

He comes closer and slips his arms around my waist. 'I was approached by a journalist from *Showbiz Online*. Said she'd been to the show a couple of times and wanted to do a feature on me as "one to watch" in the comedy world. She took my number and said she'd give me a call.'

'Wow, really?' I'm completely thrown by how unexpected this is. '*Showbiz Online* is massive. That's... fantastic.'

'Sure as shit, it is.' Shep scoops me up and gives me a smacker of a kiss, clearly so elated at this turn of events that he fails to pick up on my rather muted reaction. 'This is what I've been hoping for, Lea. It's why I came to Edinburgh, as you know. I have a real chance at this.'

'I'm so pleased for you,' I say as he puts me down and beckons me to join him in the spare room while he gets changed.

I follow him and sit down on the bed.

'This could be it, then. Your name in lights.'

He bobs his head indecisively. 'I'm still a long way away from that, but it's a big step forward.'

'Of course it is.' I pick some fluff from my jeggings, avoiding eye contact. 'So where was this journalist from – like, geographically?'

'London. Apparently, she has connections in some of the biggest agencies in the arts and culture sector. She said she might be able to get me a couple of intros.'

'Intros for what?' I ask, while Shep drops his towel and pulls on his underwear, and all I think about is how much I'm going to miss that body against mine.

'Representation. Can you imagine it? Me having an agent... doing proper gigs?'

'I really can.'

My eyes meet his, and to my horror, I feel them well up with tears. Quickly looking away, I try to hide this and the somewhat unjustified hurt I'm feeling. From the start, I knew this was how things would go. I knew Shep would move on – whether he got his big break or went home to Northern Ireland. I also knew that, when the time came, it was going to hurt. What I didn't realise was that it would feel like having my insides ripped out.

'Hey, are you OK?' Shep seems to finally clock that I'm not myself and sits down beside me on the bed.

'I'm… fine.' I stammer, head turned away from him as I try to blink away the tears that are threatening to overflow.

'You don't seem fine.' He reaches across and gently angles my face towards him. 'You're crying.'

'They're happy tears. I'm just… so delighted for you.'

'Is that really what they are? They don't look like happy tears. The misery in your face is sort of giving you away.'

'Oh,' is all I can manage in response to this.

'Lea, what's really going on? What's the craic with you and the girls? Have you fallen out?'

'What? No, they're great. Really great. I'm glad I met them, so thank you.' I decide there's no way I'm bringing up the Sal thing when he's on such a high.

Shep wipes away a tear that's managed to escape down my cheek and looks at me with concern. 'You're welcome. So, if it's not about them, then what is it? Because I don't like to see you sad.'

I genuinely don't know how to answer his question. How can I tell him that I'm basically crying over him? That I'm already grieving his departure, even though he's not gone yet. How can I tell him that I think I'm falling for him and he might just be my person? Especially when the impact of that could be just as Sal so indiscreetly suggested. I can't be responsible for Shep's dreams not coming true. No matter how much I want to tell him everything in the hope he feels the same, I know that I can't. I have to let him go.

'They're sad tears mixed in with happy tears.' I shift my gaze to the floor so he can't scrutinise my expression. 'I'm over the moon for you, Shep, I really am. I guess it's just hit home that you'll be leaving soon, and… I've enjoyed having you around. In more ways than one.' I give him a little nudge to keep the tone between us light.

He may be good at reading my emotions, but thankfully he can't read my mind. All I need to do now is keep schtum and hold it together until he leaves – though I realise the latter may be difficult in practice.

There's a short silence, during which I steal a glance at him, but I'm unable to read his expression.

'Say something, would you,' I complain. 'I feel like a right wet blanket here.'

This spurs Shep into action. He puts a casual arm across my shoulders.

'Aww, Lea, I've enjoyed it too. It's been a blast. I almost wish I didn't have to leave.'

Almost. I was almost someone worth staying for – but not quite.

'I know you've enjoyed the company,' Shep continues. 'But you've got your girls now, so you won't be alone anymore.'

'That is true. Thanks to you.'

'And we can keep in touch.'

'Of course.' I nod. 'I'd like that.'

I actually don't know how I feel about this suggestion – whether it might be too hard for me – but that's not something I'm able to voice or even properly contemplate right now.

'The sex has been dead on, eh?' He gives me a boyish grin.

'That, I can't argue with.' I grin back at him, aware that I need to lift the mood further to avoid things becoming awkward between us. 'And we do have several days of that still ahead of us.'

'Shall we make the most of it, then?' He leans in, kissing me softly and suggestively.

I return his kiss, tentatively at first then more hungrily, fuelled by a deep longing to feel close to him. Then, as we melt into each other, I can't help thinking that another week of this is only going to make our big goodbye all the more painful.

–

On Monday morning, I'm moping around the lab at work, trying to keep Shep out of my mind, when Tanya barges through the door, muttering to herself in an irritated fashion.

'Good morning,' I greet her with a curious half-smile. 'Or is that a poor choice of words?'

She practically hurls her handbag onto the table in the middle of the room, then looks at me as if she's only just noticed I'm there. 'Lea, hi. My apologies, I'm just out of a finance meeting, and frankly, I'm a little off balance after it.'

'It didn't go well, then?'

'The usual politics, as you can imagine, but that Tom has quite the nerve. I've never seen so much ruddy peacocking.'

Tanya shakes her head with a theatrical 'humph', then peers at me in much the same way she does when I tell her about a rogue result from our sampling.

'You're looking a little off balance yourself. Is everything all right?'

'Oh, I'm… It's nothing.' Feeling as fragile as I currently do, my eyes instantly well up in what I'm counting as the fifth time since I embarrassed myself by crying in front of Shep the night before.

Tanya gestures for me to take a seat at the table, then sits down beside me. 'What's upset you? You can talk to me about anything, I hope you know that.'

'I expect you can guess.' I swipe away the tears that are now running down my cheeks.

'Ciaran.' She nods solemnly, hands me a tissue from her handbag, then her expression changes to one of concern. 'I didn't cause this, did I? With all my meddling on Saturday evening? John said I'd gone too far.'

I give a feeble laugh. 'No, you didn't cause this. You were a bit… overzealous, but I know it came from a good place. Ciaran… um… Shep has been approached by a high-profile journalist who wants to do a feature on him: one that will probably attract a lot of attention and potentially even secure him an agent. It's incredible news, don't get me wrong—'

'But you think it will close the door for you and him.'

'I don't think it, I know it. He's said he wants to "keep in touch" when he leaves.'

'Ah.' Tanya grimaces. 'That is unfortunate.'

'Yup.' I exhale heavily and an involuntary sob escapes at the same time. 'Sorry, I'm so sorry. I shouldn't be doing this at work.'

'Nonsense, come here.' Tanya puts her arm around me, drawing me into her in a motherly way, which gives me some comfort. 'I'm sorry that things haven't worked out for you. If I'd only kept my big mouth shut about giving him a chance in the first place—'

'No, don't say that. You meant well. You always mean well. And I'm not sorry I got involved with him, I'm just sad that I'm going to lose him.'

'Yes, but perhaps I need to keep my nose out of some things. John certainly thinks so. Anyway, if I'm allowed to say – at the risk of overstepping again – I very much enjoyed our evening on Saturday.'

'Me too.' I sit up straight again and blow my nose. 'It was a lot of fun. It's just a shame we won't be able to do it again.'

Tanya looks baffled. 'Why ever not?'

'Because, as of next week, I'm back to being single.'

'Do you need a boyfriend for us to spend time together?'

I hesitate, unsure about what she's actually asking. 'Well, no, but... you know, that was a couples' dinner party and I won't be part of a couple.'

'Lea, you have heard of the great British invention called the pub?'

'Uh-huh.'

'Then how about we try one of those for size?' She waggles her eyebrows at me. 'Maybe a drink after work from time to time?'

'Really? You'd be up for that? I assumed you wouldn't, because you have family obligations and...' I trail off, realising that what I was about to say is a bit inappropriate.

'Because I'm old?' Tanya finishes my sentence.

I snort. 'No. Obviously not. But you are older… than me,' I rush to add as I clock the look she gives me.

'Would it ruin your "rep" to be seen out with me?'

'Of course not. Why would you think that?'

'Well, you have all those big nights out with your gal pals. Maybe you don't want to get caught hanging out with a woman who's halfway to retirement.'

On hearing this, I put my head in my hands and groan. Me and my stupid pride. Tanya is extending the hand of friendship to me – another new friendship, which I will gladly snap up – so the least I can do is come clean.

'Tanya, there's never been any "big nights out with my gal pals".'

She frowns. 'I'm sorry, I don't understand.'

'I think you assume I have a super busy social life because I'm young, but I don't. All my friends from uni have moved away, and the only one who still lives here is knee-deep in nappies and baby puke on a daily basis. I've been… lonely… and ashamed, which is why I never corrected you when you made those assumptions. I'm sorry.'

There's a short pause while Tanya takes this in, then she looks at me with such compassion that I start to cry again.

'That's why you've been working all these extra hours.'

'Yes. It was better than sitting alone in my flat, watching endless boxsets. Or talking to myself in the mirror.' I cringe at how that sounds. 'To clarify, I don't do a lot of that, it's just—'

'The odd comment.'

'Yes.' I stop dabbing at my eyes and look at her in surprise. 'How did you know?'

She shrugs. 'Because I do it too when no one's around, which isn't often in my home. Lea, I'm sorry to hear that's the situation you've been in, and I'm also sorry that I was flippant and presumptuous. It came from a place of envy – I miss being young and free. Seems like we've both made inaccurate judgements about each other.'

'Yeah, it seems so.' I give a sheepish smile. 'I have actually gained some new friends in the last couple of weeks, by the way. Thanks to Shep.'

'I am very glad to hear that. Though, do you have room for one more?'

A sense of warmth spreads through me. 'Definitely.'

'Oh, good.' She makes a show of sighing with relief. 'Because if I don't get some quality time away from my loveable but infuriating teenagers soon, I swear you'll see my mugshot on *Crimewatch*.'

Chapter 31

The next evening, having politely declined Shep's invitation to join him at The Canongate Tavern after his seven-thirty show – in a move to reduce my dependence on him – I'm surprised when he arrives back around nine p.m.

'Hi, you,' I greet him as I'm coming out of the kitchen on my way back to the living room, where I've been camped out watching a drama series I'm not sure I'm that into.

'Hiya, what's the craic?' His usual upbeat tone is distinctly absent, reminding me of the day we first met.

'Is everything all right? I thought you were staying on at the pub for a bit.'

He doesn't answer. Instead, he hangs there in the hallway, not saying anything, nor making eye contact. His shoulders are slumped, making him look like a little boy in a grown man's body.

'Come on.' I beckon him to follow me into the living room, which he obediently does.

We sit down on the sofa and, rather than putting pressure on him, I gently take his hand, then wait quietly until he's ready to share.

'My show just then – I cocked it up,' he says eventually.

I take a moment to consider this and how to respond. 'When you say you "cocked it up", are we talking a little bit or monumentally?'

'Big enough to scupper my chances.'

'Right.' I chew on my bottom lip. 'That's not good. How about you tell me what went down? You might feel better for it. Or you might even realise it's not as bad as you think.'

He scoffs bitterly. 'It is that bad.'

'OK, well—'

'I got heckled... big time. By some wee shit.'

'Oh.' I'm surprised by this. 'But you're great at dealing with hecklers. I've seen you in action. You normally wipe the floor with them.'

'Normally, yeah. I thought I could handle anything. He was a real nasty piece of work, you know? Like he and his mate came to the show with the sole intention of causing trouble.'

'Ah. I think I know the type.'

Having lived this experience with Shep and having become so invested in his success, I find myself taking on some of his pain.

'What was it about this guy that got to you so much?' I ask. 'It won't change what happened, but maybe if you can figure that out, it'll help you with similar situations in the future.'

'I've been asking myself that the whole way home.' Shep puts his head in his hands, making it evident how stressed and spooked he is by this experience. 'I think it was the intent... maybe the maliciousness of it. Most hecklers do it to appear smart, to one-up you or to look good in front of their mates... that kind of thing. They're an occupational hazard to some extent, but they can also hand you some of your best lines. This was different. It was... It felt personal.'

I'm appalled to hear this. 'But you didn't know him, right? You haven't come across him anywhere in the city before now?'

Shep shakes his head. 'No. I think he's probably nothing more than a bored bloke with a chip on his shoulder and an antisocial behaviour problem. Perhaps he can't deal with seeing others succeed. It was a constant disruption that I didn't know how to handle, and it made me look like a total amateur.'

'Surely not. Your audience must have been annoyed at the guy for ruining their experience rather than thinking you weren't up to it.'

'You'd hope, eh?'

He gives me a defeated look, which makes me want to reach across and hug him, but I sense that now is not the right moment for that. He needs to work this through first.

'Anyway, my biggest concern isn't the audience... well, not the audience as a whole. It's about who was in the audience.'

'You mean that journalist?'

He gives a hopeless shrug. 'Or other press. Maybe even a talent scout who's now crossed me off their list.'

'Of course.' I grimace. 'Though you shouldn't be hanged for the bad behaviour of another person.'

'That would be the logical view, but you know as well as I do that's not the kind of headline that sells or gets clicks online.'

'No, it's not.' I squeeze Shep's hand sympathetically. 'I guess we just need to cross our fingers that this passes without attracting any negative attention. Twenty-four hours? That's about the wait we're in for, right?'

'We?' He gives me a puzzled look.

'You think you're the only one who's affected by this?' I smile at him affectionately. 'I'm your biggest fan, you know that. Anyway, even if this does create some unfavourable coverage, people quickly forget.'

'Thanks, Lea. You're a great listener. Has anyone ever told you that?' His gorgeous green eyes lock on mine.

I bob my head noncommittally and look away, finding the intensity of the eye contact difficult. 'Maybe one or two people over the years. I'm also just as good at giving hugs.'

Opening my arms wide, I invite him to cuddle in, and it seems I've got my timing right. He scoots across and allows me to give him a big squeezy hug, then I switch my programme back on and stroke his hair while he lies against me quietly, probably still working through the pain of his unpleasant experience.

–

I'm on tenterhooks all day at work on Wednesday, waiting to hear whether Shep is in the clear. I message him a few times early in the day and he replies with different variations of 'so far, so good', which I'm relieved about. I also visit the university shop and look through the newspapers there, but there's nothing as far as I can see.

By mid-afternoon, I'm quite positive and hopeful that this situation has been less of a storm and more like Scottish drizzle – an annoyance, but unlikely to make a significant dent in anyone's plans. As Shep is now entering the peak of his day, I decide to leave him in peace and cross my fingers that his performances go well. I sincerely hope the horrible bloke from the evening before doesn't make a reappearance, and also that Shep's confidence hasn't been affected to any great extent.

I consider heading to The Canongate Tavern after work to see how he's doing, but that decision is taken out of my hands when I receive a WhatsApp message from him between his performances, telling me he'll see me back at mine later. I'm a little disappointed by this, as I don't really fancy heading home to an empty flat again this evening. Then I remind myself that in about a week's time, I'll be returning to one every night – so I'd better get used to it.

By the time I hear the flat door slam shut, signalling Shep's arrival, I'm almost climbing the walls with boredom. Having had no further news from him, I call out to him brightly.

'Twenty-four hours is up. You can relax.'

My words are met with silence, which is odd, so I hop off the sofa and pad through to the hallway to greet him properly – but he's not there.

'Shep?' I call out to him again. 'I know I didn't imagine you arriving back. Where are you?'

After checking my own room and the bathroom, I find him lying on the bed in the spare room, staring blankly at the corniced ceiling.

'There you are. What are you doing in here?'

He closes his eyes for a few moments, then opens them and finally looks at me. 'I didn't make it through twenty-four hours.'

'Sorry?'

'I think it was about seventeen when Kira came across it.'

I knit my brows together in confusion. 'When Kira came across what?'

'This.' Shep opens a web page on his phone and hands it to me.

I sit down on the bed to look at it properly, but I needn't have bothered, because staring back at me in big bold letters is the headline: 'Rising star chokes as Fringe enters its final week'.

'*Oh no*, Shep.' I put my hand to my mouth in disbelief while I read the article in full, which is by some bloke called Jonathan Watts.

It's vile. It also bears very little resemblance to the situation Shep described to me the previous evening. The fear he shared about becoming a clickbait story has come true. And what's worse, it finishes on the cruellest of lines:

> Like so many hopefuls who come to Edin-
> burgh with the dream of following in the
> footsteps of comedy royalty, it turns out Shep
> doesn't have what it takes to go the distance.
> I think I'm as disappointed about not finding
> a diamond in the rough as he must be over
> his performance. Oh well, there's always next
> year – at least for me.

Handing him back his phone, I'm lost for words.

'I never thought to check that site.' Shep spares me from having to think of the right thing to say. 'That was published at eight a.m., but it seems it only surfaced on social media under the Edinburgh festival hashtag in the afternoon.'

'Which, I'm guessing, is when Kira found it?' I ask.

'Correct.'

'I'm so sorry, Shep. This is so unfair, and… so inac-curate from the sounds of things.'

'Spinning shit is what it is.' Shep's voice is laced with fury. 'This dickhead… Jason, or whatever his name is. He's done it in just the right way to bury any possibility of me moving on to bigger things.'

'He certainly hasn't held back.' I agree. 'Though he is just one—'

'And needless to say, I haven't heard a word from that journalist who wanted to do the piece on me,' Shep talks over me, probably without even realising he's done so.

'Maybe she just hasn't got round to—'

'Oh come on, Lea,' he cuts me off again and this time I flinch. 'Do you really think she hasn't seen it? It's her job to keep up with this stuff. She probably saw it hours before I did.'

'It doesn't necessarily mean she won't do the piece at all, though.' I try once more to bring some optimism to the conversation. 'Maybe she's going to let things settle first.'

'Yeah, and a pink and green unicorn's gonna fly out of my arse.' His tone becomes sarcastic. 'What journalist in their right mind would dedicate a full-page article to someone who's taken their maiden voyage at the festival and sunk faster than the *Titanic*.'

'I was just trying to offer up a possible alternative. One where things haven't gone completely to shit.'

Shep props himself up on his elbows, his face stony. 'Why? That's not really helpful to me right now.'

Feeling his appraising eyes on me, I want to shrink away from him, but at the same time, I'm starting to feel I'm being treated unfairly.

'I don't know.' I fold my arms across my body, raising my voice slightly in a bid to assert myself. 'I don't know what else to say.'

'Then maybe don't say anything. I know you're trying to help, but maybe you've helped enough.'

'Wait a minute. What's that supposed to mean?'

He looks caught out all of a sudden, and I realise he's said something he wishes he hadn't. I fix him with an icy look.

'Come on, Shep. At least show me enough respect to explain what that comment was about.'

'Look, can we just leave it, Lea? I'm not in the head-space for this.'

'Uh-uh.' I shake my head. 'That comment was about more than you having a crappy article written about you. So, go on, spit it out.'

Shep seems deeply conflicted and like he's about to try and put me off again, but then he shrugs pathetically.

'All right, but remember, you insisted that I share this…'

I simply nod and wait for him to continue. Though I'm defiant on the outside, I can feel myself trembling, terrified of what's about to come out of his mouth.

'You rescued me at my most vulnerable, Lea, and you helped me to up my numbers at my show, which I'll always be grateful for, don't get me wrong. But let's face it, you've also…' he gives a loaded sigh, '…been a distraction that's made me lose focus.'

'What… Are you for real?' I stammer, unable to believe what I'm hearing. 'All I've done is support you.'

Shep groans in frustration and sits up properly. 'I think we both know that's not true. Do you think I don't know where you're at? Your joke about climbing the stairs when we were at Tanya's place. It might have been a throwaway comment, but it wasn't really, was it? The way Tanya spent the whole night trying to help me see that we're made for each other – she didn't conjure that up herself. It must have come off the back of a conversation you had. Then there's the way you've been looking at me. Those pained yet hopeful eyes that feel like they're begging me not to walk away from you at the end of this month.'

'This is ridiculous.' I squeeze my eyes shut to try and keep hold of myself.

'Is it? So, you're telling me I'm wrong? That you aren't hoping for more?'

'I… Oh, for God's sake, of course I've been hoping for more. Why am I the bad one for falling for you?'

His anguished eyes meet mine and he quickly looks away. 'Because that was never the agreement.'

I'm so incredulous at this statement that I get up and walk out of the room, into my own.

'Who agrees whether or not they intend to fall in love?' I shout through the wall, wringing my hands. 'Tell me. *Who?*'

'Look, all I'm saying is that it hasn't helped.' Shep appears in the doorway while I lean against the wall as I try to get myself under control. 'If we hadn't got involved like this… if I hadn't been so ripped with guilt about walking away from you next week—'

'*Then what?*' I demand with a shuddering breath. 'That wee shit from last night wouldn't have got the better of you?'

'I don't know. *Maybe.*' He runs his hands through his floppy hair in that 'stressy' way he does when he's struggling. 'My original plan was to connect with other comedians, learn more about what to expect and how to handle the challenges on stage. But I didn't do any of that because of… us.'

'Maybe I should remind you, Shep, that you were the one who wanted to kiss me first. You were the one that put the idea of you and me in my head in the first place.'

'I know that, and maybe I should never have gone there, but it was supposed to be a casual thing. No strings attached. With an expiry date.'

'Then maybe you should have drawn up a contract to that effect,' I spit back and Shep seems to power down.

'Look,' he says. 'All I know is that, psychologically, I should have been 100 per cent focused on my shows, and if I had been—'

'If it wasn't for me, you wouldn't have done your shows at all!' I finally lose my temper, unable to believe what I'm hearing.

Shep stares at me with defeated eyes. 'Yeah, well, at least if I'd gone home, I'd still have the chance to come back next year. With that write-up, it's all over, so I may as well go pack up my stuff.'

'Well, that's fine by me.' I shrug, desperately trying to keep my emotions in check. 'If I'm such a distraction, then maybe it's best you move on.'

For a moment he just stands there, then he gives a pained nod and returns to the spare room, where I hear him emptying the wardrobe, before the tears overflow and I slam my door shut.

Chapter 32

In the immediate aftermath of Shep moving out my flat feels empty, my life feels empty and my heart feels like it's been pulverised in a blender. Tanya does her best to console and distract me at work, which I very much appreciate, but it's as if a montage of mine and Shep's best moments together is running on a loop in my brain – and someone's hidden the stop button.

I'm aware that, to any outsider, the depth of my heartache might seem ridiculous and overly dramatic. On the face of things, I've only known Shep for a couple of weeks, so I can't possibly have fallen in love with him in that time. And, of course, I haven't. Not fully and completely in the sense that I know and understand every part of him. But my feelings are real and the idea of never seeing him again hurts. A lot.

I shut myself off from everyone I don't have to see or speak to. I do this to give myself time to recover from the shock of losing Shep so suddenly and to avoid well-intended but unhelpful comments about how I'm too good for him. I also just don't have enough emotional resilience to meet up with Becca, Tess and Sal in the Old Town Inn, knowing he could literally be next door. Because I'd be very surprised if he really has packed up and gone home at this late stage – he's made enough friends now to find someone to put him up for the remainder of the festival, and I can't see him not wanting to at least see things through.

To buy myself some time, I tell the girls through our WhatsApp group that I'm having a week of it (which is not actually a lie), and that I'll see them on Saturday – which is, of course, Shep's night off. My hope is that, if he is still in the city, he won't be at The Canongate Tavern that night.

Avoiding my parents isn't as easy, especially as my mum appears to have some kind of sixth sense. She's already left me a couple of voice messages, so in a bid to put her off, I let her know – via text message – that I'm really busy and that I'll call her at the weekend. This is despite the fact that all I really want to do is run home to her for a cuddle. Although I don't like to admit it, it's quite obvious that I'm also keeping them at a distance out of a (somewhat misguided) sense of loyalty to Shep, because I don't want them to hate him – though, based on his behaviour the other night, he really doesn't deserve that protection.

On Friday evening, I'm torturing myself by watching back-to-back episodes of *Love is Blind* and yelling, 'You're right, no one can understand unless they've been through it themselves!' at the screen, when I decide I need to nip this behaviour in the bud before it becomes an unhealthy pattern. As a scientist, I know that to do that, I need to change one of the variables. Just as I'm working up to texting the girls and asking what time they'll be at the pub the next day, a WhatsApp message pops up on my phone screen from Becca.

> Lea, oh my goodness, we just saw Shep
> and he told us you weren't together
> anymore. So sorry, honey. Really hope
> you're OK. I realise you might not want
> company but we're here for you when
> you're ready. Xx

This is quickly followed by one from Tess.

> Don't suffer alone, lady. Let us help. (I
> never liked him anyway – only kidding!) Tx

Then another.

> Just got told off by Becca for being
> insensitive. Soz. Tx

So Shep is still here. I suspected as much but the confirm-ation is like a punch in the guts, because it means he could easily reach out to me, but he's chosen not to. I wait for a further message to come through from Sal, and I can see her typing, but then she stops. After a couple of minutes, it becomes obvious that she's not going to comment, so I take a shaky breath and send my response.

Thanks ladies and don't worry, Tess. I know you were just trying to cheer me up. As you've probably guessed by now, Shep is the reason I've been staying away from the pub. I'm sorry I didn't tell you. Hope you understand. xx

Becca's swift with her reply.

Of course, we understand. Could we meet you somewhere else tomorrow evening? Would that be easier for you? Xx

Smiling through fresh tears at Becca's kindness and compassion, I let her know that this would be very much appreciated, and we make plans to meet at George Square Gardens. I then cross my fingers and send a message into the ether, asking for Sal to go easy on me, as it won't take much to break me in my fragile state. As I say good night to Becca and Tess – Sal having never made a virtual appearance throughout the whole conversation – I try not to think about our meet-up spot, which feels somewhat bittersweet to me. It's where I revealed to Shep that I was 'Lea no-mates', and where he made me feel safe and cared for and normal. But sadly, that happy memory is now just a reminder of what I've lost and how Shep behaved in completely the opposite way when he walked out on me.

-

Approaching the busy entrance to George Square Gardens early on Saturday evening, I'm a jumble of emotions. On the plus side, I'm looking forward to seeing the girls – though, I'll admit, the lack of interaction from Sal the evening before has me unsettled. It's also a beautiful calm sunny evening, which is already helping to lift my spirits after the last few days.

However, I'm finding it difficult to keep Shep out of my mind here. And as much as I want and need their company, I'm dreading telling the girls what happened, because I know I'm going to cry – a lot – in a public space.

'Hi there... aww, look at you,' Becca croons as I approach them, my chin already quivering uncontrollably. 'Come here, honey. You need a hug.'

I allow her to envelop me, while I try and fail to keep my composure. Tess then dives in, making it a mini-group hug, and I cling to them hard while I attempt to get myself under control.

'Let's find a patch of grass and get some drinks in,' says Tess, when we finally untangle ourselves. 'You need wine for this.'

'Yes, I do.' I nod vigorously, while dabbing at my eyes with a tissue and trying to tune out the curious-slash-sympathetic looks from the people nearby.

'Hi, Sal,' I greet her timidly.

'Hi.' She gives me a tight smile in return, which I try not to read too much into.

We find ourselves a spot to sit, then Tess recruits Sal to help her with the drinks and they head to one of the pop-up bars, leaving me alone with Becca.

'So, how are you doing?' Becca tests that the ground is dry, then sits on the grass and spreads out her linen ankle-length skirt, no doubt to minimise the number of wrinkles it will acquire. It sort of makes her look like an angel, despite the fact that the skirt is a melange of yellow and orange.

'I'm… um…' I stop and think about this for a moment, rather than diving straight into an ill-considered response.

'It's OK. You can tell me anything, no matter how bad you think it sounds in your own head.' Becca appears to mistake my hesitation for concern that she'll think I'm being daft.

'Right, I will, then.' I push my hair behind my shoulders as if I'm preparing for a challenge of a more physical nature. 'I'm… hurt… really hurt… I'd never have thought Shep and I could fall out like that, though I guess that was naïve of me. It's not like I've known him long.'

'All couples fight.' Becca shrugs. 'It's normal.'

'I know. But we're no longer together because of that fight, which shows that there really was no substance to our relationship. We were basically just friends with benefits – if even that.'

'It didn't feel like that to you, though, did it?'

'No. Not at all. Not at first, anyway. We were amazing together – until we weren't.' I let out a hefty sigh. 'I'm sad for what we've lost… what we could have had together. I just don't understand how he couldn't see it.'

Becca gives me a sympathetic look and reaches for my hand.

'Then there's the part of me that's… *pissed off*.' I crease my brow in frustration and look at her apologetically.

'You go for it.' She breezily waves me on.

'Thanks. You know, I appreciate this so much. One day, we'll do this for you and your situation.'

'I'd like that. But let's stay focused on you for now. Tell me about being pissed off.'

I pick a low-lying daisy that's escaped the lawnmower and twiddle it between my fingers, inspecting its tiny petals, before returning my attention to Becca.

'I'm angry at Shep for walking out like that. For how casual and throwaway he was over us. I'm not saying he owed me anything. When I gave him a place to stay, I honestly didn't expect anything in return, but—'

'You expected him to treat you with respect.'

'Yes, exactly.' I throw my hands up in exasperation. 'He knew how I felt about him, and instead of treating that situation delicately, he gave me shit for overstepping an agreement we never made in the first place. I can't control how I feel, Becca. I didn't ask for this.'

'Of course you can't – and of course you didn't.' Becca squeezes my hand, which she's still holding, and leans in towards me. 'Between you and me, I'm glad you're angry at him. I could tell from the way he was behaving when we saw him that he hadn't showered himself in glory. He's obviously not a bad guy, you know that, but he doesn't deserve you pining after him as if he's the one that got away.'

'You're right. I'll get over him. I just think it's such a shame. We could've been amazing together.'

'He'll probably realise that – when it's way too late… Oh, they're on their way back with the drinks. Quick piece of advice: maybe don't say too much about how you're feeling in front of Sal, especially about being angry at Shep. She's—'

'Got her own views on this situation, I know.' I give Becca a half-smile, which she returns, almost sheepishly, then she lets go of my hand. 'Don't worry, I won't poke the lady bear.'

We turn our attention to Tess and Sal, who are tottering across the grass towards us, with our drinks. While we watch them approach, I can't help wondering if that opportunity to share was engineered by Becca and Tess to protect me from a potentially unpleasant interaction with Sal. And if so, do I still need to be seriously on my guard?

Chapter 33

Once we each have a drink in our hand, Sal and Tess make themselves comfortable on the grass beside us, and we all sit quietly for a few moments, enjoying the early evening rays. The weather is glorious for the end of August, as so far north, it can often feel almost autumnal at this point. We're being treated to a mini-heatwave that's apparently due to last for up to a week – a rare stroke of luck for the tourists who have chosen to visit during this latter part of the festival.

'Don't you wish it was like this more often?' says Becca wistfully. 'This is how the festival should always be. Not the monsoon-style soaking our city's visitors have to endure so often.'

'It would be so much better,' I agree.

'Yup, defo,' says Tess. 'So, what happened with Shep, Lea?'

'*Tess*.' Becca reprimands her. 'You really need to learn some tact.'

'Oh, sorry, I was just… Well, I thought that was why we were here.' She gives a regretful shrug.

'It is why we're here.' Sal sips at her wine, her tone matter-of-fact, eyes partially hidden behind her oversized sunglasses.

'Sorry.' I take a generous swig from my own drink in the hope it'll help me relax and deflect any thorny comments that might come from Sal. 'I don't know how much Shep told you…' I pause and they make a range of gestures that I interpret as 'not much'.

'Why don't you take it from the top?' Tess urges me.

'OK… on Tuesday night he came back in a mess because of a bad experience at his show…' I proceed to fill them in on everything that happened after that, being careful to stick to the facts as much as possible so Sal doesn't have a reason to call me out.

'And you haven't heard from him since?' Tess asks, when I've shared everything right up to the moment Shep left.

'Not a peep.' I bow my head, trying desperately not to cry.

'That's shitty.' She reaches across and rubs my leg. 'A shitty way for things to end.'

'Totally,' agrees Becca. 'Regardless of the fact there was an "expiry date" on your—'

'I reckon it's better this way,' Sal unapologetically interrupts her.

I furrow my brow, wondering if I've heard right, while Becca and Tess share what appears to be a slightly panicked look.

'Why do you say that?' I ask as calmly as I can.

Sal seems in no hurry to answer, and instead shifts her position, stretching out her long tanned legs in front of her.

'This is how I see it,' she says eventually. 'You already knew this thing you had going on with Shep was likely to end. You said yourself how hard it was going to be when the final goodbye came.'

'I did.' I acknowledge this warily.

'So, firstly, you no longer have to dread that moment – it's done – and secondly, maybe it's better that he leaves with you thinking he's a bit of a shit. I assume that is what you're thinking.'

'Well, yeah.' I'm surprised by her semi-supportive stance. 'Though obviously I can't just switch off the feelings I have for him.'

'Trust me, it'll be much easier to forget a guy who's been a bastard than one you still have on a pedestal. Suck it up and move on.'

'Right.'

Pursing my lips, I'm unsure how to respond to this. It wasn't exactly said with love, but it's possibly the most supportive Sal has been towards me – which, I realise, isn't saying much. It makes me wonder if she's only said it because she's been told to play nice, but I do hope she's actually choosing to be more accepting of me.

'I suppose you're right,' I concede after a long pause.

Becca and Tess share another look, which this time I read as a hopeful one.

'Well, just know that we're here for you.' Becca gives my shoulder a squeeze and then steers the conversation onto a lighter topic, which I'm guessing she does to move on to the next stage of break-up 101: cheering me up.

Emotionally drained, I'm more than happy to go along with this, and by the time I'm on my second glass of wine, I'm feeling a bit brighter and enjoying the banter with my new friends. It might be the alcohol helping things along, but I'm also starting to convince myself that I'll be fine without Shep in my life. Our time together was incredible (before it went to shit), but perhaps he was only ever meant to be a fleeting feature in my life to help me get back on track – in the same way it seems I was for him. Maybe Tanya was right, and fate was at play, but in a different way to what she thought.

'That was honestly how it went, and I didn't know what to say, so I just smiled politely at him and walked away,' Becca finishes a story about an awkward interaction with a bloke in a supermarket, which has us all – including Sal – chuckling. 'Ugh, where are the loos? I can't hold on any longer.'

We point her in the direction of the multi-cubicle Portakabin that is the ladies', and she wanders off to join the sizeable queue outside.

Tess, Sal and I continue to chat lightly, until we're interrupted by a buzzing coming from Tess's bag. She pulls out her phone and answers it.

'Hi, little sis, what's up?' she greets the caller. 'What's that? You're really quiet... it's like you're calling from Mars... No, don't do that, I'll nip somewhere quieter...'

Tess mouths an apology to us, and holds up a finger to let us know she'll be right back.

Finding myself alone with Sal for the first time, I'm immediately uncomfortable. It's fine when we're all together, but I don't actually know Sal well enough to chat to her about anything in particular – probably because she never shares anything personal beyond her online dating updates, and Tess has already grilled her on that today. I can't talk to her about my situation with Shep either, because we all know where she stands on that.

Smiling at her uneasily, I can tell that she's equally uncomfortable.

'So that guy you went on a second date with...' I eventually grasp at the only thing I can think of, '...do you—'

'Lea, what do you think you're doing?' She cuts across me with a startlingly combative tone.

'I'm... sorry? I was just trying to make conversation.'

'I don't mean that. I mean, what do you think you're doing latching onto our group like a freaking limpet?' Sal's face contorts with such contempt that I recoil.

'I'm... Why do you... I don't understand...' I trail off pathetically and pick at a non-existent bit of fluff on my cropped trousers to avoid having to look at her.

'OK, if you don't understand, I'll spell it out for you. Don't think you're the first of Becca's strays. She has a radar for that stuff. Which is why I take it upon myself to get rid, so she doesn't get taken advantage of.'

'What are you talking about, Sal?' I can't help but reply in a small voice. 'I would never take advantage of Becca.'

'You already have,' she sneers. 'Just by being here. Poor little Lea, who clearly has no friends of her own. I bet you thought you'd lucked out. Well – newsflash – you haven't. Because her and Tess might not be wise to you, but I am, and I'm not going to let you become a sad hanger-on. You get what I'm saying?'

I dare a glance at her. She's sitting crossed-legged, with her arms folded, her expression nothing short of vicious. It's now obvious that her half-hearted show of support before was all for show.

'Do you, Lea?'

'I heard you, Sal. Loud and clear.'

'Good.' She leans in and lowers her voice. 'And don't even think about making a scene or going crying to Becca and Tess about this, because if you do—'

'What are you two chatting about?' Tess appears out of nowhere, plonking herself back down on the grass.

She's distracted by something on her phone, meaning she hasn't picked up on the fact that the atmosphere has become icier than a deep freeze.

'Not much,' Sal replies. 'Just shooting the breeze, right, Lea?'

'Right,' I force myself to say through gritted teeth and a false smile, while I'm shaking so much inside my vitals feel like they might go into meltdown at any moment.

Tess finally puts her phone away and grins at the two of us. 'Another drink?'

I involuntarily glance at Sal, expecting her to give me a warning not to accept the invite, but instead she nods, almost imperceptibly, and it takes all of three seconds to understand the intention behind that gesture: she's telling me not to run off now, as that will raise suspicion.

'Yeah, sure,' I reply in a quavering voice that could easily be mistaken for someone trying not to cry after having their heart broken. 'I can get this round in.'

One for the road, I guess. At least I can buy Becca and Tess a drink to thank them for being so kind and welcoming. Not that they'll know anything of it.

'I'll help you,' says Becca, who's also just re-joined us.

'Um… sure. I guess I can't carry four glasses on my own.' My eyes nervously flit to Sal, who shoots me another steely look, this time easily interpreted as 'not a word'.

Keeping quiet about Sal's shark attack while we get the drinks is easy enough. Becca being Becca, she's keen to use the opportunity to provide further moral support, which I appreciate more than ever, despite the fact I can barely focus on a word she's saying. It will be sorely missed, now I've received my marching orders on a nuclear scale. The one saving grace is that I'm able to cry without giving away that something else is going on.

When we return to the others with the drinks, I keep my contributions to the conversation to a minimum, and after what I consider to be an appropriate amount of time, I make my excuses.

'Aww, no, don't leave.' Tess pets her bottom lip. 'We've still got nearly an hour till our show.'

'I know.' I take a final swig from my drink. 'But I'm afraid I'm out of steam, with everything that's gone on, you know?'

'We understand, don't we, girls?' Becca slides a sympathetic arm around my shoulders and leans into me, almost setting me off again.

'Absolutely,' says Sal, a little too brightly.

'I guess.' Tess briefly continues with her play huff, then dives on me affectionately. 'You'll be OK, Lea. There are plenty more blokes out there, and at least a couple of them must have long-term relationship potential. LOL.'

'Thanks, ladies. Thanks for... everything.'

Getting up from my patch of grass, I'm thankful for my sunglasses while I say what Becca and Tess don't realise is my final goodbye to them. Then, once I've left the gardens and I'm a safe distance away, I allow the pain and distress of what's just happened to overtake me. Finding a bench in The Meadows, I settle down on it and break down in huge heart-wrenching sobs, not caring a bit that everyone passing by is staring.

Chapter 34

The next forty or so hours are probably the loneliest of my existence. It takes me until Monday evening to work up the courage to call Mum, and when I do, I tell her nothing of what's gone on. I'm aware it makes no sense at all to keep everything bottled up, but I'm still not ready to let them turn on Shep or discuss the way Sal treated me.

Sometimes my parents' love is everything I need to get back on track, and sometimes – as well-intentioned as it is – it makes me feel small and pathetic, and like I'm five years old again. If I tell my mum about it, she'll be over here like a shot, with an overnight bag, a box of tissues and my childhood teddy bear. Right now, I need to feel like a grown-up who can and will get through this without the help of Mum and Dad.

'Are you sure you're all right, love?' she asks for the third time during our call. 'You seem a bit flat and you've left it longer before calling again. I hope that man of yours is looking after you?'

'I'm fine, Mum.' I use my free hand to steady my wobbling chin as I say this. 'Just a bit under the weather. Maybe I've got a cold coming on or something.'

'OK, well get yourself an early night, then. I assumed you'd be going to watch end-of-festival fireworks tonight, but if you're not right, maybe it's best to—'

'Got it, Mum. I'll give it a miss and look after myself.'

'Good girl. I think that's a wise choice.'

It certainly won't be a difficult choice, given that I have no one to watch them with. Tanya is now my only remaining 'new friend', and she mentioned going to the fireworks with family friends, so I could hardly fish for an invite. Plus, I'm clear that Tanya is an occasional drink-after-work friend. She's not a substitute for the girlfriends I had at uni or those I've just lost (Sal excluded, for obvious reasons).

After saying goodbye to my mum, I return to my well-worn spot on the sofa, where I'm watching *Friends* in an attempt to cheer myself up, despite not having any myself. The irony of this is certainly not lost on me. However, despite it being one of my favourite shows, I'm struggling to pay attention, and my fingers keep reaching for my phone.

As I'm scrolling back through the messages that Shep and I exchanged, a WhatsApp notification appears at the top of my screen and I tap on it to read the full message from Becca.

> Hey, Lea, hope you're OK. Just wanted to try one more time to convince you to join us for the fireworks. We'd love to have you with us, but fully understand if you think it'll be a bit much. I know what tonight symbolises for you. Sending the biggest of hugs. Xx

I sigh and shake my head miserably. Why did Sal have to be such a nasty cow? What did I ever do to her? And why is she so territorial over her friendship group? I don't understand why she saw it as such a negative that I'd become part of it. Surely having more friends to hang out with is a positive thing, provided they're loyal and trustworthy and fun to be around – all of which I think I am. Becca and Tess certainly seemed to think so.

She made such unfair judgements about me – calling me a 'sad hanger-on', as if I was following them around like a lost sheep. That's not at all how things were. It was Becca who first suggested I join them, not me. How is that my fault? Unless… maybe that's the problem. Maybe Sal felt threatened by me – perhaps even by each of the new people Becca has introduced to their group. Maybe she gets rid of anyone new to prevent her power and influence over Becca and Tess being diminished. Or maybe she is just plain nasty and self-absorbed.

If Shep were here, he'd have a read on the situation and he'd probably be spot on. I so wish I could share this with him… And there was me getting ideas that maybe I didn't need him in my life.

Who was I kidding? For starters, it was Shep who created the opportunity for me to make a connection with the girls in the first place. I couldn't and wouldn't have done that on my own – and although that connection hasn't so much fizzled out as given me a life-altering electric shock, I don't regret meeting Becca and Tess for a second. I just wish Sal hadn't been such a piece of work.

Rubbing at my weary eyes, I type out a response to Becca.

> Hey Becca, thank you for thinking of me. You're right, today is a bit tough, so I'll give the fireworks a miss. Hope you all have a fab evening. Will be in touch soon. xx

Obviously, that's not true. I won't be in touch with them, and unfortunately, I think my only option if she and Tess make contact again is to ghost them. This is something I would never ever want to do, especially to people as kind-hearted as them. Feeling a real sense of injustice, I fling my phone to the other side of the sofa so it's out of easy reach and continue half-watching *Friends*, while intermittently poring over my memories from the last three weeks.

Eventually, I decide I need to eat something for dinner, if only to interrupt my runaway thoughts, so I head into the kitchen to see what I can find. Opting for beans on toast, solely due to the convenience factor, I stir the pot on the cooker while reflecting on the stark contrast between how tonight might have gone and how I'm actually spending it.

'Is this really how you want this whole experience to end?' I ask myself out loud. 'Feeling sorry for yourself because you were rejected − twice over − and probably locking yourself away for good?'

I shake my head, disappointed in myself. But then, two bites into my dinner, I decide that I don't want that − nor do I want to miss out on the fireworks purely because I don't have anyone to go with. At the very least, it will take my mind off things for a while, and that can't be a bad thing.

Abandoning my half-eaten dinner, I tidy myself up enough to be seen in public, then I battle my way across the packed city centre to find a good vantage spot. I'm not keen on the idea of going to Princes Street, because it will be too busy, so instead I head to North Bridge, where I'll get a clear view of the fireworks. I've watched them from there before − back in the day, with my uni girlfriends − so I know it's a good place to go.

Unfortunately, I arrive too late to get a front-row view, so I end up wedged between a very slushy couple (whom I do my best to ignore) and a gaggle of young Spanish blokes, who take it upon themselves to shelter me from the endless stream of people trying to get past us. There's a feeling of festivity and anticipation in the air, which reminds me a little of Edinburgh's iconic Hogmanay street party – only, it's much warmer and everyone's wearing fewer clothes.

With twenty minutes until the fireworks begin, and having nobody to converse with in that time, I end up wrestling with the unpleasant thoughts and emotions jostling in my mind, alongside the continual nudging and bumping from people as they pass, and it all quickly becomes too much. A nervy sensation pools in my stomach, escalating quickly, and I start to feel like I'm losing control. Then, before I know it, I can't think straight, my chest feels constricted and I'm struggling to breathe.

'Are you all right?' One of the Spanish guys looks down at me, having perhaps spotted me looking around wildly for some space or a means of escape.

'I'm… fine. I just… need to…' I look at him with terror-stricken eyes, unable to finish my sentence.

Without thinking, I slide into what I think is an opening in the crowd, and I'm immediately knocked to the ground by someone much bigger than me. This is all too much for my already overtaxed brain and body to cope with, and everything becomes a blur. While I hyperventilate, gasping for air, all I can hear is an urgent, angry-sounding stream of Spanish, then I'm picked up off the ground by two people, one on either side of me.

My breathing is fast and ragged and out of rhythm, but still I'm lucid enough to acknowledge my rescuers, who might just have saved me from being trampled by the crowd. Once I'm able to see around me again, I gabble a thank you to the Spanish guy who has hold of my left arm and looks extremely concerned for me. Then I turn my head, expecting to see one of his friends on my right, but to my astonishment, I discover that my second rescuer has a much more familiar face.

Chapter 35

'*Shep?*' I'm so out of sorts, I don't trust that what I'm seeing is actually real. I wouldn't be at all surprised if I'm hallucinating after what's just happened.

'Lea?' His face mirrors my surprise. 'Oh my God, are you OK?'

'I'm… I don't… know…'

'Let's get you out of here.' He expertly slips his arm around me and hoists me up so that he's taking most of my weight, then addresses the Spanish guy. 'Thanks, mate. I know her, I'll take it from here.'

My first rescuer and his friends don't seem so keen on the idea of a complete stranger wading in and carting me off. They put up a bit of resistance, and at the point when I hear the word *policía* mentioned, I haltingly manage to reassure them that I know Shep, and I'm perfectly safe with him.

Shep more or less carries me to a shop doorway on the southerly part of the bridge, and gently lowers me onto the step there.

'Are you hurt?' He cups my face, while checking me for injuries.

'No, I'm…' I'm still panting hard, struggling to catch my breath.

'I think you're having a panic attack. Try and follow my breathing… in slowly through your nose… and slowly out again... in for one, two, three, four, five... and out for one, two, three, four, five...'

He continues to coach me through my episode until I'm calmer and more in control, and the tightness in my chest subsides.

'Sorry about that.' I struggle to make eye contact. 'I've never experienced anything like that before.'

'You have nothing to apologise for.' He sits down beside me on the step. 'Crowds like that can be daunting at the best of times, never mind when you end up under them.'

Deciding I'm not ready to share that being knocked over wasn't what triggered this reaction, I simply nod in response.

'Where are the girls?' Shep asks. 'Did you get separated from them or something?'

'Eh... no.'

I shrink into myself, and Shep immediately twigs.

'You're on your own. Why, Lea?'

Because you buggered off, I want to shout at him all of a sudden, not liking being under the microscope.

'There's no way Becca, Tess and Sal would miss the fireworks,' he says, when I don't offer anything up. 'It's the perfect way to end their comedy-show marathon, which means...' He scrutinises my face, and – still very vulnerable after my ordeal – I decide I can't take this any longer.

'It means what it means,' I snap at him. 'I'm here alone. Poor "loner chick" Lea is back to having no friends.'

'But, why? What's gone on to cause this?'

'Shep, I don't mean to be rude, but it's not really any concern of yours anymore, is it?' I get up from the step, still feeling incredibly shaky, but not wanting to let him see this. 'Thanks for helping me there. I think I'll head home.'

'Wait.' He gets to his feet and grabs my arm, then releases it the moment my reproving eyes land on him.

I exhale wearily. 'What is it, Shep? What do you want?'

For a moment, it's as if time stands still. My breathing becomes laboured again, this time in anticipation of what he's going to say. His gaze is intense, and despite my impatience, I'm hypnotised, unable to look away.

'You,' he murmurs after what feels like an unbearable wait. 'I want you.'

The moment he says this, the fireworks from the castle start exploding like missiles in the sky and, although I know that I should give him a really hard time, any sense of self-control immediately escapes me. I throw myself on him, while he wraps his arms around me and returns my kiss with such urgency, it might be wise for the two of us to get a room.

We remain locked in this embrace for a good minute before reason kicks in and I pull back suddenly. 'What do you mean, you want me? Is it just for sex? No, don't answer that. Can we watch the fireworks first?'

If it is just for sex, I at least want half an hour of enjoying this experience with him and feeling like there's a possibility of something else – though that 'something else' would have to include a grovelling apology, among other things.

Shep gives a bemused look and shrugs. 'Fireworks it is, then. Though are you sure you're up to going back over there?'

'I'll cope.' I grab his hand and practically drag him back through the crowd to the middle of the bridge.

Once we find a spot where we have a good enough view of the pyrotechnics, we 'ooh' and 'ahh' at the multitude of booming explosions and the spectacularly choreographed bursts of colours in the sky. Shep slips his arms around my waist from behind and holds me tight, while resting his head on my shoulder. He's so close I can feel his warm breath on my cheek, and despite not yet having any answers or reassurances, all I can think about is how much I want this feeling to last forever.

–

Once the fireworks have finished and people are dispersing, I wriggle out of Shep's grasp and turn to face him with an earnest expression.

'OK, now we can talk.'

'Sure, but I vote for not doing it here. How about we grab a pint? Somewhere other than The Canongate Tavern or the Old Town Inn,' he adds quickly.

'Sounds good to me.'

We find a quiet(ish) bar near the junction of Chambers Street and South Bridge, and I slide into one of their high-backed booths by the window, while Shep goes to order our drinks.

As soon as my bum hits the seat, my brain switches into overdrive. What the hell just happened? How can it be that only hours ago I thought I'd never see Shep again, and now I'm sitting here waiting for him to join me?

More importantly, what did Shep mean when he said he wants me? Did he just mean it in a sexual way or is it more than that? He made it clear before that, to him, our summer fling was nothing more than a physical and very temporary thing. And regardless of the answer to that question, do I even want to get involved with him again after he hurt me so badly?

Watching him lean on the bar, chatting away easily to the barman, I feel a deep longing for us to be together again – despite his previously unacceptable behaviour. But I know it's not that simple. If Shep just wants to reunite for the next day or so, before he heads home to Northern Ireland, then I'm not sure I want or can cope with that. The idea of losing him all over again is just too painful. I may have abandoned all sense of rationality before on North Bridge, but I now need to override all that chemistry and primal biological functioning, and approach this with my head firmly in charge.

'You look deep in thought.' Shep grins at me while handing me a glass of white wine, then slips into the seat opposite.

'A lot has happened in the last hour.' I return his broad smile with a more tentative one. 'Thanks for this.'

'No bother. It's great to see you.'

'You too.'

Come on, Lea, I chide myself. You can do better than that.

Pursing my lips, I'm about to ask Shep what this is, when he fills the silence between us.

'Tell me what happened with the girls. Something's obviously gone on.'

I hesitate. This is the last thing I want to discuss right now, when there's a gigantic unanswered question sitting on the table between us.

I don't know if it's a sudden rush of courage or simply an overpowering need to know what's going on, but I decide I've had enough of waiting. Sitting back in my seat, I fold my arms and fix Shep with a stare.

'No. I don't want to sit here and tell you how everything went to shit with the girls, when you and I haven't yet discussed why everything went to shit between us. Or what you meant when you told me on the bridge that you want me. Don't mess with my head, Shep.'

His easy-going expression crumbles and I glimpse some of the same anguish I saw in his face the day he left my flat.

'You're right.' He drums his fingers on the table, betraying his obvious discomfort. 'We need to wade through all that first. I was concerned to see you on your own again, that's all.'

'Which I appreciate, but depending on where this conversation goes, that may or may not be any of your concern.'

'Battle lines are firmly drawn, then.' He chuckles, then straightens his face when he sees my eyes narrow. 'Sorry, wrong time for humour.' He pauses and clears his throat. 'Lea, I was bang out of order the other day.'

'Yeah, you were.' I keep my tone stern to hammer this home.

'I know, and believe me, I've been pretty ashamed of myself. I'd been taken down a peg or two, and I didn't know how to deal with it. I was doubting myself and whether I was good enough.'

'And you were doubting me.'

He winces. 'I know. I wasn't really, though. You have to know that. Comedy is all I've ever wanted to do and I thought my big chance was over. But that wasn't your fault, and it wasn't about you at all. I just couldn't face the reality of the situation, and that sent me into a spiral of dread for what I'd be facing from my family when I went home a failure.'

I shake my head in rejection of his self-criticism. 'Shep, one bad show doesn't make you a failure, regardless of what some jumped-up tosser writes in an online article. Look what you've achieved.'

'I know, I know.' He holds his hands up in acceptance of what I'm saying. 'I was being a daft prick. All you were trying to do was offer me something positive to hold on to – and I was so unfair to you.'

'No arguments from me on that.' I raise an eyebrow and sip at my wine morosely.

'After I left yours, I went to the pub and Kira offered me her couch for the remainder of my time here, so I could at least see my shows through to the end. Not sure that was the moving-in present her girlfriend had envisaged.' Shep pauses again to sup from his pint, eyes still on mine. 'I've spent a lot of hours lying awake on that damn thing, thinking about how badly I messed up.'

'With me or with your show?'

'With you.'

He shifts his focus to his glass, rotating it slowly on the spot, which tells me he's uncomfortable about what he's about to say next. Holding my breath, I wait for him to continue.

'When you and I got together, Lea, I had no intention of taking things beyond the end of this month, and I assumed you were in the same frame of mind. I guess you must have been at first?'

I simply shrug in acceptance of this.

'So, yeah, that was how I was expecting things to pan out,' he says. 'But then I found myself wanting to spend every free moment with you, hanging on your every word, feeling stuff that I hadn't felt for a woman in a long time – if ever.'

'You did?' My eyes widen with surprise. 'You hid that well. I mean, there were times when I thought I saw a glimmer of something there, but then it would be gone, like that.' I click my fingers to emphasise my point.

He looks sheepish all of a sudden. 'It wasn't part of the plan to get involved with you. I wanted to succeed with my stand-up so badly, and I thought the only way to achieve that was to do it alone. I'm not surprised you were confused. I was too. I was in a battle between my heart and my head. Then, when I got that bad review, I felt I'd taken my eye off the ball and I lost perspective. I'm so sorry.'

Shep hangs his head ashamedly, which tugs at my heartstrings something awful. While I'm still bruised from those poorly judged actions on his part, I now at least understand what was going on with him. He's as imperfect a human as I am – as every other person on this planet is. What I still don't have, though, is the full picture, and until that's laid bare, I'm not offering up my olive branch.

'So where are you now?' I prompt him. 'Why are we here?'

He lifts his head. 'Well, for starters, despite the dent to my self-confidence, the rest of my shows went like clockwork – I guess that's the benefit of having delivered the same set so many times. I also did hear from that journalist in the end.'

'Oh, that's fantastic, Shep!' I can't help but light up on hearing this. 'I'm so delighted for you. Your name really is going to be in lights.' I hold out my glass and he clinks it with his.

'That certainly seems like something of a possibility now, though I can't get ahead of myself.' He sighs deeply.

'I wish you'd been there. Everything turned around and you know what was taking up the most room in my head?'

'How you could now go and tell your family where to stick it?'

He laughs. 'No. It was you.' His eyes lock onto mine, that familiar electricity sparking between us once more. 'How all I wanted to do was share those incredible moments with you. And how I missed you to the point it actually physically hurt.'

'You did?' My skin prickles with anticipation, making it very difficult to continue giving him a hard time.

'Totally. It made me realise that I don't want to be telling the story of any success I have in the future, without you being a part of it.' He holds my gaze, causing my pulse to quicken, while my insides feel like they're going through a spin cycle.

'When you say "a part"…?' I trail off, encouraging him to elaborate.

'I mean I want you by my side through it all. As my girlfriend, my partner… whatever label you want to use.'

Realising that I'm being sucked in too quickly by our overpowering chemistry, I remind myself that I shouldn't forgive and forget too easily. I deserve better than all the shitty relationships I was in before I met Shep. And while I do believe this one would be different, I need to make sure that he knows there won't be a 'round three'.

I clear my throat and sit up straight in my seat. 'What makes you think you deserve another chance?'

He seems unsurprised by this question, but I can also tell he's taking it seriously.

'I don't think I deserve it. I would never act in such an entitled way. I can only hope you'll see how sincere my apology is and trust that what happened at your flat was totally out of character for me.'

'And you're sure about this? About wanting to be with me? Because I don't want to hold you back, nor do I want you to resent me if things don't go how you hope. I can't be with you if there's any chance of that.'

'Oh, I'm sure. Lea, you lift me up. You believed in me when my own family didn't, and you gave me back my big opportunity when I thought I'd lost it. You're intelligent, beautiful – literally, the best person I've ever met. And you're top-notch in bed.'

I let out an amused snort at this.

'Seriously, though,' he continues. 'I might not have known you long, but I already know that you're the sidekick I need in all this, and I want to be that person for you, too. Will you please forgive me and give me the chance to do that?'

My eyes are welling up and my throat is choked from Shep's wonderful words – I've heard all I need to hear.

'OK, I forgive you. But to be clear, I won't be so understanding if it happens again, whatever your reasons might be.'

'Got it.' He gives me a lopsided grin, which I return, then a thought comes to me.

'So, us being together and living in different cities… How will that work?'

'I figured you'd ask that.' He pulls out his phone, looks something up and hands it to me. 'Edinburgh is expensive, but I think I can afford this if I can get a job with flexible hours to work around any gigs I pick up.'

I look at the advert for a room rental on the screen and my jaw drops in surprise. 'You're going to move here?'

'I am. It's better connected than Northern Ireland, and if things go the way I hope, I'll be travelling around the UK a bit.'

'Would London not be better for that? I expected you'd want to go there.'

Shep shakes his head. 'London's too big and too expensive. Plus, you're not there.'

I'm completely stunned by all this. The most I had expected, if things were to go in the direction I'd hoped, was for us to try things long-distance. This is a whole other deck of cards.

Studying the listing for a moment, taking in the dinginess of the property from the photos, a thought brews in my mind, and I hand his phone back to him. 'It looks all right, but I don't think it's for you.'

'You don't?'

'Nah. Lucky for you, though, I know a sexy landlady with a spare room for rent.'

'Really?' Shep's face lights up with an impish grin.

'Really.' I mirror him in return. 'Only if that doesn't make you uncomfortable. It's not us moving in together, we can do the actual flatmate thing. You can pay me a small amount in rent, move your stuff across from Northern Ireland into the spare room – and if we think it's better for our relationship, it can just be a temporary thing until you get on your feet financially. Unless you think that's a terrible idea?'

'What I think is that I've just hit the jackpot. Although… what about your folks? Will your da not go back into sniper mode if he finds out we're living together – even as flatmates? Also…' Shep gulps, '…with the way I treated you, haven't I already blown my chances with him? He said I'd only get one.'

'Good thing I didn't tell him, then.' I waggle my eyebrows at him and he puts a hand to his chest in relief. 'Just you leave my dad to me. He seems to have accepted you, so I'll warm him up to it.'

'Lea, you are…' Shep climbs out of his side of the booth and slides in beside me without finishing his sentence. Then he leans in and kisses me with such intensity, I feel like I might take off.

When we eventually break apart, we gaze at each other, our happiness and relief at being back together radiating from us like heat from the sun.

'Thank you for giving me another chance.' Shep gently takes my hands in his and squeezes them affectionately. 'I am one lucky bastard. Now, how about you tell me what happened with the girls?'

Chapter 36

Two days later, and after spending every free moment together since we reunited, Shep and I have a very different evening ahead of us.

'Shep, I don't know if I can do this.' I join him in the kitchen, where he's hoovering up a bowl of chicken tikka masala.

He sets it on the counter, plonks his fork in it, and pulls me into him. 'If you don't want to do it, you don't have to. There's no pressure to go ahead with this plan.'

I suck my teeth, torn between the temptation to take the easy road and annoyance at myself for being such a wimp. 'It's not that I don't want to do it. It is important to me. Really important. I'm just... a bit terrified.'

'I hear you. Look, the girls just think they're meeting me for a farewell drink, so if you want to give it a miss, I can go ahead as planned – and I'll slip a laxative in Sal's drink when she's not looking.'

I titter. 'I know you're only saying that to make me feel better, but part of me wishes you would. She certainly deserves it.'

'She sure does.' Shep plants a kiss on my nose, then picks up his bowl and resumes eating. 'I know better than to try and fight your battles for you, though. You don't want or need a knight in shining armour to save you from the evil ice queen.'

'Don't I?' I chew on my lip apprehensively, knowing full well he's right. I'm just running scared.

'No, you don't. My job was to provide the setting and the opportunity, which is what I've done. The rest is up to you.' He spreads his hands in illustration of this. 'Remember what we talked about last night: about you burying that shame of yours and knowing your self-worth. It's irrelevant that you've not been part of their group for long, and tenure doesn't give a person the right to behave the way Sal did. If Becca and Tess can't see that situation for exactly what it is, then it's good riddance to bad rubbish.'

Shep finishes this impromptu speech with a pointed look, which I know is designed to boost my confidence. And, of course, it works.

'You're right. God, you're so right. I need to shake off this feeling that I'm a nobody, and stop letting Sal get in my head like this. It was circumstances that led to me being alone and isolated, not who I am as a person. I need to woman-up and face this, because I am better and more loveable than a nasty bully like her.'

'I'll drink to that.' Shep raises his glass of water.

'She's going to regret the day she met me.'

'Sorry to say it, but I think she already does.'

'*Hey.*' I cuff him playfully. 'Well, then, she's going to regret it even more. Because I will not be banished back to no-pals-land without a fight.'

'*Yes!*' He punches the air. 'That's fighting talk. Now let's get over there before you chicken out.'

'I won't be chickening out.' I shake my head determinedly, a fire igniting inside of me. 'I'm done with feeling inferior.'

Half an hour later, our plan kicks into action. After checking the coast is clear, I discreetly slip past the Old Town Inn and nip into The Canongate Tavern, while Shep heads inside the girls' regular festival haunt to meet them. We've agreed he'll go ahead of me, so he can get a read on the situation and check it's not unwise to unleash my counterstrike on Sal tonight.

Fifteen minutes later, my phone lights up with a WhatsApp message from Shep.

> All systems go.

I smile at his use of language, while a whirlwind of fear and dread simultaneously tears through me. It's time.

Slowly getting up from my seat, I feel my legs turn to mush and my chest tighten, as if my body is going into a similar meltdown to the other night at the fireworks.

Come on, Lea. You can do this.

This sorry attempt at an inner pep talk does little to alleviate my terror, because right now, all I want to do is run home and hide under my duvet. I really wish I could charge next door all guns blazing, but the reality is that it was so much easier to get pumped up in the safety of my flat. Sal has got under my skin good and proper, which was obviously her aim.

So don't let her win. Do what you do best: go in there and focus on the facts – then tell her that she doesn't get to treat you that way.

Now, that I can do. Surely. I *need* to do this – for every woman and girl who's ever been bullied by someone like her.

Straightening my posture, I take a deep courage-inducing breath, then I walk out of the pub.

Chapter 37

Pushing open the door to the Old Town Inn, I can see Shep sitting with Becca, Tess and Sal at a table near the back. As the place is fairly quiet, I'm spotted almost immediately.

'Lea!' cries Tess before I've even closed the door behind me. 'It's so good to see you... *oh...*' Her gaze shifts to Shep, as it clearly dawns on her that the two of us being here at the same time might not be such a good thing.

Becca leaps to her feet and rushes forward, face full of apologies. 'Hi, honey, I'm so sorry. We saw Shep briefly yesterday and he asked if we'd have a farewell drink with him tonight. We didn't want to upset you, but we also didn't want to tell him no.'

'It's OK.' I touch her arm gently. 'I knew he was here.'

'You did? But how... I mean—'

'Let's just go over there and it'll all become clear.'

I follow Becca to the table, where my eyes meet Sal's, and it's clear she's both astonished and furious that I've had the nerve to show my face again. Unable to bear her glare, I look away, my renewed courage almost deserting me.

'Hi, there,' I greet an uncertain-looking Tess, then I nod at Shep, who returns the gesture.

'Pull up a chair?' suggests Tess, looking to the others as if checking that was the right thing to say.

I shake my head. 'It's fine, I'll stand. This won't take long.'

Becca and Tess continue to look uncomfortable and bewildered, while Sal sits back and folds her arms. This is undoubtedly an attempt to intimidate me – and it nearly works – but having come this far, I now need to see my plan through.

While doing my best to tune out all the deeply unpleasant sensations rushing through my mind and body, I clasp my hands together tightly and force myself to speak.

'I'm actually here to speak to Sal.'

'Oh, right.' She tries to jump on this opportunity and use it to her advantage. 'Shall we go outside?'

'No.' I give a single shake of my head. 'Here will do just fine. I want everyone to hear this.'

Sal's face drains of colour. It seems she's put two and two together, and realised I'm about to out her. Much as I hate to admit it, this gives me a feeling of satisfaction and spurs me on.

'Becca, Tess, I want to apologise for this in advance. It's not going to be comfortable, but it needs to be said.'

Still baffled by this curious turn of events, they simply nod, eyes frantically darting between me and Sal.

'OK, so, when we were at George Square Gardens last week, and I was left on my own with Sal, she basically told me to disappear and keep away from your group.'

'*What?*' Becca looks to Sal, who now has a face like thunder.

Tess looks equally shocked, and for once seems stunned into silence.

'She's lying,' says Sal. 'Why would I do that?'

Despite my raw nerves, I force myself to look her square in the face. 'I don't know why. All I know is that you did, and that you've done it before.'

'Sal, what's Lea talking about?' asks Becca. 'And when were you two on your own? I don't remember that.'

Tess's mouth forms a perfect 'O' of realisation. 'I do. It was when you went to the loo. My sister phoned and I had to nip away because I couldn't hear her.'

'That's right,' I reply. 'And that's when you did it, wasn't it, Sal?'

'No. I didn't. Guys, she's clearly nuts.' Sal rolls her eyes and clicks her tongue bitterly. 'No wonder you broke up with her, Shep. I'd call that a lucky escape.'

Shep looks to me, obviously wanting to say something.

'Not yet,' I murmur almost inaudibly, so he sits back and lets me continue. 'All right, Sal, if it's your word against mine, then let's see if any of this rings true to Becca and Tess. They know you well enough to tell if I'm making it up.'

Feeling myself start to tremble, I lift my shoulders to fool my brain into thinking I've got this.

'You asked me what I thought I was doing latching onto your group "like a freaking limpet",' I begin to reel off her crimes. 'You told me that I wasn't "the first of Becca's strays" and you said you see it as your job to "get rid". You also threatened me to make sure I wouldn't say anything to these two.'

'Who the hell do you think you are?' Sal snorts with derision. 'I didn't threaten you.'

'Sorry, you're right. You never got to fully deliver that threat. I was so intimidated, I made it clear I understood before you could finish telling me what you'd do if I "went crying to them". My mistake.'

'Sal, is this true?' asks an incredulous Tess.

'Of course it's not true.' Sal sits up in her seat, shooting me an acidic look. 'Who are you going to believe? Me – who you've known for years – or someone you met a couple of weeks ago?'

'I don't… eh…' Tess glances back and forth between me and Sal.

While all this is going on, Becca remains silent, her expression now impossible to read.

I look at Sal and shrug. 'I'm not asking them to choose a side. That's not why I'm here. I'm here to let you know that you're not going to belittle or intimidate me – or drive me away. I'm making a choice not to be around you, because I want to spend my time with people who are kind and who care about me, and who won't try to control my actions for their own gain.' I glance fleetingly at Becca, hoping more than anything that she's not judging me poorly for what I'm doing.

Sal scoffs. 'Would you listen to this nonsense? What fucking planet do you come from, Lea? Can't you see that everyone here wishes you'd end this nonsense and get lost?'

While I no longer care a bit what Sal thinks of me, I flinch at this cutting remark.

Having clearly heard enough, Shep looks up at me. 'May I?'

I smile at him appreciatively. 'Sure.'

. He sits forward and focuses his attention on Sal. 'I don't want Lea to get lost, Sal. I also think you did what you did because she's someone you'll never understand. And because her kindness and generosity are characteristics you see as a threat to your standing in this group.'

She blanches. 'Wh-what?'

'You heard me.' He reaches out and takes my hand. 'Lea told me exactly what you did, and there was no question in my mind that she was telling the truth.'

'And now that I've said my piece,' I add, 'we'll leave you all to it. Becca, Tess, I'm truly sorry for this, but I felt you had to know.'

Shep gets up from his seat and we head for the door together, hearing Sal's furious mutterings as we go.

'Wait!' Becca calls after me, to my surprise.

We stop and turn.

She half-raises her hand in the air as if she's in class. 'I think you're telling the truth as well.'

'So do I,' Tess pipes up, following Becca's lead. 'And I think Sal's the one who should leave, not you, Lea.'

'Are you freaking kidding me?' Sal explodes. 'You're going to take their word over mine?'

'I am,' says Becca. 'Because everything Lea said sounded true, and I don't think she's someone who'd lie. That account of what happened at George Square Gardens had you written all over it, Sal.'

'So? She's been around me enough to know how I talk.'

'No.' Becca shakes her head. 'There's no way Lea could have dreamed up something so reminiscent of things I've heard you say in the past. Also, you know I've always wondered why Maria and Holly ghosted us after I welcomed them into our group. Both times I thought I'd done something wrong, but it was you. You didn't like them, so you decided they had to go, and you made sure we knew nothing of it.'

'Becca, for God's sake,' Sal spits. 'That's complete and utter—'

'Don't you *dare* gaslight my best friend,' Tess cuts across Sal with a menacing tone I'd never have thought her

305

capable of. 'You've always called the shots, which puts you in the perfect position to abuse our trust. Everything from where we go on holiday to the decision to cut all ties with the guys—'

'They treated us like shit.' Sal throws her hands up frustratedly. 'I was protecting us.'

'Your first statement is true. Your second isn't. That's more than clear now. It should have been mine and Becca's decision, but you played things so we were left with no choice.'

'You did,' Becca backs Tess up.

'It's time to go, Sal,' says Tess. 'There's no room at this table for someone so bitter and selfish and… deceitful.'

Sal is so shocked by this unexpected ambush that she's spluttering like a broken-down vehicle. The whole pub is also watching this scene play out, and it's clear that Sal is mortified by this. Snatching up her handbag and jacket, she nearly topples her chair as she vacates the table without saying anything further. Then as she passes me, she hisses: 'You'd better watch your back.'

'You try anything with Lea and the police will be involved,' Shep calls after her. 'There are multiple witnesses to that threat.'

The door slams behind Sal, and suddenly it's like I can't breathe. Big fat tears crowd my eyes, before galloping down my cheeks.

'Hey, you're OK.' Shep guides me to the nearest table to sit down, while at the same time asking the barperson to bring some water. 'You did it. You stood up to her and you've done those two a favour.' He jabs his thumb in the direction of Becca and Tess, who are making their way over to us.

'I can't believe I did that.' I wipe my eyes with my sleeve. 'I'm so glad she didn't see this.'

'It's just adrenaline and overwhelm. A perfectly natural reaction.'

'Lea, OMG, you were immense there!' Tess swoops in and hugs me tight. 'I can't believe you did that.'

'Neither can I.' I glug at the glass of water that's just been handed to me.

'That was incredibly brave.' Becca appears on the other side of me and strokes my hair. 'Thank you for doing that.'

I look up at her with pained eyes. 'I feel like I should be apologising to you. I just hurled a bowling ball through your friendship group.'

'No way. You've just opened our eyes to something we should have seen well before now. I've been very uncomfortable with Sal's behaviour for a long time.'

'Me too,' says Tess.

'You have?' Becca looks at her in disbelief. 'I knew you found her a bit much at times, but didn't think you had any major issue with her.'

'Guess I thought the same about you, so I didn't say anything. We obviously gave her a far longer leash than we should have – perhaps because we were both a bit intimidated by her and had no clue as to the extent of her bad behaviour—'

'Well, none of that matters now, I guess.' Becca brings a very guilty-looking Tess to a halt with her soothing tone. 'I'm just so glad we didn't lose Lea like the others.' She turns her attention to me. 'I'd been wondering why you hadn't been in touch. By the way, are you two…?' She hesitates, unsure whether to finish her sentence.

'We are.' I grin at her, then at Shep. 'And he's staying.'

'*Amazing!*' Tess and Becca whoop and jump up and down simultaneously, and we all laugh.

'This is something to celebrate.' Tess claps her hands with glee. 'Becca, come help me get a bottle of fizz and some glasses.'

We share a group hug and then they head to the bar together, chatting animatedly, no doubt debriefing on what's just happened.

'Seems you're a bit of a hero.' Shep sits down and slips a reassuring arm around me, allowing me to cuddle into him. 'I'm so proud of you, you know.'

'I couldn't have done it without your support,' I murmur, as he kisses me softly on the top of my head and I breathe in his scent.

'Who can do something as scary as that without knowing someone's got their back? It takes a lot of guts.'

'I suppose you're right. Well, thank you anyway, for being here and for... being you. I'm so happy we're back together.'

He lifts my chin with his finger to make eye contact with me. 'Me too. We'll make this work, I promise.'

I smile at him. 'That, I want more than anything, Ciaran.'

He gives a light chuckle as he clocks that I've used his actual name for the first time, then he kisses me properly, while a two-person cheer breaks out from behind us.

Epilogue

The following August

'Are you ready for your *paid* Fringe debut, Mr Shepperd?' I pluck a chip from the cardboard container he's holding and pop it in my mouth, savouring the delicious crunchiness.

'Am I ever.' Shep looks like the comedian that got the cream as he lounges casually on the bench we've commandeered in the Pleasance Courtyard. 'I was made for this, Lea.'

'Damn right, you were. I'm so excited that you're performing here – at one of *the* most well-known Fringe venues.'

'It's certainly a step up on last year, isn't it?'

'I'll say. It's got a real stage and everything. Between this and your other shows and having an agent now, that invite for *Live at the Apollo* must be just around the corner.'

'Slow down, would you? It's a big leap going from gigs of a few hundred people to that.' Despite giving me this reality check, Shep seems unable to hide his grin at the possibility.

'Nah, I'd rather dream big for you.' I angle my face at the evening sun, enjoying its warmth. 'You're the funniest person I've seen doing stand-up. Why wouldn't they want you on their stage?'

'Remember you're biased. You laughed this morning when I said I was gonna take a shower.'

'It was the way you said it. And also, what you did before that when we were—'

'You gonna tell the whole courtyard about our sex life?' He raises an eyebrow at me.

Looking around, I notice a few people glancing in our direction, possibly having recognised Shep from his picture on his show posters. 'Oops, fair point.'

He sits forward and stretches his upper body.

'Right, sexy lady, it's forty minutes until curtain-up. Time for me to get in the zone.' He plants a kiss on my lips and hands me the remainder of the tray of chips. 'Enjoy the sunshine.'

I wave him off with a bright smile, then as soon as he's out of sight, I ditch the chips in a bin and make my way across to the front entrance of the venue. To my delight, I see that I'm the first in the queue, so hopefully my plan will work.

–

Thirty-five minutes later, I'm parked on one of the fold-down seats in the smallish theatre space. It's a very different set-up to the venue where Shep performed last year, in that it's purpose-built and the seats are accessed from the right-hand side of the room via a set of steps that run down to the stage. I've picked the seat which is slap bang in the middle of the front row.

'How long do you think it will take him to notice us?' Tess, who's sitting to my left, taps her fingers together excitedly.

My face spreads into a mischievous smile. 'I expect not long.'

'I hope we don't put him off,' says Becca, who's on the other side of Tess.

'No chance of that,' I reply with complete confidence, my eyes fixed on the stage.

Moments later, the lights go down and the audience behind us whisper and giggle in anticipation.

'Ladies and gentlemen, can I please ask you to give a warm Edinburgh welcome to… Shep!'

We applaud enthusiastically as the most important person in my life bounds out onto the stage, grabs the mic and paces back and forth, scanning his audience in his characteristic way. He has a broad grin plastered on his face, which becomes wider still as he takes in the sight in front of him. Then his eyes land on me, and I mouth, 'I love you.'

'Good evening, how're you all doing? It's great to see you,' he booms. 'Thanks for coming to my very first show of this year's Fringe.'

There's another smattering of applause and a cheer from the back of the room.

'Thank you, that's very kind.' He puts his hands together in an appreciative gesture while still clutching the mic. 'So, this is my second year here at the Fringe, and my first not having to shake a bucket and beg for money after my shows.'

'Go on, son!' catcalls another audience member.

'Thanks, mate. You seem more pleased about that than I am,' Shep acknowledges the overenthusiastic punter with a chuckle. 'No… I am pleased, I'm chuffed to bits to be back. I just got distracted for a second there… because… you know how people who have near-death experiences describe their lives flashing in front of their eyes? Well, something similar has just happened. Walking out on stage there, I was checking out the bait in the first two rows – you know, as us comedians do… and literally every person I know is sat in those seats.'

Looking behind me, I can see Shep's audience sharing baffled expressions.

'I'm not kidding you,' he continues. 'I thought for a second I was experiencing some bizarre psychological phenomenon, but they're all here in the flesh, like some weird-ass trip down memory lane. Look, these are my folks… my brother and sister… my girlfriend's folks…' He points to each of them in turn. 'My mates from back home near Belfast… All right, lads? Beers later, yeah? My mates from Edinburgh… the pub owner from last year's Fringe venue… my postman… my urologist…'

There's a ripple of laughter and Shep zones in on one poor unsuspecting audience member.

'Lady in the red T-shirt there, you look confused. Do you not know what a urologist is?'

I crane my neck to spot who he's talking to and see the woman shake her head.

Shep gestures to the man sitting next to her. 'It's the doctor that looks up his pee-pee when he can't do a wee-wee.'

The woman assumes a mortified expression and embarrassed laughter peals through the room.

'Obviously, I'm kidding. My urologist isn't here…' Shep shakes his head with a smile. 'He's coming tomorrow night.'

The audience snickers and a few people clap at this.

'So, there you all are…' He does a visual sweep across the front two rows. 'Looking very pleased with yourselves, aren't you? I'm guessing this mind fuck is the work of my girlfriend, Lea. Here she is, everyone.'

To my embarrassment, he steps down off the stage and gets me to stand up, face blazing, while the rows and rows of people cheer and whistle.

'Thank you, I'm sure Lea will appreciate that, especially as she's now barred from this show. *Security?*' Shep gives me a quick kiss – which receives a collective 'aww' from the audience – before returning to the stage.

'Who am I kidding, talking like I have security?' he continues. 'I had to get a loan to even be here. Anyway, as you've hopefully gathered by now, I'm Shep, the bloke who robbed you of your hard-earned cash so I can repay that loan and entertain myself by manipulating you like puppets for an hour…'

He settles into his new routine, which I've heard parts of when he's practised his delivery on me. I think it's safe to say that this show, which again has audience participation as a key feature, is going to be an even bigger hit than last year's. He takes us through a rollercoaster ride that includes everything from good-natured personal humiliations to collective gasps and side-splitting laughter. The hour goes by so quickly, I'm disappointed when he wraps things up and it comes to an end.

After we've filed out of the venue into the courtyard outside, I chat away to our family and friends, with one eye on the backstage exit, until I see him appear through the door. Spotting me immediately, he beckons for me to join him, and I lollop across, wincing in case I'm in trouble.

'Am I really barred from future performances?' I ask with a sweet smile.

'Of course you're not.' He slips one arm around me, tucks a lock of hair behind my ear and looks at me meaningfully. 'That was the most thoughtful thing anyone has ever done for me. I honestly can't thank you enough. Later, when it's just you and me, I want to hear exactly how you pulled that off, but for now, just one question: how the hell did you get my family over here? I know you've been working on them these last months, but that's like taming a crash of rhinos. Look at them, they're actually smiling.'

I glance across at his mum, dad and siblings, and adopt a shifty expression. 'I might have been bombarding them a bit.'

'Meaning?'

'Covertly filming your shows and sending them the footage... sending them links to positive local media coverage... that kind of thing.'

'Wow.' Shep looks stupefied by this. 'You genuinely are the best person in the world.'

'I know.' I shrug angelically. 'Anyway, I think you need to put me down and go see your adoring fans.'

'Do I have to?' he complains, while kissing me and nuzzling my neck.

'Yes. Go see yours and I'll go see mine.'

I look over at Becca, Tess and Tanya. They're standing with Tanya's husband, John, and Byron, the infamous band member with whom Becca reunited a few weeks after Sal was banished from our friendship group. He's actually a lovely bloke, who's nothing like Sal made him out to be.

It's as if they can feel my eyes on them, because they suddenly look back at us with a range of smiles and waves. Tess even makes a little heart with her fingers and holds it to her chest.

'They really do adore you,' says Shep. 'As do I – for being generally amazing and for helping me get to this.'

He gazes around him contentedly while giving me an affectionate squeeze.

'And I'm forever grateful to you for helping me find such wonderful friends.'

'We make a good team, don't we?'

'The best.' I smile up at him with loving eyes. 'I can't wait to see what life has in store for us, because with you by my side, I feel I can conquer anything.'

'Right back at you.'

Holding hands, we wander across to our people, and as they encircle us, laughing and joking and congratulating Shep on his performance, I can't help thinking back to this time a year ago, when I felt so isolated and alone. It still seems almost inconceivable that just twelve months on, I'm surrounded by so much love and friendship, and I know I'm the luckiest woman in the world.

Acknowledgments

Stand Up Guy brings together several things that I love in life: the wonderful city of Edinburgh, stand-up comedy, writing (I especially enjoy creating the banterous dialogue between my characters) and, of course, love itself. There are few things in this world that are as natural and beautiful as two people falling head over heels for each other, and this book continues a theme I've threaded through my other published novels, which is that everyone deserves to have love in their lives (even Sal, though I think she needs to work on herself a bit first).

When I started writing *Stand Up Guy*, I was really excited by the concept of a 'meet cute' between an Edinburgh citizen and a visiting comedian – that was, until I realised I'd have to write some stand-up comedy. The idea that someone might read it and say 'Pah! That's not funny at all!' was quite daunting. But then someone close to me pointed out that, of course there would be people who didn't find it funny, just like not everyone likes the same books or movies or even stand-up comedians. That made me feel a whole lot better.

As well as having comedy at its heart – quite literally in this case – and like all of my published novels so far, *Stand Up Guy* includes some more poignant themes that are reflective of real life. This time: loneliness and bullying. I won't labour the point here, but I do want to mention that these are areas that I have personal experience with, and I expect that there are many others out there who can relate. What I wanted to do was cover these topics in a way that might help my readers get a glimpse of what it feels like to be in a situation such as Lea's – perhaps even get a sense that they're not alone if they're experiencing something similar – while keeping the tone light enough to create a humorous and uplifting read.

My home city of Edinburgh really is such a beautiful canvas for my books. I feel quite lucky to have it at my fingertips, and I especially enjoyed building this story around the events of the Fringe. Edinburgh's festivals bring such a vibrant atmosphere to the city, it was always a no-brainer that that setting would eventually feature in one of my novels. However, what you can never plan for as an author, is changing circumstances, especially in the turbulent times we live in. What I discovered once this book was already written, was that the iconic end of festival fireworks that – prior to the COVID-19 pandemic – were always the big finale, have sadly been discontinued after forty years. Having already written them into my book as part of one of the story's own climatic moments, I now see this content as a bit of a tribute to them.

Anyway, enough of my ramblings. I'll get to the point, which is the long list of people I owe grateful thanks to.

At the top of that list, as always, is my husband, James. I can't thank you enough for... well, being you (just as Shep says to Lea). You don't just support me with my writing, you truly are my everything, as well as the most selfless and caring person I've ever met. I would honestly be lost without you.

Another family member I'd like to give a great big thank you to is my sister-in-law, Angela, who helped me make the character of Shep more authentic. I also apologise, once again, for bombarding you with multiple lists of words and phrases and expecting you to play the role of Northern Irish thesaurus. Thank you also to my mum and dad and the rest of my wonderful family, who are still enthusiastically supporting me in my writing journey. You lot are the best!

To the wonderful publishing professionals without whom my books wouldn't make it into the big wide world – my agent, Kate Nash, and my editor, Emily Bedford. A huge thank you to you both for continuing to support me and help me grow as a writer, and for flying the flag for my writing. Also, to Thanhmai Bui-Van, Kate Shepherd and the rest of the team at Canelo. Publishing really is a team effort and everything you do is so appreciated.

Next up are my brilliant author buddies: Andie Newton, Fiona Leitch and Sandy Barker. I really do wonder sometimes if I'd get through this whole writing and publishing business without you. You're there for the highest highs and the lowest lows. You've bolstered my confidence, helped me during multiple moments of indecision, answered my daft questions and picked me up off the metaphorical floor more times than I can count. For all of that and so much more, thank you.

Finally, a heartfelt thank you goes to all my fabulous friends, colleagues and readers who continue to support me. Writing is something of a lonely business so it helps immensely to have you cheering me on.